HUNTING THE ELEPHANT IN AFRICA

ELEPHANT IN UGANDA

This elephant was one of a herd of about a hundred, all of which were close round
him in the bush although invisible to the camera.

HUNTING THE ELEPHANT IN AFRICA

Foreword by Theodore Roosevelt

Captain C. H. Stigand

Peter Capstick, Series Editor

St. Martin's Press
New York

To the Reader:

The editors and publishers of the Peter Capstick Adventure Library faced significant responsibilities in the faithful reprinting of Africa's great hunting books of long ago. Essentially, they saw the need for each text to reflect to the letter the original work, nothing having been added or expunged, if it was to give the reader an authentic view of another age and another world.

In deciding that historical veracity and honesty were the first considerations, they realized that it meant retaining many distasteful racial and ethnic terms to be found in these old classics. The firm of St. Martin's Press, Inc., therefore wishes to make it very clear that it disassociates itself and its employees from the abhorrent racial-ethnic attitudes of the past which may be found in these books.

History is the often unpleasant record of the way things actually were, not the way they should have been. Despite the fact that we have no sympathy with the prejudices of decades past, we feel it better—and indeed, our collective responsibility—not to change the unfortunate facts that were.

—Peter Hathaway Capstick

HUNTING THE ELEPHANT IN AFRICA. Copyright © 1986 by Peter Hathaway Capstick. All rights reserved. Printed in the United States of America. No part of this book may be used or reproduced in any manner whatsoever without written permission except in the case of brief quotations embodied in critical articles or reviews. For information, address St. Martin's Press, 175 Fifth Avenue, New York, N.Y. 10010.

Library of Congress Cataloging in Publication Data

Stigand, C. H. (Chauncey Hugh), 1877–1919.
    Hunting the elephant in Africa.

    Originally published: New York : Macmillan, 1913.
    1. Elephant hunting—Africa. I. Title.
SK305.E3S68   1986   799.2′761′096   85-25024
ISBN 0-312-40158-2

First Edition

10 9 8 7 6 5 4 3 2 1

EDITOR'S NOTE
TO THE REPRINT EDITION

HE lay motionless, six-foot-four inches of steel muscle and wire tendons watching the sun rise before his dark, bloodshot eyes. Under his right hand, sand just shaken lightly over it to kill a growing glint, lay seven feet of hand-hammered iron, as keen as steel and as straight as bamboo. At his side he felt the smugness of three feet of fighting sword, loose in its rawhide sheath. His shield lay under his chest. He was nineteen and unafraid. He was an Aliab Dinka, the Fearless Ones of the White Nile. He knew that in a few moments he would kill. Or be killed.

The Equatorial Battalion, in battle square formation, was marching, the dull swish of their puttees soggy against the tall greening-gold of Kor Raby, in the Mongalla Province of Sudan. Under his thick coating of wood ash, the Dinka heard the men approaching. It was time to attack. Time to kill. Time to be a warrior.

Through the grass, he saw, off to his left, a lone man. From the pips on his shoulders, an officer. The Aliab Dinka marked him as his target. The man must be mad, he thought, fooling as he was with paper and marking the terrain. . . .

Captain (posthumously Major) Chauncey Hugh Stigand was off to one side of the British squares, just begging for a sticking. Stigand knew that war with the Dinkas could be avoided 99 times out of 100. But of that 100th time, Stigand wrote: "It all starts with that other ninety-nine, but either the enemy is unfamiliar with firearms or enjoys a particular superiority of men or both." Then, as Stigand related with an eerie forethought: "Nothing is seen of the assailants except a few flying men. Suddenly, there is a rush in thick grass and the little column gets massacred." Ironically, Stigand has written here of the manner of his own death. And this brings us back to the grass of Kor Raby, where a sweating spearman waits for a sweating officer in the growing heat.

The ash-smeared naked warrior is not alone; against the few British Battalions are more than 1,000 Aliab. He has noted his mustached target; that one off to the left, bending over his papers and scribbling notes.

It is the hundredth time. With a wild whoop and screech, the thousand Aliab charge through the deep grass. Off to the side, Stigand Bey, *the governor of Mongalla Province, drops his papers and starts to kill men. A nearby warrior takes a round through the brain from the great marksman. Another. The early sun catches the gleam of brass as it is ejected from the .303. The nickle-plated slugs punch neat and deadly holes*

*through the small shields, but the sleet of spears is un-
avoidable. Sergeant Macallister drops, vomiting blood
as the long iron lances his chest; Commander White
falls with three lengths of razor staves through his lungs
and guts. But what of Stigand. . . ?*

That Stigand will die is inevitable.

Captain Chauncey Hugh Stigand, O.B.E., counted
among his honors the Order of the Nile, War Medal,
and Victory Medal, and memberships in the Royal
Zoological Society and the Royal Geological Society.
Just before his death by burnished iron, he was also the
Bey or governor of the Mongalla Province of Sudan.
Not bad for a man who also spoke a dozen languages,
several well enough to be a certified translator.

Born in 1877, Stigand was considered the most
physically powerful officer in the British army and
wrote many works in collaboration with Denis D.
Lyell (who may well lurk later on in this series). Theodore Roosevelt, who wrote the Foreword to this book,
complains with good nature that it was as tough to get
Stigand to tell his adventures as it was for Grant to
recount his.

Stigand was noted not only for his bravery and his
skill with a rifle, but also for his unusual understanding
of native peoples and their languages. Yet he remained a hunter of men, and his prisoners numbered
into the hundreds. How many men he personally

killed is unrecorded, but the number unquestionably ran to many score.

Chauncey Hugh Stigand was probably the unluckiest of all the great hunters, having been mauled almost to death by rhino, lion, and—this not being mentioned in *Hunting the Elephant in Africa*—also by old Jumbo himself. The telling of the third encounter cannot but add to the flavor of this book.

The incident happened after *Hunting the Elephant in Africa* was published, but there is very little detail of the event in contemporary literature. The source in which I found the most reliable information is the very rare and valuable book by D. D. Lyell, *The African Elephant and Its Hunters* (Heath Cranton, Ltd., 1924). Lyell, having been a lifelong friend of Stigand, wrote:

An elephant had come to raid some native crops, and Stigand, not wishing to shoot it, had gone without a rifle—rather a reckless proceeding. [Stigand habitually carried a .256 Mannlicher.]

This elephant, I believe, had probably been wounded by a white man or a native, and was in a nasty frame of mind; for as soon as it saw Stigand it charged him and knocked him down. It drove one of its tusks through the fleshy part of his thigh and then picked him up and threw him some yards through the air. One account I read said twenty yards, but I doubt if it was so far as that. Having flung him away, the animal again came for him; but Stigand, knowing it was his last chance, kept still, and the elephant, after smelling him with his trunk, ran away and left him.

As he had received a very severe wound he had to come home for treatment, but after some time recovered his health and strength. During the years he lived in Africa he seems to have gloried in risks. Whether all were justifiable is a question I need not discuss, except to say that it would be good advice to the beginner to say that it is best when going near dangerous animals to be prepared for any eventuality, as it is impossible to foretell what a beast will do under the circumstances.

Stigand recovered at the home of *Sirdar* General Wingate.

Stigand married an American, and the couple had one daughter. It was Mrs. Stigand who had the graves of her husband, Macallister, and White moved from Kor Raby to Kaji Kajo, where they were buried under selected stone.

Hunting the Elephant in Africa is an extremely rare book: not only for its lack of supply, but for its invaluable content and delightful style. In it, Stigand speaks not only of the elephant, but of other dangerous game as well—much of which caught him, often causing horrible wounds when it did. Stigand is perhaps my favorite writer of Africana, with his casual yet vivid characterizations of the chase: the chase of both men and other dangerous game.

I think it is now time to return to the burnished grass of Kor Raby, where Chauncey Hugh Stigand has but a few moments to live.

The warrior who has marked Stigand as prey has slithered off to his left in a silent, serpentine motion, bunching with his fellow warriors for a rush through the heavy grass—just as Stigand predicted. A low bird call swells into a bellow of battle as the spearmen and the Equatorial Battalion join, hand-to-hand. Steel squeals on iron but the squares of the British refuse to rupture. Stigand, however, is not in one of the squares. Dodging a sleet of spears, he runs, firing, as the Aliab surround him and the first fluttering, humming, fluted blade slices home; perhaps the blade of our ash-covered friend. Maintaining his balance, Stigand somehow keeps firing.

How many Dinka were killed by Stigand *Bey* and carried off, smears against the grass and abandoned spears? If a dozen spears were found, you can bet the rent money that Stigand killed ten or a dozen. He was, after all, one of the finest marksmen in all of Africa.

I think you will find appropriate here the letter from F. C. Roberts, *Bimbashi* of the Equatorial Battalion and a Victoria Cross winner, to Mrs. Stigand. It gives as good an account of the battle of Kor Raby—as reconstructed by the battalion—as can be found. Bear in mind, however, that all is conjecture. Nobody actually saw Stigand killed.

Dear Mrs. Stigand,

It is with great sorrow that I am writing to give you the details of Stigand Bey's death. I am sure that you will wish me to tell you everything. In the beginning of November the Aliab Dinkas on the western bank of the Nile round Tombe rose. Stigand Bey did his utmost to settle matters peaceably, but to no purpose. The Equatorial Battalion was ordered out, and up to the 5th December had a certain amount of fighting. On this latter date the column again commenced operations with Stigand Bey as Political Officer. I own that it was not right for the "Governor" to come with us, but unfortunately no one else was available owing to sickness. Stigand Bey had also by this time made up his mind that half measures were of no use, and that the Dinkas required severe handling. He himself showed the greatest keenness in all the arrangements; and I am afraid from the start took unnecessary risks, always being well in front or on the flanks of the column reconnoitering, and taking bearings for a future sketch of the country marched through. At 7.15 a.m. on the 8th December the head and flanks of the column were rushed in very thick grass, by what I estimated to be a thousand of the enemy (in order to explain things better I am enclosing a rough plan of our formation, and where Stigand Bey was at the moment the rush came). Personally I was at the head of the right flank guard, saw him with his rifle to his shoulder firing as hard as he could and attempting to stop the backward rush of the advance guard and the carriers, which threatened to break up our square formation. No one I can find in the battalion saw him killed, but it must have happened within the first two minutes. His end I know was an extremely gallant and a happy one, by the smile on his face when we picked him up. From the spear wound through his chest he must have died instantaneously and have suffered no pain. All of us know that he gave his life to save the column from utter destruction, which would have been certain unless he had stopped the first rush before too many of the enemy got inside the square. We afterwards picked up about a dozen of his empty cartridge cases, which I think speaks for itself. At dusk the same day we buried him and Major White, our Commanding Officer, who was also killed, fifty yards to the N.W. of a small clump of trees at a place named Kor Raby, where we had spent the night of the 7th/8th December; this spot will be well remembered by all on the patrol, and you must not worry about the exact position not being found in the future.

It is impossible for me to tell you how all, British and Native officers, non-commissioned and men, feel for you in your great loss; your consolation is that he was one of the most gallant officers and the finest man the Sudan or Africa has ever known, and I feel certain that his death was the one he would have chosen above all things—giving his life for others.

With deepest sympathy,
Yours very sincerely,
F. C. Roberts, Bimbashi, a. O.C. Equat. Bn.

Mongalla, 21st December, 1919

—PETER HATHAWAY CAPSTICK

NOTE

The original edition of Hunting the Elephant in Africa *contained a chart of elephant and elephant tusk measurements that, regrettably, could not be reproduced in the Peter Capstick Library edition.*

FOREWORD

FOR three-quarters of a century there have been capital books written on big game hunting in Africa, — one of the best being the earliest, that by Captain Cornwallis Harris. Of course the only type of big game hunter who can write a book really worth reading is the hunter who is also at least to a certain extent an out-of-doors naturalist. In addition, he should thoroughly enjoy the strange desolate scenery of the African wilderness, and have a sympathetic understanding of the wild men who accompany him on most of his hunts. More and more of late years the best type of big game hunter has tended to lay stress on the natural history and ethnology of the regions into which he has penetrated, and to make his book less and less a catalogue of mere slaughter.

Captain Stigand is one of the most noted of recent African big game hunters and explorers, and he is also a field naturalist of unusual powers. His studies of the tracks of animals have been almost unique. The only studies approaching them are those about the tracks of the game of continental Europe, in the German hunting books of the seventeenth and eighteenth centuries. He has the keenest appreciation of the vivid and extraordinary beauty of the teeming African wild life, and has made close first-hand observations of the life histories of very many species of big game. In the past there have been many big game hunters who wrote overmuch of their own exploits, so that it becomes wearisome to read the endless lists of the animals that they killed. With Captain Stigand our quarrel is the direct reverse. He tells too little of his own achievements. He has, as I can myself testify, the reputation among all first-class African hunters of being himself one of the foremost. He is equally fond of venturing into unknown regions and of the chase of dangerous game, and is an adept in the especially difficult art of wood and bush tracking and stalking. Three times he has been nearly killed by his quarry: once by a rhinoceros, once by a lion, and once by an elephant. It is unfortunate that he will not give us more minute and extended accounts of his own personal adventures — one of the excellent features of the books of that other great African hunter Selous is that he does give such extended accounts of his personal experiences. But it is as difficult to get Captain Stigand to tell what he has himself done as it was to get General Grant to talk about his battles. After this manuscript was in my hands, Captain Stigand was nearly killed by an elephant. It was in the Lado, and he was taken down to Khartoum; but his letters to his friends at home touched so lightly on the subject that they had to obtain all real information from outside sources.

However, Captain Stigand more than makes up for
this reticence about himself by the keenness and wide
range of his observations about the life histories of the
big game, and by his sympathetic and understanding
appreciation of his native allies and companions.
Modern biologists have grown to realize the prime
scientific value of such first-hand field observations.
There are but a limited number of men who combine
the opportunity and the power to make these observations about big game.   In this limited number Captain
Stigand stands high.

Like Mr. Selous, Captain Stigand has made much
field study of the subject of protective coloration as
applied to big game.   Scientific men are no more immune from hysteria and suggestion than other mortals,
and every now and then there arises among them some
fad which for quite a time carries even sane men off
their feet.   This has been the case with the latter-day
development of the theories of protective coloration
and of warning and recognition marks — but especially
the first.   Because some animals are undoubtedly
protectively colored and take advantage of their coloration and are served by it, a number of naturalists have
carried the theory to fantastic extremes.   They have
applied it where it does not exist at all, and have en-
deavored to extend it to a degree that has tended to
make the whole theory ridiculous.   Most good observers are now agreed that in the higher vertebrates, that

is, in mammals and birds, the coloration of probably the majority of the species has little or nothing to do with any protective or concealing quality. There are some hundreds of species which we can say with certainty are protectively colored; there are a great number which we can say with certainty are not protectively colored. As regards others we are still in doubt. There have not been sufficiently extensive observations made of wild animals under natural conditions to enable us to speak with certainty as to just the part played by protective coloration among large numbers of the smaller mammals and birds. We are, however, able to speak with certainty as regards most big birds and especially most big mammals.

Captain Stigand has shown that as regards most of the big game of Africa protective coloration plays not even the smallest part in concealing them from their foes. This is especially true of the animals of the plains, the giraffe, zebra, hartebeest, oryx, eland, roan and sable antelope, wildebeest, topi, gazelle, and the like. As to these animals we have a sufficient number of first-hand observations to warrant us in saying that the extreme theories of Professor Poulton and the Messrs. Thayer have no basis whatever in fact. It is much to be regretted that there are not more scientific writers with the clear scientific judgment displayed by Messrs. DeWar and Finn in their "Making of Species."

The big game animals of the plains do not seek to

elude observation and are not helped by their color in the struggle for life. It is astounding that some of the closet theorists who have written on this matter should have failed to understand what the conditions actually are. For example, it has been seriously asserted that zebras, oryx, and the various plains antelope are protected by their colors at their drinking places. No such statement would ever have been made by any man who had ever seen these animals approach a drinking place. They make no attempt whatever to hide, and if they pay attention to cover at all, it is merely to avoid it, because it may hold their great enemy, the lion. They often come in great herds to drink. They are in motion of course — otherwise they could not get down to drink — and anything in motion at once catches the eye of any beast hunter. They move forward, now at a walk, now at a trot; halt, wheel, and run backwards; and often do not come down to drink until there have been half a dozen such false alarms. Occasionally, especially if they suspect the presence of a foe, they make their final rush at furious speed, gulp the water hastily down, and rush off again. The coloring of the different species is infinitely varied, and this although they are living under precisely similar conditions. It is varied in some species even between the male and female, who live in the same herd. Yet those species like eland and roan antelope, whose general tint does often shade into the landscape, make no more effort to hide than such animals as the sable and the wildebeest, whose coloration is advertising in the highest degree. There is no reason to suppose that the species of one type are helped or the species of the other type harmed by their coloration. The coloration of the zebra, giraffe, and of many of the antelopes so far as it has any effect is of a revealing or advertising quality. Of course there are circumstances under which any type of coloration, no matter of what conceivable kind, is concealing; but with most of the African big game the coloration must reveal them much more often than it conceals them; nevertheless the circumstances of their lives are such that neither the revealing nor the concealing quality of the different coloration patterns has any effect upon the life of the species.

Mr. Wallace does not go to the extremes of the ultra concealing coloration men. But in a recent volume he has strained the recognition mark theory to an impossible point by claiming that the horns of certain African antelopes are useful as such recognition marks. He gives several pictures of these antelopes. In most of the species thus pictured only the adult males have the horns which he describes, and it can hardly be seriously contended that there has been a development of "recognition" marks to the exclusion of all of the animals of one sex and of half of the animals of another, including all the young. Among the species Mr. Wallace enumerates as having horns which serve as recognition marks are hartebeests. Now the harte-beests have relatively small and inconspicuous horns, whereas their bodily shape is unmistakable. They live under conditions which make it certain that they must see one another in the immense majority of cases at dis-tances such that their shape would identify them and their horns would not, and in the remaining cases they would be so near that they could not fail to identify one another even if they were absolutely hornless.

When leaders of scientific thought develop theories of this kind it is natural that many good observers should be unconsciously influenced by the opinions of those to whom they had been trained to look up as authorities. In consequence, even good outdoors men have committed themselves to statements on this subject which will not stand investigation. It is one of the merits of Captain Stigand that he is among the observers who have set forth the facts so clearly as regards big game that there is now no excuse for further mistakes or misstatements in the matter.

In short, Captain Stigand has written a book which ought to appeal to every believer in vigor and hardi-hood, to every lover of wilderness adventure, and to every man who values at their proper worth the ob-servations of an excellent field naturalist.

THEODORE ROOSEVELT.

CONTENTS

ILLUSTRATIONS

HUNTING THE ELEPHANT IN AFRICA

HUNTING THE ELEPHANT IN AFRICA

CHAPTER I

ELEPHANT HUNTING

THERE is something so fascinating and absorbing about elephant hunting that those who have done much of it can seldom take any interest again in any other form of sport. It seems so vastly superior to all other big game shooting that, once they have surrendered themselves to its charms, they cannot even treat any other form of hunting seriously. Everything else seems little and insignificant by comparison.

The lot of the elephant hunter is now a hard one. Girt about on all sides with exorbitant and restrictive licenses, and with most of the elephant now driven into unhealthy and impenetrable country, he must needs be an enthusiast who would become a devotee of this sport.

Sometimes when struggling waist deep through a swamp or forcing a way through tall grass and noxious vegetation reaching far above his head, with a blazing sun and in a fever-stricken locality, after having paid £50 for a license to shoot two elephant, he must think bitterly on the accident of birth which brought

him some fifty years too late into this world. He
would hardly be human if he did not think with envy
of those who had been able to shoot an unlimited
number on no license in a gloriously healthy climate,
and moreover in country so open that the pursuit
could sometimes be carried out on horseback. There
is one thing, however, for which the modern hunter
has to be thankful, and that is the accuracy, lightness,
and power of his weapon; in all others he is handi-
capped.

In the early days in the East African Highlands
things must have been much the same as in the old
days in South Africa, except that the healthier parts
were never so famed for elephant as the more tropical
and unhealthier climes of Uganda and the low country
to the north.

The late A. H. Neumann must have had a glorious
time in the Meru country and the Highlands north
of Laikipia, the latter a place in which elephant are
seldom met with now.

The difficult and forbidding country about Lake
Rudolf is at least open and absolutely devoid of vegetation. The accounts of how elephant were met with
day after day in perfectly open country by Count
Teleki in his discovery of Lakes Rudolf and Stephanie,
a country which is now almost elephantless, read
almost like a fairy tale to modern hunters.

I have never met elephant in such open country

as this, but, coming as I do amongst latter-day hunters, I have perhaps little to grumble about, as I have often found them in quite favorable localities where it is possible to move about easily. In another forty or fifty years perhaps it will sound equally like a fairy tale, that elephant could ever offer a clear and open shot at a hundred yards' range.

The only place in which I have come across elephant in a cold and temperate climate is on the Aberdare range, and there it is often too cold to be pleasant. Owing to the thickness of the vegetation, the scarcity of shootable bulls, and other circumstances I was not successful.

The first time I visited these hills was in 1906 in company with a brother officer, Captain Olivier. The elephant appeared to consist chiefly of herds of females and young and had a sufficiently bad reputation. Shortly before, a hunter had had his arm broken by being flung aside by an elephant, whilst others had spent unpleasant moments with them.

We decided to be very careful and cautious; so when we located a herd on the lower slopes we spent some time investigating them, and trying to spot a bull from a safe distance. They were screaming and trumpeting, a sign that they were chiefly females and young. They moved along the lower slopes inside the bush belt rapidly, and where they had crossed the numerous watercourses coming down from the mountain they had pushed aside bushes and branches which had closed again over their path.   In such places as these it was often necessary to crawl on hands and knees to pass the obstructions.

Finally they moved up into the hills and started grazing, and we were not able to get a good look at them. The wind was bad, and we manœuvred about for some time without seeing them, being only aware of their presence by the sounds of breaking branches.   As they appeared to be slowly coming down the hill again, we decided to wait till they reached a spot in which the bushes were shorter and where we would have a better opportunity of being able to locate a bull if there was one with the herd.

When one has a license only permitting the shooting of two elephants, one has to be very wary in approaching big herds in thick country, and cannot afford to run the risk of being charged by or shooting a female or small bull.

Whilst we were waiting, sleet began to fall, and we took refuge under a big shrub.   The sleet presently turned to hail, and we cowered under our shelter. Meanwhile we heard the elephant breaking branches and feeding uninterruptedly a short distance away. During the storm an elephant with about 30 or 40 pound tusks appeared not 40 yards from us down wind and apparently quite unconcerned at the sleet.

We tried to shoot him, but we could hardly see for

hail, and it is a difficult matter shooting with another man when always accustomed to shoot by oneself. We each put a shot into him, but between us bungled him. He turned and raced to the edge of a steep nullah about a hundred yards off, and appeared to fall over the edge. We ran out from our retreat, but at that moment the hail redoubled in intensity, and came down the size of small marbles, so that we were absolutely unable to stand up to it. With one accord we turned and fled to a tree close by, and pressed ourselves against the trunk.

The hail continued for about an hour, we were bitterly cold, the altitude was 8000 feet, and we were only dressed in the usual hunting shirt and shorts. I got a fit of ague and my teeth chattered so that I could not speak. While in this condition I peered round the trunk of our tree, and there, close to where the elephant had been I saw two rhino standing and calmly surveying the scene. The noise of the hail on the trees and ground, and the chattering of my teeth prevented my being able to tell Olivier of my discovery, but I nudged him and he peered round and saw what I was trying to tell him.

I fired, and one of them dropped on his knees; when trying to reload, — I was shooting with a mannlicher, — a big hailstone got into the breech and jammed it. Olivier finished him off with a shot, whilst the second one turned and ran off.

Soon after this the hail stopped and we went to look at the place where we had last seen the elephant. We found that he had fallen, picked himself up again, and made off. The ground was so thickly carpeted with hail since he had passed that it was almost impossible to follow his spoor, and we were so cold and miserable that we abandoned it, and returned to camp.

Next day we went to take up the tracks; the hail had melted to a certain extent, although still lying thick in the shade. The whole herd of about 40 animals had, however, passed over the spoor of the bull whilst the ground was wet and slippery, and had cut it up to such an extent that the original spoor was effectually obliterated.

We stopped a day or two longer in the vicinity and saw a herd again but could not find a shootable male in it. On another occasion we saw an elephant on an opposite hill. After marking down the position we spent an immense time pushing through a tangle of vegetation, and when we at last reached the spot we found that he had moved on, and we were not able to catch him up.

A few months later I was surveying in the same neighbourhood, and after a fortnight's work decided that I was due for two off days at the rate of one Sunday per week. I got hold of two Kikuyu who knew the hills well, it being their trade to look for honey and take it down to sell in the villages on the east side of the range. I also took three porters to carry a waterproof sheet, a blanket, and a canteen for me. One of these porters was an old man, who, according to his own account, was so well fitted out with charms and spells that he could tackle any dangerous beast with impunity and move amongst them unharmed. I was told that if a lion was lying here and another there, two spots about five yards apart being indicated, he could come and sleep between them and continue on his way next day unmoved.

The honey-hunters led us by elephant paths up the hills till we reached the bamboo forest. The whole mountain is covered with a network of these paths and the back of practically every spur, ridge, and col is crowned by an elephant road following its highest part. In places we met salt licks, either banks of red earth or old white ant-hills, on which could be seen the tusk marks of elephant who had come to break off lumps of the salt earth. All these marks, however, were of females or young and there were no impressions of big tuskers.

We had just descended a steep bamboo-covered hillside, crossed a mountain torrent, and were slowly climbing the steep opposite side of the valley when we heard a noise from the slope behind us. On looking back we at first only saw the bamboo moving by some unseen agency. Every now and again there would be a trembling in a clump of trees and the top of a stem would bend over and disappear with a cracking sound.   On looking through my glasses I could distinguish here and there a black trunk soaring upwards to reach for a high branch, and occasionally a glimpse of part of a black body between the bamboo clumps.

After watching for some time I made out what I took to be three bulls on the right of the herd.   Knowing that I should not, in all probability, get another sight of them, once I left my coign of vantage on the hillside, I took careful stock of their position and of any big trees on the way to serve as landmarks.   Then I descended to the bottom of the valley again, crossed the stream, and began the steep toil up the slope.   When I finally arrived at the spot at which I had seen them there was nothing but their spoor left; the whole herd had moved on and there was not even the noise of cracking bamboo to be heard.   I followed the spoor a little way, and, as I could see or hear nothing of them, I returned to the porters and arranged a site for our camp.   Having done this I went after the elephant again, taking the Kikuyus with me, and we came up with them about sunset, busily feeding in a valley covered with bamboo forest.   It was too late now to try and find where the males were, so we left them and returned to camp.

The waterproof sheet was pitched on the side of the hill in the middle of the elephant path, there being no flat spot in which to put it and indeed no other place clear enough.   I brewed myself some cocoa, which was very comforting, for the night was chilly, and we were at an altitude of about ten thousand feet. The rest of the repast consisted of cold meat, biscuits, and some honey the Kikuyu had found during the day. After rolling myself in my blanket and making myself as comfortable as I could on the very sloping pathway, I fell asleep, thinking how awkward it would be for us if the elephant wanted to pass by this same way during the night.

However, they did not come our way, but next morning we found them still breaking bamboos in the valley in which we had left them the evening before. We could not see them, and, as the wind was blowing down the valley we followed along one side of the slope and descended below them. Here we found a network of fresh tracks, quantities of elephant having been feeding off the bamboo, which was greener in the valley bottoms, whilst the upper slopes and the backs of the ridges were covered with old bamboo forest.

We had nearly reached the stream at the bottom of the valley, and we could still hear the herd busily feeding up-stream on our right when there was a stampede to our left, and we could also hear another herd beyond them charging off, crashing and crackling through the bamboos. We waited till the sounds had passed away in the distance, and still we could hear the crack, crack of bamboo from our herd feeding undisturbed.

We cautiously made our way up the valley towards them till we could locate them by the moving of the bamboos. As they were not to be seen we circled round to try and get a view and mark down a shootable bull from the hillside above them. As we did this we gave our wind to yet another herd who went crashing off with such a clatter and crackling of bamboo stems knocking against each other and breaking that we thought it must disturb our herd, but when we listened we again heard the reassuring crack, crack, showing them to be still grazing. Again we circled round, and this time stampeded a fifth herd.

We then descended a gentle slope towards our herd. A few tall junipers were dotted about in the bamboo here. I was with one of the Kikuyu and the old porter; the others I had left behind on first hearing the elephant. The old porter climbed up a tall and conveniently sloping tree to reconnoitre. Whilst he was up the tree I could hear a herd coming towards us, having evidently become uneasy from hearing the other one stampeding. I took refuge behind a tree with the Kikuyu as they appeared. They passed at about fifteen yards' distance, one female or unsizable male after another.

Now a tree is all right to stand behind when it is between you and the elephant, but when some are one side and some another, one begins to wish for a tree to grow up behind one as well as in front. So when about five had passed close by and were standing just behind me, and the remainder of the herd began to come towards my tree with the intention of passing on both sides, I felt it incumbent on me to make some sort of demonstration. The next elephant was a young male who came swinging along straight towards our tree, and there were others on each side of him, so at about ten yards I planked him in the forehead and he dropped dead, whilst the herd turned and went back the way they had come.

I was just looking at the fallen elephant and regretting the accuracy of my aim when another herd appeared on the scene, so I ran back to the shelter of my tree whilst they trooped past at thirty yards' distance. In the middle of the herd was a sizable bull, but he was surrounded on all sides by females and young. I got a momentary clear view of his head, and had a snap shot, and he fell. Instantly the rest closed round him, heads inwards, to lift him up with their tusks, and there was nothing to see but a ring of sterns. I ran out from my shelter to try and get another shot, but the next moment they had got him on to his feet and, surrounding him on all sides, so that it was impossible to get even a glimpse of him; the whole herd bore down on me.

They were not charging, they were only stampeding, and I happened to be in the direction they had chosen. I did not wait, but turned to run, and looking over my shoulder saw a perfect avalanche of flesh bearing down upon me.

As often happens with elephant, they did not go far, but suddenly stopped dead and listened. I looked round and saw that they had stopped, but could not see the wounded male. Just by me was a small tree with sloping trunk and a fork about twelve feet up. I thought that they were unlikely to come my way again, but would go off another way now, and that if I could reach this fork I might be able to get a glimpse of the bull over the backs of the others. It was a ridiculous thing to do, because twelve feet is just about level with the elephant's eye, and one would have been a very conspicuous object there.

Anyhow, I commenced clambering up this tree as best I could with my rifle in my hand. There was another wild rush in my direction, and just as they reached within a few yards of my tree I caught hold of a rotten branch, which broke, and I fell heavily to the ground, not more than a few yards from the feet of the nearest elephant.

This strange fruit dropping off the tree so startled them that they swerved away at right angles and crashed into the bamboo, pushing and jostling to get in front of each other. As they could only pass between the clumps and they all chose the same two clumps, it was almost half a minute before the last of the herd had passed. The hind view of them charging and pushing each other, all trying to get the same path, reminded me more than anything of a scrum in a Rugby football match.

I saw my wounded bull again, reeling like a drunken man, but by the time I had picked myself up and got my rifle he had passed, and there were a number of small ones bringing up the rear who successfully blocked the view.

The sleeper with lion during these events had taken himself to the top of his tree, from which safe eminence he directed operations. The Kikuyu, however, had remained close by me during the first part of these proceedings and only made himself scarce when we found ourselves in the road of the herd. He shortly appeared, and we went back to the dead elephant, and the old man descended from his perch, but no sooner had he come down than a herd came rushing through the bamboos towards us and we ran again. They came up to the dead elephant and then returned.

I began to wonder how many herds there were around us and climbed up a tall tree to investigate. Owing to the thickness of the bamboos I could see nothing from there, but heard what I took to be the wounded elephant staggering and stumbling about a little way down the slope of the hill. I decided to investigate, but the sleeper with lion preferred to remain up his tree, and he did not come down again during the rest of the morning.

I crept towards the sounds down an elephant path in the bamboos and presently saw the back of the head and part of the body of what I took to be the wounded one.

I tried for the back of the ear, but could not get a clear shot; however he dropped to the shot and then there was a wild screaming and breaking of bamboos as a herd came rushing towards me. I hurriedly put another shot into the fallen elephant, and then scrambled back up the slope to the top of the hill, where the ground was level and one could move about better.

They appeared by the sounds to have reached the spot where the wounded elephant lay, and then moved off. I waited till all was quiet again and then returned to investigate. The wounded elephant was no longer there, but I heard bodies moving about in the bamboo but could not see more than a few yards, owing to its density. Close to where the elephant had been lying there was a sapling, and I clambered up this to try if I could see anything. When I reached a fork about ten feet up three female elephant appeared and passed and then returned, and stood about thirty yards below my tree with their trunks curling in the air, testing the wind. They moved backwards and forwards several times, and then passed out of sight, and I returned again to the dead elephant.

I then called for the porters I had left behind to come and cut it up, and while doing this we went back a little way and heard other elephant unconcernedly feeding at the bottom of the valley. The porters arrived after making détour to avoid them, and I sat down and made some cocoa, thinking that I would give the elephant time to clear off before following the wounded one.

After the operation of cutting up the elephant had been proceeding for about an hour, there was suddenly a wild rush, and trumpetings in the bamboo close at hand. We turned and fled, I leaving my cocoa on the ground. A herd rushed up close to the dead elephant and then returned back into the thicker bamboo. After all was quiet again we came back, all of us very jumpy by this time.

After finishing my cocoa I thought I would have another try to find the wounded elephant. My men tried to persuade me not to, and stood by the dead elephant howling to me to come back all the time, but it seemed a pity not to have another try. So I returned to the place at which the elephant had fallen, picked up the blood spoor, and began following it. Every now and then I heard some big body moving in the bamboos, and, when after going a little way, I heard elephant moving on both sides and in front at the same time, I got an attack of cold feet and returned to the dead elephant, where my men were shouting lustily for me.

Taking the fat and some meat we then started to make our way back, but on all sides we heard the cracking of bamboo from different herds grazing unconcernedly, as if nothing had occurred to disturb them. When we finally got through the ring of elephant and left the sounds behind us, we all breathed freely, as they had got on our nerves. We had run into elephant at about 6.30 or 7 o'clock in the morning, and they had been close round us on all sides from that time till we left at about 1 o'clock, although several shots had been fired, one elephant killed and another wounded, and they must have had our wind often enough.

I have never experienced or even heard of anything like it before or since, and, if a stranger had told me that anything of the kind had happened to him before this occurrence, I should have most certainly doubted his veracity. As a rule, one shot or one whiff of a human being is enough to stampede a herd or group of herds right out of a neighbourhood.

We made our way down the hill and back to my camp at the foot of the mountains. On the way one of the porters got lost, and after shouting for him for about half an hour we went on. Suddenly there was a loud clatter and rustling amongst the bamboo which made us all start, and the old sleeper with lions nearly jumped out of his skin. Someone said "Baboon," and we all laughed except the old man, who asked indignantly, "Who is afraid?"

We got back to camp just after sunset, and I sent a search party out along the foot of the hills with a lantern to look for the missing porter. They returned with him shortly; he had dropped his load, and his clothes were torn to ribbons. He said that he had missed us about an hour or so after we started back and had taken a lower path down the side of the hill, where he had come into another lot of elephant, and had run away from them, hence the loss of his load and his torn clothes.

It is difficult to combine the absorbing task of hunting elephant with a conscientious performance of one's work, and, if one tries to, the chances are one does both badly. In this case I was unable to devote another day to the following of the wounded elephant. "It was the two paths which defeated the old hyæna," said one of the Swahilis to console me for my disappointment, referring to a folk-lore story in which a hyæna came to the fork of two paths and could not make up his mind which to take. Finally his right legs tried to take the right-hand path and his left legs the left-hand one, and he split in two.

My survey work subsequently took me to the highest peak of this part of the range, and I was camped for two days at an altitude of about twelve thousand feet. I also crossed the high road back at the other end of the range, but I came across no more elephant, and I was too occupied with my work to be able to leave it and go off to hunt. Moreover, as we had just come to an end of the porters' food I had to hurry on to the Kikuyu villages at the foot of the range.

CHAPTER II

As it seldom falls to the lot of the white man in Africa to find an instructor of his own colour, he generally has to pick up a knowledge of bushcraft through long, and sometimes bitter, experience, with the help of the natives he is amongst. As the latter are seldom able to impart the information they possess, he must needs learn from them by observation and deduction. Some white men appear to have not only picked up what bushcraft they know from contact with natives, but also their sporting code from the same source. All is grist to the native mill, and he generally tries to entice his master into indiscriminate and senseless slaughter. He has no idea of the sporting instinct, as we know it, and only hunts with the idea of getting unlimited meat.

In tracking, however, he is often very proficient, but different tribes and different natives vary enormously in this respect, and it makes a great difference to the sportsman what sort of natives he first gets hold of.

There was an old man who engaged himself to me as a tracker in my early days, whose methods puzzled me for a long time. On finding a track he used generally to follow it back a few hundred yards and then branch off at right angles to it. It was only after he had been with me a month that I discovered his actions were not instigated by reasons so subtle that they were incomprehensible, but that he was an absolute duffer.

In British East Africa there appears to be an utter dearth of trackers. During three years of trekking in the country and constantly trying new natives, I never hit on a single one who was any use whatever. Even men who lived by hunting were nothing wonderful in their own forests, whilst once they left these they were perfectly useless. The latter, though, have one great point to commend them, and it is that they hunt in silence. They refrain from talking loudly and tread lightly and silently. Many of the best trackers amongst other tribes seem to imagine that all game is stone deaf. Nothing can induce them, as a rule, to keep their mouths shut, and many of them walk clumsily and noisily.

Often when I have been trekking along with a party of men or porters, I have turned to a boy orderly or gun-bearer and said, "Tell them to keep their mouths shut or else there will be no meat for them to-day." The individual so addressed generally turns and yells at the men behind him, expatiating on the virtues of silence at great length, and in a voice sufficiently loud to scare any game for miles round.

Perhaps it is, however, that each native thinks he himself possesses a soft and gentle voice and that it is only his fellows who are loud and raucous. As the Swahilis say, "A baboon sees not his own stern callosities, he only sees those of his fellows."

I was quietly fishing on the Loangwa River one afternoon when a Puku put his head out of the grass on the opposite bank, and then came down to drink at the river. To see a wild animal drink is a sufficiently rare sight to be worth watching. As a rule, they only drink at night or very early morning. This was in broad daylight, at 3.30 in the afternoon. Fortunately the native tracker with me did not see him at first. When he did he gave a long-drawn Oh! and then an Ah! followed by an Ogwe! all noises expressive of interest and astonishment, but which had the effect of sending the Puku back to cover before the completion of his drink.

In Nyasaland and North Eastern Rhodesia practically all the natives are fair trackers, and some are very good. Almost any man picked out at random from one's porters, soldiers, or servants would be better than the best tracker I have met with in British East Africa. At Fort Mlangeni there used to be a man whose speciality was sable. It really was marvellous the way he always managed to find them.

I was out with him one day and we found the old tracks of a bull, perhaps they were of the evening before.

He followed them a short way and then struck off and made for a little round hill, an underfeature to a range. Climbing this, he made another native with him sit down on one side of the hill and told him to watch the opposite slope. He then posted himself on the other side and we sat quietly and waited. We had been there perhaps an hour when along came a fine bull sable. He told me afterwards that it was the same as that of which we had seen the tracks. I had no means of verifying this, but I quite believe him, as he knew the hills and the sable and their ways upside down.

I was very fortunate in my trackers for the last two years I was in Nyasaland. I had three in constant use, whose names were Ulaya, Chimalambe and Matola. Ulaya was a real genius at tracking. In the early morning or the beginning of a track he was wonderful, but he soon got disheartened and bored, and then he was perfectly useless. He had none of that "infinite capacity for taking pains," most erroneous description of genius, which poor old Chimalambe possessed in his pig-headed, plodding way.

For the first hour or so Ulaya used to fly away with the track; he was practically never at fault and not a sign escaped him. If after that time the track was still old, he generally used to sit down and say it was no good, and nothing would induce him to take any further trouble over it. Chimalambe then took up the spooring and for hour after hour he would slowly and painfully worry it out, making frequent mistakes, losing the track, and returning to pick it up again, but he was prepared to go on in the same way all day. Meanwhile Ulaya used to follow with a bored, disinterested air; occasionally when the spoor was lost he used to point it out with a pained expression, but more often he sat down and watched Chimalambe muddle it out.

Matola was my orderly; he was neither the brilliant genius nor the pig-headed plodder, but just a sound, sensible fellow and a good soldier, as I will try to show later. When it came to close quarters with elephant, rhino, and buffalo it was always a case of "please step in front Private Matola," whilst Ulaya and Chimalambe used to dally behind to explain to each other how it really ought to be done.

In 1904 I trekked up to Lake Bangweolo with these three. I managed to get specimens of the black Lechwe, and hoped also to get Situtunga, but in this I was disappointed. I could not get any of the local natives nor my trackers to realise that I was serious in my desire to lead an amphibious existence in the swamps and spend a lot of time and trouble in the hope of getting this one animal. From their point of view, it must have seemed ridiculous. The flats were swarming with Sassaby and other game to be had for the shooting. To leave all this meat walking about, and court certain discomfort and every probability of disappointment in the swamps, on the very off chance of getting another kind of meat, must have appeared sheer madness to them.

Hence whenever I asked about Situtunga the natives replied that there was much meat on the plains and they did their best to put me off. It was not only because they thought of themselves and the meat they would miss, but also they thought that they would save me disappointment by feigning entire ignorance of Situtunga.

I took Ulaya out in a canoe in the swamps one day, but his pained and resigned look was so depressing that I never did it again. Without the whole-hearted assistance of the natives of the country, and Ulaya, who was the only one that knew their language, it was impossible to do much, and the ways into the swamp were difficult to find. After I had spent all the time I could spare and only just penetrated the fringe, we moved on northwards.

We crossed the Chambezi River, and here I got news of elephant. One day I started out at 5 A.M. from a place called Chimutu. After a round unproductive of any result we struck a village at about noon. As we had been a long détour in the bush I thought that it could not be so very far from my last night's camp, so sent back for it and then proceeded again.

We got back to this village in the evening, but there was no news of the camp, so I settled down to make myself as comfortable as possible under the circumstances.

The chief produced food for my men and I had my canteen with me. I got a mat from the village and spread it before a fire and brewed myself some cocoa. I also had a camp pie and some bread, so I proceeded to open the former.

It was in one of those tins that open with a key which rolls off a strip of tin. As so often happens with them, directly I started turning the key the strip of tin broke off flush, leaving nothing for the key to get hold of. It was then necessary to cut a tongue of tin to give the key a fresh bit to grip on, a proceeding somewhat damaging to one's hunting knife.

Having done this, I placed my knife on a tree stump by me and tried again. The new strip broke away, so I had to have recourse to the knife again. As I was cutting away I heard someone come quietly up behind me, and looking round, saw that it was Matola standing to attention. Having prepared a new strip I was putting the knife down again, when a hand came forward to hold it for me. Again the strip broke and the hand reappeared with a knife, but this time it was his knife, and not mine, which was blunted on the tin.

This quiet thoughtfulness often shown by the Bantu native is a very pleasing trait. The above incident reminded me of a time, when in Somaliland, I had asked a Somali to lend me his knife to cut something with, not a tin, but a bit of string or something which could not possibly have done any harm to it. The Somali did

BELGIAN POSTES IN THE LADO
The top picture shows the station of Yei and the bottom that at Loka.

not proffer his knife, but commenced to haggle with me as to what I should give him, if he allowed me to have the privilege of using it.

The Somalis are the most grasping natives it has been my misfortune to meet. In 1900 I was at Berbera with Captain Bruce, R.A., who was afterwards killed in that country. We were engaged in sending caravans up country. It was very hot, and we found the Somali extremely trying to the temper. When we were very upset we used to relieve our feelings by writing eulogia on the Somali character. The only one I can now remember anything of was one that began, "Courteous, brave, generous to a fault, the Somali, etc."

To continue, having successfully opened the tin and fed off its contents, I made myself comfortable for the night on my mat. Shortly afterwards I heard the cheery voices of my porters singing in the dark, and presently they appeared. Having resigned myself to spend an uncomfortable night, it was very pleasant to see the sudden and unexpected arrival of all the comforts of civilisation. As I sat on my mat watching everybody bustling round to minister to my comfort, I felt that my position was somewhat analogous to that of the slave-raiding ant with all his attendant slave ants waiting on him. One was putting up the camp table and chair, another the bed, a boy called the hyæna had got out a box of cigars, guessing that they would be the first thing I would want, another was preparing the coffee pot, Matola was getting out the rifle oil and cleaning material, others were putting up the tent.

It was late before we got fixed up, and then I had the dinner I so nearly missed.   Next morning we did not get the loads packed up and started till 8 o'clock.   After going two hours we found spoor of the night before. Fortunately there was water quite close, so leaving word for the porters to pitch camp there, we started off.

The spoor seemed fairly fresh at first, and got older in appearance as we proceeded.   This is caused by the difference in the effect on the spoor of the sun.   It was perhaps six hours old when we found it, but it had passed those six hours in the shade.   As the sun mounts up and gets stronger, spoor of the same age looks much older and drier.   Leaves dropped and grass and shoots crushed down or kicked up look quite fresh after lying all night in the cool air with the dew on them.   A few hours of sun, however, soon shrivels them up.

Many elephant had been about, and the grass was dry and the ground hard, so it required considerable discernment to hold our track amongst all the others.   As usual, Ulaya was very keen for the first hour or so, and worked out the spoor at a rapid pace.   After that he grew disheartened and bored, as we seemed to have rather lost than gained, and so for the rest of the day Matola came in for the lion's share of the work.

At one o'clock the wind came in puffs from different directions with distant thunder, a hopeless state of affairs when after elephant. The track was of three animals, a bull, cow, and young one. As we followed I noticed at one place that the bull had passed between two trees only about a yard apart at their bases, a circumstance from which I did not draw the deduction I should have done.

At four o'clock the spoor was still old, we had not halted since we had started eight hours before, and we were all rather done and had given up hope. We had just stopped by a tree which had been pulled down, and were feeling the leaves that had been dropped to see how dry they were, and I had half decided to abandon the hunt. At this moment one of the men who had gone forward a little whistled, and immediately everybody made themselves scarce.

The elephant were returning along their tracks. A young bull was leading; behind him I could see the ears of another, but not what sort of tusks it had.

The young bull walked straight towards me, but stopped twenty yards off and began pulling a tree down. I hoped that those behind would come up into view before he had finished, but the one behind him went off to one side and I could not see it clearly because of the branches.

Presently the small bull commenced coming towards me again; if I crossed to look at the other, I must give him my wind. This I decided to do, and ran across to the other one, hoping to see it and get a shot before the alarm was given. The small bull gave the alarm, and ran back to the second elephant, who pricked up its ears. I then saw that it was a female, but it had very big tusks for a female. I took a shot at her, but I was unsteady with my run and the whole day in the sun, and did not knock her over. She crossed, and I fired a couple more shots at her. At the same time a terrific trumpeting was heard from just behind.

I thought that I was all alone, but at this moment Matola appeared and said "Don't go that way, that is father and he is a Nyungwa (tuskless bull)." He had seen him whilst I had been engaged with the female. Matola had the most wonderful way of vanishing entirely and always appearing again when he was wanted.

We hurried after the female and the Galongwa (young bull) and the other men with me reappeared from behind trees and ant-hills in the most miraculous way. Presently they all fled again. The Galongwa was coming back on our wind. Father was screaming in one direction and the female had gone off in another. What made this youngster leave his mother and come straight back up the wind at us I cannot imagine, unless it was pure deviltry.

I did not want to shoot it, so got behind a tree as it came trotting up. Matola had vanished, as usual, whilst I saw Ulaya and Chimalambe running away for all they were worth. It struck me that it would be intensely amusing to see the Galongwa chase them, as he was going in their direction, and was just passing my tree.

However, I did not have the satisfaction of witnessing this hunt, as he pulled up sharp ten yards from my tree and turned on me, a contingency I had not expected. The only thing to do was to down him, and so I reluctantly fired at his head and dropped him. I went up in front of him, but he was not dead and commenced to get up again. I put another shot in his forehead, but it did not reach the brain, and the next moment it was I who was being chased, besides being defrauded of the sight I had looked forward to, of seeing fat Ulaya do the hundred at his best pace with the Galongwa after him.

I dodged sharply to my right, thinking that the elephant would pass, and I would get a side shot as he did so, but I tripped over a fallen tree, perhaps one he had pulled down earlier in the day. I went sprawling, dropping my rifle, and just managed to seize it by the muzzle as the elephant was about to tread on it. I then dived head foremost into the branches of the fallen tree.

I made frantic efforts to crawl through, but a stout branch resisted my progress, and at the same moment the Galongwa pushed in after me, and pushed me through the branches to the other side. Two drops of blood from his forehead fell on my shorts, one on the thigh and one on the knee. Instead of pushing me straight through in front of him, though, he kicked me sideways.

The impetus he gave me bent aside the stubborn branch, and the next moment I found myself crawling out on hands and knees on one side of the tree, with rifle still grasped by the muzzle, whilst the elephant was executing a dance and stamping up the ground the other side, five yards from me, evidently thinking that I was under his feet.

I quickly changed my rifle round and discharged it into his stern. It was the last cartridge in the rifle. Having fired, the rifle was taken out of my hands, and I found Matola, who had counted the shots, standing beside me, serving me the second rifle as a waiter might offer a dish. By some oversight it had not been loaded, and I had given strict orders that none of my men were ever to load or unload my rifles. Being a good soldier, Matola had not disobeyed this order, even under these extreme circumstances, but had gone the nearest to loading it he could. The breech was open, and he was holding the clip in position with his thumb just over the magazine. All I had to do was to press it down, as I took hold of the rifle, close the bolt, and I was ready to fire. The elephant was turning round, and I shot him in the brain, dropping him dead.

The story has taken a long time to tell, but of course it all happened in a moment. I think as an example of a combination of pluck, discipline, and presence of mind in a sudden emergency, the behaviour of Private Matola would be difficult to beat.

We returned to camp, arriving after dark. Ulaya and Chimalambe were full of the day's adventures, and told the story of how we had been chased by the Galongwa over and over again to an admiring audience. I noticed that Matola's name did not figure at all in their narration. A listener would have thought that Ulaya and Chimalambe took a prominent part in the day's proceedings, whilst Matola, if he had been present at all, had been a distant spectator. Matola, having cleaned the rifles, retired to sleep, and did not take part in the discussion.

About the third time they got to the point at which the elephant rushed up to them, I put my head out of my tent and asked if they had seen what happened. Of course they had, how absurd; were they not present ? "Well, you must have very good eyesight," I replied, " because after it was over Matola and I looked for you everywhere, and at last we thought that you must have run all the way back to camp."

It was rather mean of me, because they had not really run very far, and, neither of them having the second rifle, there was no real reason for them to stop. It annoyed me, however, that Matola, who had behaved so well, should be left completely out of it. Moreover, Matola's lack of interest in the matter might easily have been interpreted by those who had not been present as shame or chagrin at not having shared in the glorious doings of the others.

CHAPTER III

ABOUT RHINO

A RHINO is generally a very easily killed animal. If you can get him broadside on with a big bore he almost always sits down at once. Facing he is less easy to kill, and if moving, often a very difficult shot indeed.

In British East Africa, where he is plentiful and can be found in open country, there is nothing in killing a rhino. In Nyasaland and North Eastern Rhodesia, however, where he is more scarce and always found in thick grass or bush, he is really a very sporting animal to shoot. The natives there fear him more than any of the dangerous game, partly because he is really dangerous in their country, and partly because, owing to his scarcity, they have not grown accustomed to him. They have not had a chance to cultivate a sufficiency of that familiarity with him which breeds contempt. In the latter countries he seems to walk much farther and has to be generally tracked up all day like elephant, instead of being come upon by chance as in East Africa.

I have shot a good many rhinos in East Africa and in the Lado, when under the Belgians, during the ordinary course of trekking, either when in want of meat or because they came uncomfortably close to one's porters. Less often I have killed them to make up my license or because I thought the horns were good. However, I have never taken any interest in shooting them; it always appeared tame and uninteresting, with the exception of the few occasions when they came through my porters, in which case it was too disconcerting to be pleasant. In Nyasaland and North Eastern Rhodesia, however, the hunting of rhino was quite different, and killing one seemed a feat quite worthy of accomplishment. No doubt this was largely due to the difficulty in finding him.

Whilst hunting near Lake Bangweolo I followed one for the greater part of the day, and finally crept up, closely followed by the faithful Matola, within five yards of where he lay, heavily breathing in thick grass. Even then it was so thick that I could not see him properly, and bungled the shot, and he crashed off with a noise like an infuriated steam engine. We tracked him till dark, but did not come up with him again.

This particular rhino followed close to the edge of a grass fire for several miles. I have often read, and been told, of wild animals' fear of fire, but never myself noticed anything to corroborate this idea. In fact, rather the reverse. I have often put up game lying peacefully quite close to a bush fire. These grass fires are of yearly occurrence, and the game must be well accustomed to them.   It is only when surrounded by a fire ring that they lose their heads, and indeed this must be a very alarming occurrence, especially if there are hundreds of natives at the same time shouting from all sides.

In Nyasaland and North Eastern Rhodesia the elephant are often very bold at night, and after the harvest calmly walk into the villages, pull the roofs off the nkokwes, or grainstores, and help themselves to the maize cobs.   When this happens, or they have been very persistent in entering the plantations at night before harvest time, the natives make large fires in their fields, and spend the night shouting and beating drums to frighten them away.   Even this often does not deter them, and they visit the fields all the same.   When, however, they are kept off, I fancy the shouting and the drumming have more effect than the fires.

To return to the rhino, after the case with which one has shot him in other places, it seems odd to read the pages of one's diary and notice the long tracks after him, the excitement when he commenced nibbling thorn, which showed that he would soon lie up, and the trouble one took to bring him to bag in Nyasaland.   As I have said, he travels much farther there and in North Eastern Rhodesia, and one has to follow him for long distances.   As often as not one picks up his night's tracks at a water hole.   He often goes tremendous distances to and from water, and perhaps his grazing grounds are seven to ten miles from the place at which he drank.

In 1905 I was looking for elephant in the vicinity of
Fort Manning. I had no thought of rhino, but was
anxious to shoot the elephant on my new license, as the
old one had just expired. I was following an old elephant track across a dambo, or open grassy flat, when
I met a fresh spoor crossing at right angles. The grass
was very thick, and the track showed as a beaten down
lane of grass, but it was not immediately apparent what
had caused it, as the grass was too thick under foot for
any spoor to be seen. I turned up the track for a few
yards, and then bent down, parting the grass so as to see
the tracks under it; I had a few Angoni with me,
but they were some yards behind on the old track.

Before my investigation was complete, I was left in
little doubt as to the owner of the tracks, as I heard the
engine-like puffs of a pair of rhinos close at hand breaking down the grass. Evidently they had been lying
up close to the spot at which I had hit their track and
had now got my wind.

The next moment a great behorned head burst out
of the grass a yard or two from me. I had no time to
think, but just shoved my mannlicher in his face and
pulled the trigger. He swerved, but I do not know
what became of him after that, as at the same moment
I became aware of the second one bearing down on me
from my left. There was no time to reload, so I tried
to jump out of his path, with the usual result in thick
stuff, that one tripped up.

He kicked me in passing, and then, with a celerity surprising in so ponderous a creature, he whipped round,
and the next moment I felt myself soaring up skywards.
I must have gone some height, as my men on the elephant track said that they saw me over the grass, which
was ten or twelve feet high.   However, they are so very
unreliable in their statements that it would be quite
enough for them, if they heard what had happened, to
imagine that they had seen it.   Anyhow I fell heavily
on my shoulder blades, the best place on which it is
possible to fall, partly by accident and partly from practice in tumbling in the gymnasium.

On looking up I saw the wrinkled stern of the rhino
disappearing in the grass, at which I said to myself,
hurrah! for I thought that he might continue the
onslaught.   Somehow I had the idea that he had been
playing battledore and shuttlecock with me for some
time, but when I came to think it over I could only
remember going up once.   Possibly being kicked first
gave me this impression.

Next I looked round for my rifle and espied it on the
ground a little way off.   I picked it up and examined it
to see if it had been injured.   While doing this I suddenly
found that a finger nail had been torn off and was bleed-
ing.   Directly I discovered it, it became very painful.

Whilst examining this injury some of my men appeared and uttered cries of horror.   I could not make
out why they were so concerned till I glanced at my

RHINO

Trotting past my caravan in the Lake Rudolph country.

chest and saw that my shirt had been ripped open and was covered with blood whilst there was a tremendous gash in the left side of my chest, just over the spot in which the heart is popularly supposed to be situated. Small bits of mincemeat were also lying about on my chest and shirt.

This was a new problem to think out; I was in rather a dazed state, so I left the consideration of my finger and began to consider my chest. I felt nothing at all except a rather numb sensation. It struck me that it must have pierced my lungs; I would soon know if this was the case, as I would be spitting blood. I waited a short time and nothing of the sort occurred, so I concluded that the lungs were all right.

Just at this moment there was a rustle in the grass; it appeared that the rhino had come back. One of my men helped me up and another put my rifle in my hands, and I awaited them, but presently we heard them tearing off again.

I was only about thirty miles from Fort Manning, and so I sent off a native to tell the other fellow there, Captain Mostyn, that I had met with an accident. Then I started back to the nearest village. After walking some time I felt faint, and so my natives cut a pole and trussed me on to it, fastening me with my putties. This was, however, so very uncomfortable that I had myself untrussed again and performed the rest of the journey on foot.

Having arrived at the village, I sent off for my camp, which was at another village, and sat down to await it patiently. After a few hours it turned up, and I dressed my wound as best I could and lay down. I calculated the time the news would take to reach Fort Manning and the distance out and came to the conclusion that Mostyn could not possibly send help before about noon next day.

I had a sleepless night till, about two in the morning, I heard voices, and then the stockaded door of the zariba being pulled down, and presently Mostyn appeared. He said that a native had arrived at sunset with the information that the white man had killed a rhino, to which he replied "Good." The information was repeated and the native seemed in a greater state of agitation than the news seemed to warrant. Then he said that a rhino had killed the white man.

This was quite a different thing. He was so agitated that Mostyn could not get out of him what had really happened, and so, thinking there must have been an accident, he got the Indian Hospital assistant, and the two set out. They covered some twenty to twenty-four miles in the dark on a bad track between 7 P.M. and 2 A.M., a very fine bit of marching, especially as they did not know for certain where I was and had to knock up villages on the way and ask for news.

The Indian, whose name was Ghulam Mohamed, was so done up when he arrived that I told him he had better rest till morning, but he insisted on attending to me at once, and stitched up the wound most skilfully. He was a first-class doctor, and the job could not have been done better, for three weeks later I was well enough, though still in bandages, to start on a 240-mile march, which I performed in ten days.

I think the country in which I have seen most rhino was that about the south and southeast of the Ithanga Mountains in British East Africa in 1907 — I add the date, as game in a locality differs often from year to year; I was surveying there and quite frequently met about ten whilst trekking along.

One evening, coming home in the dark from sketching, I almost walked right into one standing quite motionless. Another day in thick thorn two rushed up the path we were following. The porters threw down their loads and dived into the thorn right and left, whilst the rhino passed right up the line without damaging anybody or anything, although they must have passed within a few yards of thirty men in all.

I find in my Diary for 5th November, 1907, "Came near to Maboloni Hill. Saw seven rhino grazing near the hill and steered the caravan safely past, leaving four about a hundred yards up wind and three about four hundred yards down wind." The next day I find "Met twelve rhino all in our immediate path. Two were lying down close to where I wanted to set up the plane table. After great difficulty they were persuaded to move, and I began setting up the table when another appeared. Leaving here we came on a party of three lying down near a river bed, one bull, a cow, and a calf. I watched the bull making advances to the cow, which were not favourably received, as she got up and prodded him away. They lay down again, and then suddenly all three jumped up and rushed off; I do not know what alarmed them. Going up a narrow spur I met one, and steering round to avoid him came suddenly on two others lying just over the edge of the ridge.

"The cook went down to the river and said that he saw eleven and had to get up a tree."

On the next day I met two rhino on a spur, the farthest one of which started walking towards us. It was very comical to see the man carrying my plane table, who had only seen the latter, hurriedly put down his load and bolt from the farther one right into the arms of the nearer one, which he had not noticed.

On the day following this I was out early after lion, and hearing a noise behind me, saw a female rhino and small calf racing towards me, so I hurriedly got up a tree and let them pass.

Later in the day when trekking along with my porters the same thing happened again; a female and calf appeared out of some thorn and raced after us. Loads were hurled down and there was a general *sauve qui peut*, but they turned off again when they reached the loads and dashed back into the thorn.

Just after that I saw one with an immensely long posterior horn, much longer than the anterior, standing under a tree in our road. I went forward and shouted and whistled till it moved on, and then we proceeded, only to find another about a hundred yards down wind of where we wished to pass.

We were so bored with making constant détours to avoid these animals that we waited till he had grazed on about another 150 yards and then made a slight détour up wind so as to pass about 350 yards from him. When the leading part of the caravan got up wind of him, he went on peacefully grazing, but when about half had passed, he suddenly got our wind.

Instead of going away he came towards us. I had shot my two rhinos for the year before we met any of the above-mentioned animals, and so I had been trying to avoid them as much as possible. I now stationed myself in front of the caravan, hoping that he would turn off, but he came steadily on.

When he got to about 80 yards distant he still had his head up. I fired, missing him on purpose, hoping that it would frighten him, but it seemed only to encourage him, as he then put down his head and came in earnest, wavering slightly from side to side to keep the wind. His head and horns covered his heart and brain, so at 50 yards I put a shot into the side of his shoulder, and at 30 yards I put another, which fortunately disabled his right shoulder so that he stumbled. He picked himself up and came on again, but now slowly, and the danger was past, as he was disabled and could be easily dodged.

As I was surveying, and not shooting, and had no intention of shooting at a rhino, having shot all I was allowed, I had only three cartridges in my rifle, which I had now fired. My pockets were so full of pencils, notebooks, etc., that I had handed over all my cartridges to a Mkamba guide, who could be found nowhere.

I called out for more cartridges, and meanwhile the rhino came slowly stumping on and I retreated before him. He had just reached the spot at which the porters had thrown down their loads, and I expected to see him begin to amuse himself with them, when my dog, who had only been a spectator so far, thought it about time to join in. He rushed barking at the rhino and the beast turned round and round, facing him, while the dog rushed round and round trying to get at his heels.

Whilst this diversion was in progress the head man discovered the Mkamba guide up a tree, secured the cartridge bag, and came running up with it. Getting a convenient side shot, I finished the rhino. We cut off the horns with a hatchet to hand in at the next government station we passed, and continued our march.

I have only mentioned a few of the rhino incidents which happened when I was sketching in that country.

It must be remembered that we were not looking for them, but rather trying to avoid them, as they delayed our marches and hampered my work.

In the same country a rhino suddenly started up and came rushing towards us. When we shouted at him he thought better of it and turned round to make off, disclosing the fact that he had no tail. This seemed to tickle the porters very much, and as he disappeared with his small stump, in place of a tail, sticking straight up, he was sped on his way with shouts of derision. They seemed to imagine that his lack of a tail made it specially impertinent of him to have attempted to come for us.

Once when I was sketching on a hilltop to the south of Embu where lion had been heard for several nights, after finishing my work, I sent my men back to camp with the instruments, and myself made a détour, hoping to meet a lion. Whilst passing under a tree, I noticed a rhino coming slowly towards me. The tree was easily climbable, and my first impulse was to get up and take some photographs, but then I remembered that I had no camera. So I moved a little out of his path and watched him. He came slowly up to the tree and lay down underneath it. I regretted very much the absence of my camera; one could have taken a splendid illustrated interview from a perch on the tree.

Rhino, in spite of the thickness of their skin, appear very subject to sores. There are almost always large

sores on the chest or stomach, and often enormous festering sores on other parts of the body. They frequently, too, are cut and gashed about, these being probably caused by fighting together. A female I shot once,
amongst other gashes, had one vertical one extending
from the centre of the back almost to the stomach.
That is to say, it went nearly halfway round her body.
It seems almost inconceivable that such a wound could
have been inflicted with a prod of another's horn, and
yet I cannot think of any other cause to which it could
be attributed.

When I was hunting in the Lado Enclave in 1908, I
found the white or square-lipped rhinoceros very common about Wadelai and close to the Nile for some days
to the north. Although I never looked for them or
followed up their spoor, I was constantly meeting them.
As it was a grass country, they could not be seen so
easily as in a country such as that described above, so
they must have been even more numerous than they
appeared. It was curious that on no single occasion
did my Baganda porters recognise what they were when
they saw them in the grass, but invariably said, "There
is an elephant." The same held good with the spoor,
as they always said that it was elephant spoor.

I suppose that as they are not met with in Uganda
proper they had never seen them before. One would
have thought that after seeing them once or twice and
cutting them up, they would have learnt to distinguish

them from elephant and that they must have noticed how different the spoor was from that of the latter. This was the more remarkable in that they were really very good at detecting and spooring elephant. I have always noticed that, however good a native may be at hunting and tracking the game he knows, directly he meets something new to him he is not only hopeless, but makes the most wild and impossible shots. One would think a trained tracker would be too cunning to go so hopelessly wide of the mark as they do. The tracks of a waterbuck and hartebeest are often very similar, but a good Nyasaland tracker would never be in error about the two.

I have never heard a tracker on meeting a spoor new to him say, "This is a spoor I have never seen before." He always finds a name for it amongst the animals he knows and generally chooses one that has no likeness to it at all. The first time I saw the spoor of Lesser Kudu I at once recognised it from its likeness to that of the Greater Kudu, but my tracker, who had come with me from Nyasaland, where there are none of these animals, said "Mpala." Yet I cannot pretend to anything like the knowledge or the ability of these men, which proves that they hunt more by instinct than anything else, and do not use their heads.

CHAPTER IV

THE best elephant country I have struck was the Southern Lado Enclave and the southeastern edge of the Welle district at a time just after the stations of Wadelai and Dufile had been abandoned by the Belgians. The number of elephant there then was marvellous, but the country was unhealthy and the travelling difficult, although the actual hunting was generally easy. Later the district became so overrun with poachers that the majority of the bulls were either shot out or moved westwards.

In 1908 my friend, Captain R. S. Hart, and myself, having been fortunate enough to obtain permits from Brussels, took out our licenses at Mahagi, and then separated to hunt. Had we known more about the country we should have come earlier in the year; as it was, we wasted much time in Uganda before we could find shootable bulls, and reached the Congo as the grass was beginning to get long. Shortly afterwards the heavy rains broke, filling up the swamps and making the rivers often impassable.

Hart proceeded northwards from Mahagi, whilst

I came down the Nile, bringing with me a large canoe I had bought on Lake Albert. The first day after I commenced operations and had been trekking all day, I came across a small herd of females and young, and so leaving them, returned to my camp on the Nile at 5 P.M. I had started out at 5 A.M. on three boiled eggs, and on my return found that the cook had been unable to buy anything, so I had to dine off a soup tablet, some rice, and beans.

If I had known how poverty-stricken the country was, I should have brought some tinned food; as it was, the greater part of the time I was in the enclave I was hard up for meat, and my porters for food. Although there were plenty of elephant, small game was very scarce, and I seldom had the time to hunt it, and moreover was always loath to fire for fear of disturbing any elephant that might be in the neighbourhood.

Next day we managed to buy a few chickens from the Uganda bank and then trekked inland and saw no fresh spoor, but got information of elephant at a place about 25 miles farther on. We trekked on to this place, and found that the news was old, but I managed to shoot a buffalo, which was very fortunate, as I was able to exchange the meat for flour from the villages for my porters.

There was so little cultivation in the country and the natives were so unwilling to sell any food, that it was only by this exchange of meat for flour that we were able to feed our porters at all. Now and then we were able to buy a pound or two for salt, but the natives generally treated the rest of our trade goods with supreme indifference, and always declared that they had no food to sell.

When an elephant or rhino was shot we had to guard the carcass till the people had brought us flour. Generally, however, they turned up in such quantities for the meat that this was impossible, and we then had to cut off all the meat we could secure and take it on with us to the next village or group of villages, and there change it for flour. As nearly every village was in a state of war with the adjoining one, the people in the next village who were eager for meat would have been unable to get any from the carcass.

All the natives were ready to help find elephant and bring in news, as they were unable to kill elephant for themselves. The Madi and Lugware, amongst whom we did most of our hunting, are extremely timorous about elephant, and seldom seem to kill them with spears as other tribes do. Once an elephant had been killed they took no further interest in finding them till the bones had been picked clean, every scrap of meat had been devoured, and moreover till they had had sufficient time to recover from their gorge.

So it used to be our practice to cut out the tusks as quickly as possible, and at once move off to the next hostile village, where the people would still be suffering from meat hunger and ready to bring in news of elephant and help one in finding them.

On the day following the shooting of the buffalo we started at sunrise and reached a village about 8 miles on. Here we were told that the whole village had gone on to the next one to join in an elephant hunt. The people here were Alurs, who were not so timorous with elephant as the Madi.

We went on to the next village and found the chief, who was the only able-bodied man left in the village. He said that the elephant had been seen close by and that he would take me to the place. I wanted to take on my camp part of the way, but as he said there was no water ahead, I left it, and took one of the head men on with me. We marched for two hours, and then came across the old site of a village. As this was a pretty certain indication of the presence of water I looked round and found a water hole, and so sent the head man back to fetch the camp on to this site.

We then went on, the chief, myself, and a guide I had obtained from the Uganda side. After going for another two hours without seeing any sign of spoor, the chief suddenly sat down and said that it was very far to the place and that we had better go back. I said that if it was very near four hours ago, it could hardly be very far now, and anyhow I would go on. The chief said that we could not possibly reach the place that day. However, I persisted, and we started off again.

After going for a bit we came on elephant spoor, which we followed, and it led us to the identical place where I had seen the small herd of females and young close to the Nile some days before. The spoor then took us up the valley in long grass, not real elephant grass, but only about breast high, with isolated higher stalks. By the tracks it would appear that it was an enormous herd we were following.

Suddenly we heard numbers of natives yelling and shouting from the side of the valley; this was the elephant hunting party. Apparently they had headed them off, and this had the effect of driving the whole herd back on us. In another moment the grass all round us was seething with elephant. There must have been about two or three hundred split up into little herds of twenty or thirty animals in each.

They were charging up and down in the grass on all sides, alarmed by the shouting from the hillside and not being quite certain which way to go. There were no big tuskers, but plenty of males of about 50 and 40 pounds.

It was the first time I had been in the middle of a big herd with an unrestricted license, and I am afraid that I rather let myself go. Fresh herds came surging up out of the grass, and I had an exciting five minutes. When they went off I ran after them, till the last one I fired at disappeared, and racing after him, I heard him gurgling on the ground in front of me. I was exhausted after my long day and running, and threw myself down at a muddy pool of water to drink, thinking that he was done for. When I got up he had gone and I never caught up with him again.

I then returned to make certain of any still breathing and count the bag. There were in all eight, most of them shot from my original position, but three I killed whilst running after them. I had been shooting very well that day, and I believe the only one I hit and did not get was the one who fell down and afterwards got up again and went off. At any rate no other blood spoor was found after a minute search by myself and many natives. There was such a seething mass of elephant, however, and I had to fire so quickly, that it is very difficult to tell for certain.

The native hunting party then descended with loud shouts and cries and fell on the meat whilst I set off back to my camp. I was met by porters with the lantern before it got dark, and arrived shortly after sunset. As I had been going for over twelve hours without food or rest, I was glad to tumble into my chair and start to work on dinner, which consisted of some excellent buffalo tail soup, buffalo marrow and heart.

Next day we moved to the scene of the disgusting slaughter and I sent for my canoe, which I had left at my first camp on the Nile, as it was impossible for my porters to carry all the ivory. The canoe proved an absolute godsend later, as I should not have been able to proceed without it.

Just at present, however, it was not of much use, as I had been unable to obtain any paddles with it and the two natives I had hired from the Uganda bank to manipulate it now insisted on returning, as they said that they would have to go back through hostile country if they came on any farther with me. With no paddles and no natives who understood its management, it was little use, so I had to proceed down the Nile by short marches, sending back the porters after each march to fetch the remaining loads.

In this slow and stately way we continued towards Wadelai, at which place I had promised to meet Hart on a certain day, while I occupied the time of enforced delay in hunting. I killed an elephant near a village and was lucky enough to be able to exchange some of the meat for a paddle, and then made two of my porters learn how to manage the canoe.

Two days later, while waiting for the canoe to be brought down, I followed a herd of elephant, and they took me past the spot at which the last elephant had been killed. This is a thing I have frequently noticed when after elephant, — how often their spoor leads you past an old skull or the spot at which one has been killed. This happens so often that I think it must be more than coincidence. Very possibly they are

really following some old path or elephant track which
has been habitually used by elephant, and which they
recognise, whilst it appears to us just like any other
part of the bush if the path is overgrown.

By this time I should have been at Wadelai, so I
sent on my head man with a letter to Hart, telling him
of the predicament I was in and asking him to send
some of his porters to help me.   The man returned and
told me that Hart was not at Wadelai, and so I did not
hurry unnecessarily.   It afterwards appeared that the
man, with extraordinary ingenuity, had crossed the river
and made his way to British Wadelai, at which place he
naturally did not find Hart, nor could he have been expected to, since we left him inland of us.   Meanwhile
Hart had been waiting for me at Belgian Wadelai as
agreed, and as I did not turn up he left the day before
I arrived.

When we got within ten miles of the place we met fresh
spoor of two big elephant on the path, and so I sent the
camp on whilst I followed the spoor.   It led us inland
and then into the immense tall grass and reeds which
covered some low, wet, and slushy country on the banks
of the Arua River.   After going for an hour or two
through water and mud we heard them the other
side of a belt of very thick grass.

We came through this and into shorter grass the
other side, and I got a glimpse of one of them 150 yards
off, as I was on a little rise.   I made my way to a tree

sixty or seventy yards nearer, from which place I could have got a good shot. Just as I was about to fire, I saw for the first time a second elephant beyond him. As he tossed up his head for a moment I caught a glimpse of his tusks, which were a bigger pair than the first. I could not see him well enough to fire at him from where I was, so decided to get nearer. Between me and the first elephant was a shallow dip so that if I advanced at all, I must advance almost up to where he stood, as I would pass out of sight directly I left the higher ground near my tree.

I descended the dip, and had to move very slowly as the grass was long and dead, and rustled as I moved. I got up to within 25 yards of the first elephant, and could only see him imperfectly through the tall grass, while the second I could not see at all from my new position.

The first one was breaking up a small tree, and I advanced again, but this time he heard me moving in the grass and suddenly whipped round and stood listening with ears outspread. In another moment he would have been off, so I had to fire hurriedly through the grass, although I could not see well. I gave him both barrels of my .450, and he crashed off into the thick grass and reeds

I followed his spoor, which after a few hundred yards began to show a lot of blood. He passed through very thick reeds, and I followed till I heard a noise in front.

Climbing up a convenient ant-hill high enough to enable me to get a view over the tall grass, I saw an elephant standing under a tree in front. He immediately
moved on and downwards, and passed out of sight, and
then I heard a rustling noise which I could not make out
for a moment, but I suddenly realised what it was. It
was water splashing; he must have descended into a
stream, perhaps the river that I had heard was between
me and Wadelai.

There was not a moment to lose, so I slid down my
ant-hill and raced as hard as I could down the spoor.
I came out suddenly on a dense belt of reed, through
which the path led as a narrow lane. The next moment
I was on the river bank with a dense mass of reed lean-
ing well out over the water on either hand and prohibit-
ing a view up or down stream; just below me in midstream was not only my elephant, but a herd of about
25 in number, all bulls, slowly making their way across
the stream, which was coming down in flood.

Never had there been such a chance, as I could see
the steep bank on the opposite side of the crossing, up
which they must clamber one by one, exposing their
heads to a vital shot as they did so. It is the sort of
situation I have dreamed of often enough, but never
hoped to realise. Bringing up the rear was my wounded
elephant, presenting only a stern shot to me.

Now I come to think of it, I undoubtedly ought to
have waited till the leading elephant began climbing

the opposite bank, which was not more than 40 yards away.   What I did was to blaze into the stern of my wounded one.   He immediately turned round and began coming back towards me, whilst the whole herd stopped and marked time in midstream.   The elephant turning round gave me a chance of firing into his chest, which I did without delay.

I have said that, although on the river bank, I was in a narrow lane of tall reeds.   I could see across the river and the landing on the other side clearly enough, but owing to the reeds at the water's edge, reaching far out over the water, I could not see either up or down stream, but only the narrow strip of water straight across the river.

The stream was coming down with great force, and as I fired into the elephant's chest he seemed to be carried down-stream by the current and passed out of sight behind the reeds.   The same thing had happened to the whole herd; whilst marking time in midstream they had lost ground and been taken a few yards down-stream, which was sufficient to take them out of my sight, although I could hear them not 20 yards off.

I rushed back through the reeds and charged into the belt another 10 or 15 yards down-stream and fought and pushed my way through till I stood on the edge of the steep bank; but here my position was worse than before.   I could hear the elephant just below; the nearest could not have been more than ten yards or

ELEPHANT IN THICK BUSH

He has just become uneasy and is testing the wind.

TAME ANIMALS AT KAGULU. [LADO ENCLAVE]

From left to right they are : female waterbuck, male waterbuck, and Uganda kob.

at most fifteen yards from me, but so dense was the mass of reeds growing outwards from the bank over the water that I could not see a square inch of the water at my feet, far less the elephant.

It seemed the most maddening thing possible; if I could only find an open space, I might shoot any number; and here I was, absolutely defeated by a mass of reeds. The sounds passed down-stream, and I crashed through the reeds again and ran down the bank about 40 yards before making another dive into the reeds. I rushed in with such impetus that I fell down a steep bank, ramming the muzzle of my rifle into the soft earth as I fell.

After scrambling out again I had to run back along my tracks till I found the porter with my second rifle who had dallied behind. I seized this and dashed down the elephant path again, which followed along outside the reed belt, and after going for about a couple of hundred yards there was a break in the reeds, trampled by elephant. It was at a bend of the river, and I came out on to the bank and got a clear view of several hundred yards up-stream. There was not a sign of any elephant, not even the wounded one, nothing but the muddy river frothing down in flood.

I then returned to the crossing and waded in to see if there was any sign of the wounded one. The stream was tremendously strong, and I had to move very carefully. When I reached the edge of the reeds and could

look around the corner, the river was up above my
waist. To my relief I saw the side of the elephant
rising as a little island about a foot above the water.
I managed to reach it, almost neck deep, and climb on
to it, but the head was below water and the stream was
too muddy to be able to see the tusks; I could only
ascertain what they were like by feeling them.

As I knelt on him he moved; I thought for the
moment that he had come to life again; the next moment
I realised what had happened. The river had risen
another few inches, which had just floated him off the
bottom, and I was commencing to float down-stream on
top of him.

I hurriedly left him, and tried to reach the shore
again, but the stream was so strong now that I could
make no headway against it, and would certainly have
been carried down if one of the local natives, who had
accompanied me, had not reached out to me the end
of his long spear whilst he himself was standing in shal-
lower water and holding on to the reeds. With this
help I regained the bank, leaving my elephant majesti-
cally sailing down-stream. The next thing was how
to recapture the elephant. I had visions of him sailing out into the Nile or being eaten by crocs whilst his
tusks sank to the bottom and were lost forever.

We hurried back down the river to fetch ropes and
assistance, but there was no telling where he might land
up, and the banks were so thick that it might be al-

most impossible to locate him. Also I thought that if the natives got hold of him they would cut off all the meat in the water and let the skull and tusks sink to the bottom, as these bones did not interest them at all.

An hour or two's walk brought us to a big village on the river bank. It was here that the path to Wadelai crossed, and I heard with a certain amount of satisfaction that all my loads had passed over to the other bank in safety, although it puzzled me to imagine how this had been accomplished, as the river was coming down at a prodigious rate, and was reported to be over a man's head at the middle of the ford.

When I said that I wanted to cross, a few of the villagers tested the ford by entering the river a couple of hundred yards up-stream, and proceeding diagonally across with a funny little skipping and bobbing motion. They held their hands straight above their heads, and as they neared the centre each skip carried them about 20 yards down-stream to one yard across. At one time their heads disappeared under water, and only their hands were above the level of the river.

On arriving at the other side they ran up the bank again, and throwing themselves into the water came swimming across like fishes and pronounced the ford practicable. Then taking my rifles, ammunition, field glasses, and camera they held them high above their heads and bobbed and skipped across the river with them. Although the men carrying them were at one time wholly under water my goods reached the other side safely and dry.

I learnt that all my loads had been taken across the river in this wonderful way, but the water had not been quite so high then. Only one load had got a little wet containing trade goods which were soon dried again.

We got into the old Belgian station at 3 P.M., where I collected my porters, and taking some rope set out to find the truant elephant. We followed up the river bank on the Wadelai side as, owing to the bend of the river, it was not so far up this side. To my relief we met a native carrying a bit of trunk; the elephant had come to shore then and the natives had lost no time in nosing it out. Presently we heard the sound of many voices, which guided us to the spot, and we found a number of people in the water busily cutting up the carcass.

The first precaution I took was to moor the tusks to the bank so that there should be no danger of their being washed down-stream or falling to the bottom of the river after being cut out. The porters worked well, and by shortly after sunset the tusks were out, and we started back again. We blundered along in the dark and overshot the station, as there were no stars out to guide us. Finally we ran into a village and got a native to put us on the path.

We did not get in until about 11 o'clock at night, however, and I found dinner ready for me in the old Belgian mess, which was in quite good repair. I had been on the move since sunrise and been twice wet through and had my things dry on me. So it was with some relief that I got a change, and then had a feed and came to anchor.

CHAPTER V

AFTER the events described in the last chapter I took a day's rest at Wadelai. The old Belgian station was built on an elevated site overlooking the river, which at this spot narrows to·about 200 yards broad and is quite picturesque, as its banks are hilly. The houses were of brick, thatched, and still in quite good repair, although when I passed a few months later most of the roofs had fallen in.

I spent the afternoon in the canoe on the river, more by way of coaching the crew than anything else. We were returning slowly up-stream, past a few hippo who were disporting themselves about a hundred yards or more away. One of them raised his head and shoulders out of the water and looked steadily in our direction; it is probable that he did not really see us, as these animals are very short-sighted, but that he had our wind.

After a prolonged stare he dived under water, and then we saw a V-shaped ripple on the surface slowly approaching the canoe, showing that he was swimming under water towards us. As the ripple approached nearer and nearer, I felt that he should be discouraged, and got my rifle ready, expecting every moment to see his head pop up. However, nothing of the sort occurred, but the ominous ripple still approached till there was a tremendous crash, the end of the canoe was raised a yard in the air by some unseen agency and then fell heavily to the water again. As the canoe rolled I clutched my rifle and the sides of the canoe, expecting every moment to be deposited in the river.

The bottom of the boat filled with water, and I anxiously looked for the yawning hole which I felt sure must exist, thinking that the only thing to do would be to sit on it by way of caulking it. However, no hole could be seen and it dawned on me at last that all the water had come over the end or the sides. The great massive log of wood which we called a canoe had successfully resisted the shock.

It was really a fine canoe, the best I have ever seen on the Nile, and its carrying capacity appeared unlimited. We started by loading it gingerly with six or seven loads, but before we had done with it, it was often carrying half a ton.

Meanwhile the V-shaped ripple was slowly retreating. The old hippo, having had his little joke, was going off without even offering a shot. I did indeed get a glimpse of a broad back just after the shock, but I was then too busy clutching on to the sides to attempt a shot.

Next day we proceeded down-stream again. The

ivory and extra loads, such as a supply of food we had obtained from the pleasant Chief Ongwech of Wadelai, were put in the canoe, while the porters proceeded by land.

After my unpleasant experience of the day before I felt nervous about trusting my ivory to the tender mercies of any hippo who might feel facetiously inclined. So I made a buoy for the canoe and fixed it by a rope to the stern or bow (we never knew which end was which, as they were both square) and also decided to travel in it myself.

Ongwech gave me two men, one to go in the canoe and one with the porters so that we might both arrive at the same place.   For below Wadelai the river enters into a sudd region traversed by a few channels.   Once one gets out from the shore there is no telling where any channel may lead to; it may come out on one bank of the river or the other, or it may proceed for miles with dense sudd between it and the shore, or end in a *cul de sac*.

So we proceeded down-stream in the canoe, a very sumptuous way of travelling after the continuous walking here and in Uganda, till we arrived at the appointed place for camp.   It was a little village on the shore, the first spot at which our thin winding channel reached terra firma.

The village was the first Madi one we had struck. I went up to it and could only find one man, on whom I sprung the only phrase of Bangala I knew well at that time, which was "Are there elephant?" He stared at me in doubt for some time, and I repeated my stock phrase several times in different tones and in the most ingratiating way I could.

At last I could see a dawn of intelligence glimmering over his features, and he spoke rapidly in a strange language, pointing inland. This was enough for me; I returned to the canoe and got my bandolier and rifle. Then, telling the canoe men to await the arrival of the porters and choosing a site for the camp, I invested my new-found friend with the bandolier and pointed in the same direction as he had, repeating elephant, elephant. He explained something at great length, and he appeared to be reluctant to go, as he pointed to the village several times, but I pushed him on, repeating elephant at intervals and making signs that he would get a reward of calico.

So we set out and made for the foot of the hills, and here he pointed to the spoor of elephant which had been eating the crops the night before. This was all I wanted, so I took up the trail and started, following it into the hills. They had been far since their night's feed, and the day was hot but the going was good. The grass was short and the country gently rolling, whilst at intervals we saw bushes bowed down with heavy loads of a black berry the size, shape, and colour of a blackheart cherry and with the taste and consistency of an enormous

bilberry.   This fruit is called uba by the Madi.   With
these we refreshed ourselves from time to time till
at about three o'clock, as we were on the side of a
rolling slope, my companion pointed out a small
herd of elephant about 800 or 1000 yards distant on
the other side, I being too engrossed in the tracks to
notice.

Having pointed these out to me, he considered his
part of the programme complete and, with a satisfied
sigh, he resigned himself to rest under a tree whilst I
carried out the only part which remained.

This was the first experience I had of the Madi, and
later I was astonished again and again not only at their
timidity with elephant, but their absolute ignorance of
the beasts who were found in such numbers in the vicinity of their villages.   Even the most timorous native
knows, as a rule, that an elephant is not dangerous at
800 yards with the wind right.   Moreover, he knows
enough about them to pose to the uninitiated as quite
brave, as he realises exactly how far he can go in complete safety.

Not so the Madi, however;   I beckoned him to come
on, as there was no telling where the elephant might
lead me to, and his services would be useful later in
finding the best way back, but he absolutely refused
to come a step farther.

So I proceeded after the elephant, and presently got
to an ant-hill about 50 yards from them.   The biggest

was hardly worth shooting, but there was always the food problem of the porters to be faced, so I decided to shoot him, which I did and he fell on his side. The others, instead of moving off, stood by him. They had useless tusks, and I did not want to fire again, so waited some five or ten minutes, but they would not go.

I thought if I shouted they would go, but it seemed so ridiculous to shout all by oneself that I refrained. Then I bethought me of my guide; he would be an objective to shout at, so I descended from the eminence of my little ant-hill and started shouting for him. I looked back, and the elephants were still standing, and I thought what a much more penetrating voice a native has, and that I must get my guide to do some real shouting.

After going about a hundred yards back, I looked round and saw the elephant moving off, and then I saw my guide cautiously descending the slope towards me. As the elephant had gone, there was no real reason why he should not be with me, and moreover I wanted him on the return journey, so I walked to meet him, as he came down the slope a few yards at a time listening and reconnoitring carefully.

When he was about forty yards from me the fallen elephant emitted a dying gurgle and he stood still, meditating retreat. I shouted at him again, and he evidently thought that I was in urgent need of more ammunition, as he had taken off the bandolier and held it out invitingly to me.   Presently he advanced cautiously again, but just as he reached me, the elephant, now some three or four hundred yards behind me, emitted another terrific gurgle, so thrusting the bandolier into my hands he fled up the hill again.

I then returned to the elephant and cut off the tail, and presently my friend appeared, reconnoitring again in the distance.   He saw me standing by the elephant, and so at last prevailed on himself to come near; but he would not come right up to it.

We then returned to the village, and found that the porters had arrived, camp was pitched, and better still, dinner was ready.   It was after sunset, so I knew that no natives were likely to cut up the meat that night, as my guide would be much too timorous to take them back in the dark.

Having suffered from the difficulties of obtaining porters' food, I thought that I would make certain of laying in a goodly store of flour next day, to harbour up against a run of blank days when no elephant, and hence no food, would be forthcoming.

So I sent word to all the villages within a reasonable distance to say that we were going to make a cordon round the elephant next day and that no one would be allowed inside this ring to cut up the meat unless they first paid a fee in flour.   Therefore they were to accompany me to the spot with their flour, and it would be taken over by my porters and they would then be allowed access to the carcass.

Early next morning I captured my guide, to make certain that he did not go off and show the place where the elephant lay. Soon an immense crowd collected round my tent—Men, women, and children, and even little tots of about seven years of age, carrying gourds of flour as tribute, and baskets in which to place the meat. Spears and knives were being sharpened in all directions, whilst the crowd mustered. I marshalled the porters with sacks ready for the reception of the flour, and then with my guide of the day before I led the way, followed by many hundred people of all sexes and ages, carrying the most varied assortment of weapons and receptacles.

I felt so pleased with myself as I reviewed my army and thought of the goodly stock of flour that was presently to be laid up against a rainy day.

Now to find one's way about in a trackless bush is a peculiarly difficult and rare feat for a white man to be able to accomplish. Moreover, this was a very uniformly rolling country, of shallow valleys and gentle slopes, all exactly alike, with no general feature to recognise about any of them. In one of the several hundred little bottoms within a ten miles' radius of camp lay my dead elephant.

On my return journey the day before I had taken careful note of the route. I did not then know how wonderfully ignorant of the country just round their villages were these Madi. I afterwards discovered that they seldom dared go more than a mile or two from their homes for an exaggerated fear of the bravery of the next section of the tribe and their ferocious conduct should they meet with any stranger. At the time I had only wondered at the circuitous route by which my guide led me back.

We started out by the same route, and if I had been solely responsible for leading the way, I should probably have been able to find the way back to the dead elephant by following religiously our return march of the day before, on which I had noted numbers of small landmarks, such as the holes in the ground, peculiar shaped bushes, branching elephant tracks, etc.

After proceeding about a mile, my guide branched off from the old track. I pointed to the way we had returned, but he spoke with great volubility and pointed with his spear. Anyhow, I thought, it was a roundabout way by which we had returned; it was his country and he had known it all his life, and who was I to dispute his knowledge? He had probably thought of a better and shorter way.

So we proceeded with our immense following and walked and walked and walked, but not a sign or vestige of the dead elephant did we see. The women and children carrying the flour and baskets presently got tired and returned home. Then the men began

going off in different directions, and at last the guide
sat down and said he was defeated. We then wandered
over these hills and inspected numberless little bottoms
each exactly like the other.

At last I decided it was no good making blind shots,
so I set back to strike the track by which we had returned the day before near the village. Seldom have
I felt so small and humiliated. We must have been
miles beyond the spot at which the elephant had been
killed, for it was late afternoon when we reached the
old track, and then I decided to return and await the
morrow.

In the evening, some of my porters who had left me
came in with the news that they had found the elephant and secured the tusks. I had not the face to
try again to exchange the meat for flour, but nevertheless they brought me in a certain amount of their own
accord, whilst my porters brought in sixteen loads of
meat. These I sent over in the canoe, to the Uganda
side of the river, where they were exchanged for flour.

While waiting for the return of the canoe, I had another hunt after elephant on the hills behind. After
walking about a couple of hours, I came on the tracks
of an immense herd. They were spread over a front-
age of half a mile or more, grazing as they went. As
the wind was across their line of advance, from right to
left, I followed them, always keeping to the left hand
one of any branching tracks till I at last caught up the

extreme left of the line. I could only see females and young, and they were moving at a fair pace. Following on, I came up close to a little detached group on the left consisting of four elephants, two female and two young. As they tarried behind the rest of the line, I had to wait till they moved on, and being quite close to them, about 30 to 40 yards, I had a good opportunity of observing them. One of the two females had most peculiar and abnormally shaped tusks. Whilst watching these, I suddenly heard loud talking from down wind. The African native is a noisy talker, and the Madi are no exception, rather the reverse, as they have a most peculiar way of lowering the voice and expelling the last word of each sentence with prodigious emphasis.

The elephant heard them and trotted off. I waited to see who the natives were, and found that they were just two men walking along a pathway having a friendly conversation; they had no idea that there were any elephants in the neighbourhood, and it was most extraordinarily bad luck that they should arrive at this exact spot just at this moment, especially as natives so seldom leave their villages in this part to go so far.

On following on, I found that the whole herd had taken alarm and moved off. I had a tremendously long journey after them, and at last came up with them again in the afternoon. They were moving down the centre of a marshy valley in a solid phalanx, and there must have been 500 of them closely pressed together. I followed parallel to them, slipping and slithering about in the mud and having to run every now and again to keep up with them. Out of all that big herd I could not see one animal worth the shooting.

After proceeding some time, I perceived an ant-hill which they must pass, and ran to reach this place before they approached, so as to have a good look at them once again as they passed. The phalanx marched past me, the nearest about 150 yards distant. So closely pressed together were they that it was only possible to see those nearest me, but there was nothing worth a shot amongst these.

As they reached abreast of me, two females had a quarrel, and one pursued the other out of the herd, prodding her with her tusks. They both came towards the ant-hill and stopped at about 50 yards' distance. This was too much for the two Baganda porters who were with me, and they turned tail and fled, making a prodigious noise, squelching and splashing through the mud and pools of water. The two elephants pricked up their ears, and the one which had been prodding the other came straight towards me at a brisk trot, evidently to see what it was.

Had I been in Uganda I should have had to fire in the air or lie down and hope for the best. In the Congo, however, it is no crime to shoot a female, so as she came close up to me I dropped her. At this the whole herd turned off and stampeded through the swamp. At the same time I caught a glimpse of another enormous herd at the top of the rise on the other side of the valley, a herd which must have contained a couple of hundred animals, so at one and the same time something like 700 elephant were in sight.

A very remarkable coincidence was that the female who had run at me in this way, out of all that vast herd, was the identical one I had noticed so specially earlier in the day and whose abnormally shaped tusks were unmistakable.

As this herd had been alarmed now for the second time, it was no good following it any farther, and indeed there appeared to be nothing worth shooting in it. This being the case, I thought perhaps I might come up with the second herd I had seen, but they too had got the alarm, and I never succeeded in coming up with them. However, in their tracks I found two rhino peacefully slumbering, and shot them both. I was now far from camp and did not get back till long after dark.

I have said that we were extensively fitted out with trade goods, but that the natives did not care much about them. This was only the case when we tried to purchase anything, such as chickens or sheep, but they were quite pleased to receive our goods for nothing. The only thing we possessed that they really seemed to hanker after was salt, and this was especially the case when we got farther inland. There they would con-

IN THE NILE SWAMPS NORTH OF WADELAI

The upper picture shows two natives crossing on a raft made of ambatch poles, and
the lower a floating island of sudd.

sider a spoonful of salt quite a fit remuneration for a
day's work after elephant, whereas they would hardly
be grateful for 10 or 20 times its value in beads or
calico.

Amongst our varied goods was a bundle of frock and
tail coats, articles that we were told were indispensable
in Congo travelling. These were really very fine
goods, some of them were second hand, but some were
new with the tickets on. If I remember rightly, we
bought them at an average price of 3 rupees or 4/ –
each in Kampala. It seems rather unfair that the
Uganda native should only have to pay 4/ – for a
frock coat whilst we have to pay seven guineas.

These gifts were reserved for great occasions, some
chief who had been very useful, or some native who
had brought exceptional news about elephant. Practically everybody in the interior was completely naked.
When a clothesless savage was invested with a long-
tailed morning coat, he presented the most comical
appearance. He looked so very well dressed when
walking away from one, whereas, when coming towards
one it only accentuated his nakedness.

However, fashions in the bush are often as fastidious in
their way as those in civilised countries, and even these
royal presents did not always meet with unqualified ap-
proval. One Madi had really been very useful in bringing in news, and so when I parted from him to trek
onwards, I produced a magnificent kind of redingote.

He immediately donned it and pirouetted round, looking over his shoulder to judge the effect of the back view.   He hit the long tails once or twice with the back of his hand and appeared dissatisfied with the fit.   I asked him what was wrong, and he said that he did not like these, flapping the tails.   It appeared that for ordinary bush wear long tails were not being worn, so I told him that he could cut them off if he did not like them.   "No," he said, "that would not be the same"; he wanted a coat exactly the same as the one I was wearing.   Now in this matter I could not oblige him, as it was the only coat I had, except a rough one for evening wear, and in its way it was quite unique.

Hunting day after day through bush and thorns soon tears one's clothes to pieces.   I had been very hard up for a coat shortly before leaving Nairobi, and had got hold of some heather-coloured, very strong kind of khaki material which struck me as peculiarly suited in colour and texture to hunting.   As I was on trek at the time and was not able to be measured, I sent the material in to a Goanese tailor with an old khaki uniform jacket as a pattern.   While giving explicit instructions as to the number and position of pockets and manner of buttoning, I trusted to the aforesaid khaki jacket for general size and shape.

Unfortunately, however, this same khaki jacket was very old and very shrunk, whilst the frayed edges further took away from its length.   The result was that when I received the coat in question it fitted more like an Eton jacket than anything else, whilst the sleeves were halfway up the forearms. As the material was strong and durable, and there was no one to criticise my appearance, I was undaunted by these defects and took it into general use. It was this coat, then, that was envied by my native guide, and I had a good mind to let him have it and myself wear the tail coat. The only thing that dissuaded me was that the latter was really too dressy, and moreover had no loops for cartridges or convenient side pockets.

Another great feature of our trade goods were some gaudily coloured bandana handkerchiefs that Hart had obtained. They were most attractive looking, but the first man to whom I gave one returned shortly to know how he was to wear it. It was not large enough to meet round the waist, and I was confronted with the problem of how to dress a naked man in one pocket handkerchief. After profound thought I devised a way. The handkerchief was knotted round the neck and hung in a graceful fold over the left shoulder. Later on the sight of men ornamented in this way grew quite common in the Lugware country, and Hart and myself always recognised at once from this any village which the other had visited.

My cook, a coast Swahili, took great pleasure in extolling our wares. I remember him once trying to entice a man to sell a chicken by a display of the goods we had to offer. "A beautiful silk handkerchief," he said, producing one of these bandanas. The man pawed it over and did not think he cared for it. "A chain of the purest gold," said the cook, bringing out a penny brass chain. The man fingered it some time and did not seem pleased with it. The cook held up his hands in supplication, and besought Allah to note the ignorance and depravity of these savages, who could not appreciate the rarity and worth of such costly articles as these.

The same native whom I decorated with the tail coat was carrying my big bore for me one day, whilst I had the mannlicher. I wounded an elephant, and raced after it downhill. It was one of a small herd, and they performed a semicircle on the hillside amongst a lot of scattered bush clumps, finishing up by going down wind. I raced round the corner of a clump of bushes almost into their arms, as it were, for they had suddenly brought up standing. An irate female rushed out at me, having got my wind. There was no time to get away, and indeed I was out of breath, so I steadied her with a shot in the forehead, at which she turned and rejoined the herd, and they went off again.

The native, who was not as yet tail-coated, had left me hurriedly when this little incident happened. To make up for his conduct, when we came a little later on the wounded elephant standing, I saw him twice raise the big bore, shut his eyes, give a tremendous pull on the trigger and a prodigious jump at the same time. As the safety catch was fortunately on, his efforts met with no response from the rifle, and I finished the animal with my mannlicher.

He was inordinately pleased and proud of himself, and told me that it was he who had shot the elephant. When I denied this, he was most indignant, and stoutly maintained that I had to thank him alone for obtaining this elephant. His face of astonishment and chagrin was a picture when I opened the breech and showed him the two cartridges comfortably lying in their chambers unexploded.

To exonerate this man from a charge of showing an excess of bravery I must explain that he was partly Alur and not wholly Madi.

CHAPTER VI

THE buffalo, perhaps above all big game, loves the true, wild, uninhabited country. He loves not man, his habitations, his fields, or anything to do with him. In North Eastern Rhodesia and Portuguese East Africa I found him very wary, and moreover in these countries it was excessively hard to pick a good bull out of a herd, owing to the length of the grass they lived in.

After the long track up, one would, time after time, come on them lying down in the grass for their midday rest, with one or more cows standing up as sentries. The horns of the latter would be visible, but however one might manœuvre it would be impossible to see a bull without giving the alarm to the sentinels. Once the alarm was given there was a general stampede, and in the rush and confusion the odds were very much against being able to see or pick out a good bull. They appeared to be much more wary in those countries than in East Africa or the Lado, where I have often seen them staring interestedly at one, or even coming a little nearer to have a better look.

On two occasions in the former countries I have been

following buffalo when a honey guide has attached himself to my party, and owing to the incessant twittering given the alarm to the herd. I do not ever remember such an occurrence when after buffalo in other parts, but I have several times been close up to elephant accompanied by a honey guide and they have not taken the alarm from it. Perhaps if they were on the alert, they would do so, but before being alarmed elephant are generally very dense and deaf.

I see that Colonel Roosevelt has assigned to me the statement that I consider buffalo the least dangerous of the five dangerous African animals, lion, elephant, rhino, leopard, and buffalo, a statement I certainly made, but with certain qualifying remarks which rather alter the point of view. The question as to which is the most dangerous game animal is always being asked and answered in different ways, but it has so many aspects, and the conditions are so varied that it is impossible to answer it definitely without many saving clauses.

In the case I refer to I stated that, judging by the cases of death and maulings with which I was personally acquainted, I would put down the risks run in the following order; lion, elephant, rhino, leopard, and buffalo. That is to say, that I have known or heard of more men being killed or mauled by lion than I have by elephant, more by elephant than by rhino, and so on. Thus one who visited the same countries as I have and shot under the same conditions would probably take his risks in that proportion. However, I went on to explain that since the extermination of buffalo by rinderpest, there were two factors which tended to keep his average down, one was his scarcity and the other that in many countries he was considered royal game and so, not being hunted, the hunter did not put himself in the way of being mauled by him.

During the last few years he has become more numerous, and in most countries the restrictions on shooting him have been modified or removed, with the result that he has once more come to the fore as a dangerous animal.   Since writing about him in the " Game of East Africa," there have been numbers of cases of buffalo maulings.   Judging by the same standard as before, and counting only the last few years, he would perhaps come first, but on the other hand I have not been in a good lion country during these years.

The question is really like asking which is most dangerous, steeplechasing or motor racing. A jockey would perhaps say that the former and an employé at Brooklands that the latter was most dangerous.   A lighthouse keeper would not be in much danger of losing his life in either of these pursuits.

Elephant shooting is so apart from all other things that it is impossible really to draw a comparison. With the lion and the buffalo we can lay down a few general rules.   Neither the lion nor the buffalo, unless the lion is a man-eater on the prowl, is generally dangerous unwounded. If wounded, both of them will probably make off for thick cover. However, there is a possibility of the lion charging when hit.

Both animals are very dangerous to follow when wounded, the more dangerous the thicker the cover. If you get within 20 yards or so of them, under these conditions, the chances are that they will charge, and the nearer you get to them the greater the chance that they will do so. However, both of them will as likely as not break away again before you get within this distance. They will both have the advantage of being able to hear or see you coming whilst themselves remaining motionless. The lion will be the harder to detect as he will probably be crouching and completely invisible. On the other hand, the buffalo will be the harder to stop of the two.

In a country like British East Africa you will only be allowed to shoot one buffalo a year, but there is no limit to the number of lions you may shoot. On the other hand, you will perhaps have less difficulty in finding your one buffalo than your first lion.

Finally, it is impossible to say which is really most dangerous, and it depends a lot on the carefulness or recklessness of the hunter. Personally I am more afraid of the buffalo, because I have not yet been mauled by him. The closest thing I had with one was when I shot one charging with my muzzle touching his chest.

Once I was out hoping to get a buck or two, to eke out my porters' rations, at a time when we were very hard up for food.   We had done a trek that morning and I was just going for an evening stroll round camp with only soft-nosed cartridges.   I was with my gun-bearer Tengeneza, and we were on an open plain beside a stream.   Suddenly we saw the top of a black back coming up from the dip of the stream towards us.   I sat down on the plain behind a tuft of grass which would hardly have given shelter to a rabbit, whilst Tengeneza knelt beside me.

Presently the owner of the black back loomed into sight, an enormous old solitary buffalo, strolling towards us.   He was coming so dead on that it was difficult to get a good shot, but finally I took aim at the side of the shoulder and fired.   He immediately put down his head and came straight towards us.   There was nothing to aim at but his massive skull, and I put my second barrel into that.   I found out afterwards that the soft-nosed bullet did not penetrate more than the horny boss.

At this he snorted and looked round and then trotted to a position about twenty yards to our left and stamped the ground and looked from left to right.   Tengeneza put my mannlicher into my hand and I gave him a shot in the shoulder; at this he turned round and again came towards us, whilst I put another ineffectual shot in.   If he had gone on past us another ten yards, he must have had our wind.

Meanwhile Tengeneza had reloaded the big bore, which by the way was very old and worn, and not a hard hitter, and exchanged it for my mannlicher as coolly as possible. The buffalo now came trotting across our front, still looking for us, whilst I put a shot in his right side, and then as he passed, another oblique one behind the shoulder. He looked round again, only now rather staggered, and I took the mannlicher and put another oblique shot in, which finally brought him down.

Directly he was down I went to examine his eyes, as from his not having seen two figures at twenty yards on the open plain, I could only assume that he was stone blind. I found that his eyes were perfectly sound, and how he did not see us whilst I fired seven shots and exchanged rifles three times I cannot imagine. At every shot he snorted and looked round, and every moment I expected to see him come tearing at us. My generous thought during these moments was, "I hope he takes Tengeneza first, as it will give me a chance of putting a point blank shot into his side."

Tengeneza was one of Neumann's donkey men. He was afterwards a porter on the East African Survey. My first acquaintance with him was when I was starting from the Ithanga Mountains down the bank of the Tana. He had been sent from another party to me with a letter and arrived just as we were breaking up camp. As all my porters had loads I gave him my water bottle and cartridge bag to carry.   On the morning's march I wounded a lion.   He showed such intelligent interest in following up the spoor, so unlike the usual professional porter, and was so cool and collected when we suddenly came on it in thick thorn, that I made him into a gunbearer from that moment.

Since then he has trekked with me over a considerable part of East Africa, through Uganda, in the Lado Enclave, and through Abyssinia, and he has always been staunch and reliable, as the above incident will show. Most *bona fide* gunbearers would have either fired or cut and run under similar circumstances, but Tengeneza was only a porter.

It would seem as if the northern buffalo were more dangerous than those of the south.   I refer to the Cape buffalo in both cases.   I do not remember hearing of any accidents occurring with buffalo in either Portuguese East Africa or North Eastern Rhodesia, and certainly the ones I shot in those countries never showed any fight.   I omit Nyasaland, as the buffalo was preserved there whilst I was in that country.   Selous too did not consider the buffalo a very dangerous animal, and in the old days when thousands of buffaloes were shot in South Africa fatalities were very few.

In the north, however, I have heard of numbers of accidents occurring in British East Africa, Uganda, and the Sudan, with the same buffalo, the Cape buffalo, although in some cases it was not definitely proved which

species of buffalo it was. Also in the north I have
seen time after time that impudent stare, and the coming nearer to have a better look which I do not remember in the south, although the sentinels would of course
stare till they had made out what you were, and then
they were off like lightning.

The Abyssinians have a great respect for the buffalo,
and used, I believe, to count the killing of a buffalo as
equal to that of six men in their awards for valour.
Their buffalo is of course the Abyssinian buffalo, which
bears a smaller head than the Cape one.

I brought a very fine Cape buffalo head through
Abyssinia, from south to north, which I had shot on
the way up. Everybody we passed on the road used
to stop and turn round and stare at it as it was carried
along on a porter's head. They were greatly astonished
at its size, and one Abyssinian offered to exchange it for
his mule.

The safest and easiest way I have ever heard of
shooting buffalo was that practised by some Abyssinian
hunters. There is an oasis called by the Borana
"Gamra," which I discovered in the desert south of
Abyssinia. It consists of a pool of water welling out
of the sand. There is no other water for many miles
in every direction, and the game come from very far to
drink at this spot at night.

A party of Abyssinian hunters had made a stockade
on a little patch of dry ground in the middle of the pool,

inside which to await game. The bones of lion, buffalo, and Oryx lying all round testified to the success of their manœuvre.

Towards the end of 1911 there was an outbreak of what was said to be rinderpest, which swept down the east bank of the Nile north of Lake Albert. About Nimule and Gondokoro the natives lost 80 or 90 per cent of their cattle. At the same time quantities of buffalo collected at the north end of Uganda between Gondokoro and Mongalla, and probably hundreds died in quite a small area.

Where all the buffalo collected from is not known, but for a few days there was a great number, and the district was dotted with dead carcasses. Then they disappeared; the natives said that they had collected in a great herd, and all trekked off towards Abyssinia. At the beginning of 1912, however, buffalo were observed to be in their old haunts again, though probably in reduced numbers, so these collected together must have broken up again.

Of late years there has been a lot of hair-splitting in the subdivision of buffalo into countless different varieties judged by differences in shape or structure of the horns. I do not pretend to have scientifically studied the subject, but any practical naturalist who has observed and shot buffalo will agree that in any herd of buffalo there are many different shapes of horns, and that moreover the appearance differs enormously according to the age of its possessor. When one reads that the length of the smooth tips of the horns is indicative of one variety, the extreme flatness of the basal portion of another, shorter tips another, massive bosses, tips rapidly diminishing in diameter, tips long and tapering and so on and so forth, each distinctive of a variety, one becomes a little sceptical if such characteristics really do denote different varieties. Not only are all the characteristics above displayed in the buffaloes of one herd but a single old buffalo may have, at different times of its life, answered to all or nearly all these descriptions. He starts with the smooth horns, which gradually get more corrugated at the bosses. They then become horns with long, smooth tips; later the coruscations reach farther up the horn and the bosses become more massive, whilst the points are long and tapering. Later he will, by fighting or digging up salt earth, blunt, wear down, and shorten the tips till they are rapidly diminishing in diameter, and finally, if he lives long enough, or fights incessantly enough, he will wear the bosses of his horns smooth and flat.

I admit that horns are as a rule wonderfully good indications of varieties and species, as is instanced by the varieties of grant and hartebeest, which can usually be detected by their horns alone. However, in the case of the buffalo, any such deductions should be based on a great mass of evidence, that is to say, numbers of horns from each area suspected of producing a variety.

Perhaps amongst all the hollow-horned ruminants the buffalo is most variable in the shape of the horns of individuals and of the same individual at different times of its existence.

Again the case of the points turning upwards, downwards, inwards or outwards is also adduced as typical of varieties. With an animal who knocks his horns about so much as a buffalo, I hold that some small deviations in the direction of the points are due to accidents of youth. A slight dent or chip at the tip, when the horn is growing, will often tend to make it take a slightly different direction, although I admit that any great variation in any direction from the normal is unlikely to have been caused to both horns identically.

The Dinkas usually have a pet, and perhaps half sacred, bull in every kraal. This animal, from the time it is a calf, is treated quite differently from all others. It is tied up in a special place, especially looked after and fed, and is the playmate of the children. It can be recognised at a glance, as the tip of one horn grows downward and the other upward. This growth is caused by cutting or shaving off the underside of one horn and the upper side of the other when it is a calf.

Similarly, I take it, in a buffalo a chip or bruise on the horn tips in early life would materially affect the subsequent growth of the horn. Also a buffalo given from an early age to dig up earth for salt, or perhaps one

A SHADY CAMP

In the background is my tent and in the foreground a number of loads, including water-barrels, bags of porters' food, trade goods, and the skull of a pugnacious buffalo, described in this chapter.

living in a locality with especially hard soil would have materially blunted and shortened horns.

Perhaps the critic might say that all buffalo living in a given locality would be affected equally by such a consideration, but such is not the case. Apart from the buffalo, the African ruminant that is in the habit of blunting its horns to the greatest extent is the roan. In the same herd I have shot a roan with long, tapering tips and one with horns perhaps six inches shorter than they would have been if allowed to grow naturally, — horns tapering almost like a sable's, and horns blunted to a stump.

The females and young of buffalo are, as amongst most game animals, lighter coloured than the adult male. This is not so noticeable with the Cape Buffalo as it is with the Congo, in which species the young are of quite a reddish colour whilst only the old bulls show up as black.

The buffalo is perhaps more dependent on water than any other game animal, save those types which are more or less amphibious, viz., Lechwe and Situtunga. He is seldom found far from water, and when the sun is hot often drinks several times during the day.

Nearly all game seem to object to the smell of the human being much more than the sight. As said above, the buffalo will often stare in an interested way on seeing one. When he finally decides to go off he will perhaps only go a short distance and then wheel round again to have another look. This seems to be especially the case in the north.

Whilst following elephant spoor in the Lado once, through a bamboo country, I met a herd of buffalo walking towards me. I was unwilling to make a noise for fear that the elephant might be near, and for the same reason I did not wish to stampede the buffalo up the elephants' tracks, as they often make a tremendous noise stampeding, especially in bamboo. So I waited to one side of the track, and when the leading ones came level with me, I showed myself, hoping that they would go off to a flank.

However, after having gazed at me for a bit, they stampeded back up the elephant track in a leisurely way. After proceeding a few hundred yards I found them grazing, this time a little to one side of the track. I waved my arms at them, but they only stood and stared, and it was not till I got well within the hundred yards that they went off again. Not far on, I met them again for the third time, but this time they went off to one side and left the elephant track. On the other hand, if they smell one, they generally stampede in earnest and sometimes even the smell of one's tracks is enough to set them off.

I believe that the sense of smell is in much more direct connection with the brain than the sense of sight. Even with us human beings, who have lost this sense to a great extent, there is nothing like a scent to suddenly and vividly recall forgotten memories. A sound and sight will appear familiar but the mind will generally have to grope after what it recalls, whilst with a scent the memory is an instantaneous flash. Perhaps this, then, is the reason why the duller-witted beast responds so much more quickly, and is so much more affected by the sudden, noxious smell of the human being than he is by his sight.

CHAPTER VII

IN most parts of tropical Africa the year is divided into a dry and a wet season. During the dry season the land is parched, the tall grass dies and is burnt, and the bush fires shrivel up the leaves of the trees. The air is full of dust and ashes, the sun shines in a cloudless sky, and long marches have to be made between water-holes, which as often as not contain nothing but foul mud.

At the beginning of the rains all is changed, the trees put out fresh leaves, green grass springs up everywhere, at first not long enough to be a hindrance, and the air is cooled by the first showers. As the rains continue, however, the grass grows up rank and tall, all low-lying country turns into swamp, through which the traveller has to wade ankle or knee deep in mud, sometimes for hours at a stretch, and the numerous rivers and water-courses in flood form serious obstacles to progress. This splashing through slippery mud is most fatiguing and exasperating, besides being conducive to fever, rheumatism, and ruination of boot leather. One of the most unpleasant treks I have made was down the Nile bank in the Lado Enclave at the end of a very wet year.

Every few miles one had to cross a broad swamp, and as often as not, on arriving at the current or stream which fed it, one would find, if there had been heavy rain during the last day or two, that it was too deep to ford, and one must raft all one's things across.

I was coming down from Mount Wati to Dufile, which station then had been abandoned by the Belgians only a few years back. On reaching the Koshi River I found that it was in flood. The local natives produced an ambatch raft and after two and a half hours' work everything was got safely across. We then marched on for three hours and rested, and then did another hour, which brought us to an enormous swamp in our path, lying in a flat-bottomed valley filled with water and reeds.

We started crossing at 2 P. M., and after two hours of slipping and struggling in the water and mud, sometimes chest deep, and sometimes only knee deep, we had the satisfaction of seeing the solid, dry bank of the other side only a few hundred yards off. In another ten minutes, I thought, the wretched porters who had been going all day and who had been wallowing through miles of mud without being able to put down their loads, would be able to have a rest.

However, at this moment we suddenly struck the current or channel of the original watercourse which supplied the swamp, and it was over one's head. I called a halt and they had to stand with their loads on their heads, waist deep in water, whilst I reconnoitred up and down to see if I could find a fordable place. The men carrying tusks had the laugh over their fellows, as they were able to stand their burdens up on end in the water.

I tried in several places, but without result; once I suddenly slipped into deep water and sank like a plummet, and only managed to pull myself up again by clutching at the reeds. I never made out the reason for this, as I did not come up after reaching the bottom; perhaps the water bulged out my open shirt and acted on the principle of the parachute reversed. Meanwhile, the sun sank inexorably; now there was only another hour of sunlight left and two hours of swamp behind us if we were to retrace our steps to the bank we had come from.

Whilst wondering what to do we heard the sound of a drum from the hill above us; there was evidently a village there. It was no good shouting, as the people were so timid and suspicious of strangers that it would only have driven them away. They appeared always in constant fear of attack till their fears were allayed. As nearly every village was at that time hostile to its neighbour, we found it almost impossible to get any accurate information about the people ahead, or the route, and generally had to go blindly on in the direction in which one wished to go. Moreover, on suddenly appearing in a new village, there was always the uncertainty of how one would be greeted. Sometimes, every soul in the village would fly into the bush. At other times, the women would go and the men remain and be just sulky, refusing to do anything for one; occasionally they would be most friendly. They were always friendly in the long run, but it sometimes took a few days to accomplish this result.

I was the only one amongst my whole party who could swim, so the alternatives which offered were, that I should swim across and try to get help, or that we should all return. As the porters were chiefly affected, I put it to them, "Shall we go back and camp the other side and have all this crossing to do again to-morrow, or shall I leave you here and see if I can get help?"

They one and all decided on the latter, so I took off all my clothes, excepting a thin vest, swam across, and made my way up the opposite hill in the direction from which the drumbeats had seemed to come. Presently I saw two men walking along; they had not seen me, so I followed them quietly till we came in sight of a village, and then called to them. They stared for a bit and commenced to run.

At any rate, it would be a difficult business to rush into a strange and possibly hostile village and make the natives bustle out immediately to help one out of a predicament, especially when only knowing a few words of a language, which they might or might not also know. It seemed almost impossible that I would be able to prevail on them to bring help to my unfortunate porters before dark. The native is usually so slow and wants to talk such a lot first, and now every minute was of importance. Moreover, one cannot be said to be quite at one's best when making a first appearance in a new society practically naked. I called again to the two men, and they seemed half inclined to stop, so I hurried on and entered the zariba of the village just behind them. There were several men standing about, and fortunately I saw a log of ambatch lying on the ground, so I pointed to it and trotted out the few words of Bangala I then knew. "Porters, big water, presents, calico." I then jostled the man I took to be the chief out of the village and pointed towards the swamp, and in five minutes I was on my way back with twenty or so men and ambatch enough for a raft.

We reached my porters just after sunset and got everything across the intervening space of deep water, which only proved to be about twenty yards wide, before it was quite dark. The villagers played up well, and it was very lucky that they were a willing and intelligent lot.

I took good care after this experience to obtain some ambatch of my own, as soon as I reached a spot where it was procurable, and after that always trekked about with sufficient to make an emergency raft. The ambatch is a kind of thorn tree which grows in water or swamp. Its wood is a sort of pith and so light that what appears to be a great baulk of wood can be balanced on one finger.

One reads in the boys' story books that the hunter, when he comes to a river, cuts down trees and makes a raft on the spot. In Africa any wood that I have tried, freshly cut in this way, immediately sinks to the bottom or floats under water. Fallen and dead trees are eaten by white ants or burnt in the annual bush fires, and so the chances are that there is no dead or dry timber available.

I used to carry eleven poles of ambatch, two of which were cut in half. This made a load for one porter. When we came to an unfordable stream, if the current was not too swift, we used to lash these into a raft with the porters' sticks as crosspieces. The nine full length logs were lashed together at the base, whilst the four halves were built up in a platform at one end, as in the diagrams.

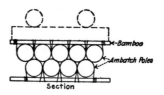

Section

This would just take one load high and dry out of the water lashed on to the platform, or one porter lying along the raft, with the water lapping over him. The raft is propelled by a man swimming behind. The reason that the load is lashed on the forward end and not the middle is that the swimmer rests his hands, and part of his weight, on the rear end, which counter-balances the load.

Naturally, crossing the loads one by one was a very slow process, and if the river were at all wide, lasted

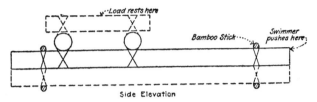

Side Elevation

most of the day, as at each crossing the raft would be taken by the current to a point on the opposite bank several hundred yards down-stream of its starting point.   It would then have to be taken out, carried up-stream again, and crossed back to the near bank.

I was coming up the Uganda bank of the Nile once, when I reached a river so heavily in flood that it was then impossible to cross.   As I was in a hurry, I con-ceived the project of rounding the mouth in canoes by way of the Nile.   The next thing was to procure canoes. The native is always very chary about lending his canoes in this part, and hides them in the sudd.

I struck a village on the bank and the natives said, as usual, that they had no canoes.   I knew that they had, as I saw fish and fish traps in the village.   After hours of discussion and promises of presents, they admitted having two and said that they would bring them for me. They assured me, however, that I had come to quite the wrong place for canoes, the place for them being a village on the Nile the other side of the impassable river. Not only had the chief there an unlimited number of canoes but he had big ones which would hold many men. The land flowing with milk and honey is always just ahead according to the native.

After a long and aggravating delay, finally a small and very leaky canoe was produced. I decided to go on in this and found that it would just take my tent, one box, and my cook besides myself and the paddler. I told the head man to try to procure more and come on with them, whilst I would try and get some ahead and send them back.

It was impossible to tell how far it was to our destination, as the channels in the sudd wind so and sometimes take one right over to the opposite bank, several miles distant, and back again, to progress only a mile or two up-stream. We started in the afternoon, and by nightfall found ourselves in the middle of the Nile with several miles of sudd between us and the bank on either side. The only thing to do was to push into a clump of papyrus, and wait there till morning.

If I ever spent a more uncomfortable night I cannot remember it. The various holes in the canoe had been stuffed up with mud, which came out in the dark, and we had to spend all night baling whilst sitting in a few inches of muddy water at the bottom of the canoe. The mosquitoes buzzed in clouds, and the hippopotamus splashed round, and there was always

the uncomforting reflection that one might get inquisitive and investigate our craft. I had no tobacco
and no food. To add to our misery it commenced
to rain, and the clouds made the night absolutely
dark.

At the first streak of dawn, we had a final bale out
and plugged up the holes once more and then set sail
and reached our destination in a couple of hours. No
sooner had we got the tent on shore and commenced
putting it up than a fearful thunderstorm burst, all
the villagers fled for their houses, and left the cook and
myself wrestling with the tent in a gale of wind.

It only lasted half an hour, and then the sun came out
and I got hold of the local chief. He pursued quite
different tactics to the others. Yes, he had a few
canoes, they would be here in a minute; we waited an
hour, and no canoes came. "Where were they?"
"Oh, just coming." Another hour and nothing came.
Meanwhile I was foodless, and my porters patiently
awaiting the arrival of the canoes I had promised to
send, and probably not liking to help themselves to
their rations as I was not present to give them out.

I hate using drastic methods with natives, but there is
a limit to one's forbearance. At the end of the second
hour, I asked where the canoes were. The chief said
"just coming," so I caught hold of him, and holding his
arms behind his back, told him that if he did not tell
his people to produce the canoes at once, I was going

to beat him till he would be unable to walk or stand or sit ever again.

The canoes appeared like magic, and were despatched for the porters, and then I set to work to lay all the things in my box out to dry in the sun.

Fortunately my papers on the top were dry.

The reader may ask why I did not bring a box of food instead of the tent or papers. There was only room for a couple of loads in the canoe. I took the tent, making sure we should arrive that night, and I did not relish spending it in the open as it was then raining every night. The box contained my money, diary, and writings, and I never parted from it. I obtained a chicken at the village which I cooked spatch-cock, and some dura flour which I ate out of half a gourd.

In the evening my things turned up, everything wet through, gun cases, trade salt, porters' food, trade goods, but this was only what had constantly happened before. One of the canoes containing porters had sunk on the way, at least it had filled with water and remained floating with its gunwales level with the surface and the porters holding on to it, till they were rescued by other canoes.

The African canoe is always the dirtiest, most leaky, and ramshackle conveyance imaginable. It is cumbrous, yet seldom stable. At every crossing one holds one's breath as the rocky, leaking vessel containing one's hard-earned tusks or box of valuables meets the current, and rocks too and fro. It is always with the greatest relief that one lands the last load on the far bank.

Near Nimule there is a crossing at a narrow place where the stream of the Nile is very strong. The canoes are very narrow at the top, and broaden out below. The opening at the top is but a narrow slit and the passenger has to squirm in sideways to get his hips into the body of the boat. He then takes his seat in the usual two inches of muddy water at the bottom, and the canoe is pushed out into the current, swaying dangerously. The traveller, however good a swimmer he may be, must now sink or swim with the canoe, for if it capsizes he is successfully pinned inside, caught by the hips, so that it would be impossible to slip out. There appear to be no new canoes in Africa. They are all of vast antiquity, the wood is rotten and cracked, and they all leak. I only remember one exception, and then by the extraordinary fatality which insists on the smaller African canoes being the height of discomfort, I was not enabled to have a clean or dry passage.

I was on one of the rivers which flow into Lake Bangweolo (this lake is called Wemba by the natives), and wanted to cross to the other side, so the head man of the village took me down to the river's edge, and hailed one of two canoes which were fishing a little way off

FLOATING MY TENT ACROSS A SWOLLEN RIVER ON A RAFT

THE AFRICAN CANOE PROPELLED BY A POLE

the shore.   It came into the bank, and behold it was a brand new one, clean and dry, the first I had ever seen.

Whilst marvelling at this, the fisherman went off to the village with the paddle; it never struck him that we should require a paddle with the canoe. The head man rushed after him and I waited, contemplating with pleasure the first dry canoe journey I was to have.

At this moment a native from the village arrived at the river's edge with an enormous gourd with which to draw water.   The water was shallow and muddy near the bank, and seeing a canoe to hand he stepped into it and walking to the far end, leant over and filled his gourd from the deeper and cleaner water.   Having done so, he turned round and fell flat on his face in the bottom of the canoe, breaking his gourd and filling the bottom with water.   This is the nearest I have ever been to having an absolutely dry canoe journey, except on those rare occasions when one meets a canoe big and stable enough to carry one sitting on a tent or box.

The natives about Bangweolo did not seem to have the same objection as those of the Nile to lending their canoes.   They were always ready and willing to do their best.   At one place, the Lulingira River, I gave out one evening to a miserable little village that I wanted to cross next day.   As they only had one canoe, they immediately sent word to the villages up and down stream to send their craft, and in the morning I found a fleet of four drawn up ready, the best that could be produced in the locality.

The flagship had nothing particularly wrong about it, except that it leaked badly. It could carry two of my porters across at a time. The next best would take one man and one box. The third seemed to have been torpedoed, as there was a great gap on the starboard side. However, it would carry one man if he leant out to the port side, so as to keep the broken part out of the water. The fourth and last had its bow broken away. This would also hold one man if he sat right aft, so as to tilt the broken nose above water.

So long as a canoe can be plugged or made to keep above water at all, it never occurs to the native to make another. One would think that a tribe or village that subsisted almost entirely on fish would be careful always to have a serviceable canoe; but they prefer to go on for years with half a canoe, rather than go to the trouble of making a new one.

One of the most trying native paths I have ever walked on, I think, was one across the Bangweolo flats between these rivers flowing into the lake. It was only from four to six inches wide and worn to about the same distance below the level of the surface. It was much worse than walking on a railway line, as the path was waggling and one had to lift one's feet so high. Walk one ever so wisely, every few steps one would kick one's own ankles and stumble against the side of the path. Yet was the path preferable to the country on either side, which was all hummocks, tufts, and sun cracks.

The native idea of fishing is very comical to one accustomed to the fly and wary fish. The possibility of the fish being frightened away never seems to occur to him. He does not walk up the stream and find some quiet, secluded nook in which to practise his art. He takes a thick, home-made bit of cord, fastens to it a clumsy great hook, by means of a series of knots which form a lump as big as a marble, and goes down to the public drinking place, the ford, or the ferry.

He then hooks on a bit of meat or pulse, throws it into the river, and sits down to await results, as likely as not holding the line with his toes. That four or five men are splashing and bathing in the same spot, a constant stream of women washing and filling their water pots, a crowd of people shouting and talking, and canoes passing backwards and forwards, only adds to the cheerfulness of the scene. It does not, in his opinion, militate against his chances of success.

Perhaps he is right; he manages occasionally to catch fish, and possibly this is how the fish like their bait offered. These fish are so wonderfully unsophisticated in some ways and yet very shy in others; perhaps they are used to the noise and the splashing and shouting at the fords. I know that in the secluded nooks I have often found them very shy and ready to dart off at once if one's shadow falls on the water. Here, probably, they are on the lookout for crocodiles and other enemies.

In the ford when one is wading across with a large party of porters, they are sometimes so little alarmed that they come and nibble at one's toes. I remember once on the Tana River, when wading in with a mob of shouting porters to pull out a hippo, everybody was dancing as the fish were tickling their toes.

The only place where I have seen anything like scientific fishing is on the Victoria Nile. There the natives cut long, tapering rods, almost like fly rods, and fish with very fine lines. They bait with grasshoppers and throw the insect out almost like a fly, and then keep it moving in the water to make it look as if the animal was kicking. I have watched them fishing like this at Fajao, just below the magnificent Murchinson Falls. Even with this display of science, they do not appear to be very successful and perhaps only catch three or four half-pounders during an afternoon's fishing.

Just below the ferry at Fajao there used to be, and perhaps is still, a most remarkable number of crocodiles. There was one little bay where they used to lie out on the bank in hundreds, closely packed together. If one suddenly came round the corner, one's first impression was that the whole bank was slipping down into the river. This effect was caused by a living mass of perhaps several hundred disturbed crocodiles, hurrying back into the water.

Of other methods of native fishing, the most usual are netting and spearing. The Dinkas are very good at spearing. A canoe is paddled silently round the creeks and corners of the sudd, the paddler sitting at the stern, whilst in the bow the spearer kneels motionless with weapon poised. Directly he sees a ripple on the water, indicative of a fish being suddenly disturbed, he hurls the spear. The haft is fastened to the bow by a bit of rope, so that it can be recovered after each throw. Of course he does not hit his fish every time or nearly every time.

The basket-work kind of lobster pot is very common in Africa. It resembles an enormous safety ink-pot made of wicker. This is placed in running water in a narrow channel, and the rest of the channel is blocked with stakes or hurdle work. The fish follow up the obstruction to find a way through, meet the aperture of the lobster pot, swim in and cannot find the way out again.

Sometimes an arm of the river is staked across during the rains. When the dry weather comes, the water dries up or recedes and the fish are unable to get out. The throw net is used on the Nile about Khartoum but not by any of the more savage tribes. It was probably introduced by the Arabs and requires considerable dexterity to use well. It consists of a square, flat net surrounded by weights and with a bag or pocket in the middle. The skilful thrower gathers it together and throws it so that it spreads out flat in the air and descends over a shoal of fish. The weights hold the edge of the net to the ground, and the net is then drawn in with a cord and the fish who have failed to swim under the edges are found in the pocket.

CHAPTER VIII

CONTRASTS AND CHANGES

ONE of the features of African travel, which has a fascination of its own, is the extremes which one suffers, extremes of heat and cold, exhilaration and despondency, comfort and misery. If it were not for the times of hunger, thirst, weariness, and discomfort, one would never appreciate to their full extent the more favorable periods.

I once read of a traveller trekking across the sweltering plains of Mexico and meeting with a clear, cold stream fed by Orisava's snows. Often while trekking in sultry climes, I have wished that nature would be more generous in this provision of iced drinks for tropical regions, and have longed to experience the same sensation. Then one day I met with the same phenomenon. Whilst trekking across the open, glaring plains south of Embu, I met with a clear torrent from Mount Kenya, so cold that it was almost painful to drink.

Perhaps the best natural drink I have had before that was on one hot, scorching day when meeting with a cold stream from the Muchinga Mountains in North Eastern Rhodesia.

Once, whilst escorting a convoy of baggage camels up the Sheikh Pass in Somaliland, I had to return again and bring up those that had given out on the way up. It was a very hot day, and as I nearly reached the summit for the second time, I espied a little karia perched on the side of the mountain, so vertically under a steep wall of rock that the sun had not yet touched it, although it was mid-day. I sent down to it, and a vessel of beautiful cold milk was brought up to me.

It is very pleasant, after a sojourn in an arid, parched, low country, to climb the hills and experience the cool mountain breezes. After hunting in a temperature of 104° in the Loangwa Valley, nothing can describe the exhilaration felt, after performing the long climb, to find oneself on the top of a range like the Muchinga. The sun is indeed hot at these altitudes, but there are shady trees under which to rest, and be refreshed by the cool breezes.

Sometimes the extremes of heat and cold are too marked to be pleasant. When elephant hunting in Uganda, one faces daily a cold shower-bath, while pushing through the long grass dripping with dew before the sun rises. A little later the sun is up and one is scorched and dry.

Often in the Lado, I have been wearily dragging myself along, wet through with perspiration, after a breathless day, with eyes aching from the glare, when one of those thunderstorms which roll up so quickly have suddenly broken. They are preluded by a violent hurricane and accompanied by a terrific downpour, and in a moment one is wet through and shivering with cold.

The change from dejection to pleasure when one suddenly sees one's camp fire, whilst stumbling along in the dark, is worth undergoing much discomfort to experience. One moment one expects to have to lie down wet and hungry in the bush, and the next, one knows that food, a hot bath, and a comfortable chair are close at hand.

Whilst travelling down the Nile, I proceeded in my invaluable canoe one day, leaving my porters to come by land. As the natives, at the village from which we started, were not on friendly terms with those of the next, we could get no information about the country ahead or the winding channels in the sudd. We started gayly in our canoe and the channel soon took us out into the centre of the papyrus swamps, some miles from the shore on either side. We travelled down and down but could not get into the shore.

At last we espied a hippo run or path through the sudd, which we thought feasible, and with immense labour pushed and propelled our craft through the obstructing reeds till we came out on a lagoon in the swamp. We crossed this and saw the rising bank of the shore not more than a few hundred yards from us; but between us and it was a dense mass of reeds through which we could find no way. By dint of hacking at the reeds and pulling and pushing, we at last managed to get in to the shore after a couple of hours' hard work.

The two Bagandas in the canoe had their food, cooking pots, and blankets, but I had none of the creature comforts which are necessary to a white man in a tropical country, so I left them in charge of the canoe and set off to look for my camp.

I reckoned that we must have come a good deal farther than the porters, and so my search must be conducted up-stream. After a few minutes I came on a path which led me to a village. I could get no information here about my camp and so took a path leading southwards.

It was now well on in the afternoon, and about two hours' walking brought me to one of those very unpleasant swamps which abound beside the Nile in this part, and are especially bad in the rains. This one was half a mile or so across, and like most of them consisted of thick reeds and papyrus through which wriggled a narrow path, sometimes only ankle deep in mud, but generally with a foot or so of water over the mud.

These "paths" consist of a number of uneven holes made by the feet of elephants. It is impossible to see one's foothold, owing to mud and water. At one moment one sinks into a deep hole and the next one strikes a mound under water. Worse still is it when one treads just on the edge of one of these deep elephant foot-prints and slides suddenly to the bottom, clutching wildly at the reeds on either side. On recovering one's balance one's hands are covered with a downlike growth of hundreds of minute little hairs, which have come off the stem of the reeds and enter the pores of the skin sufficiently to cause irritation, especially when any-thing is handled. To remove these, a pair of tweezers and a few hours to spare are necessary.

Progress is slow in these swamps, and as I reached the centre and saw the sun set, my position was not of the pleasantest. I was two hours and a half from the last village, wet, tired, hungry, and alone, up to my knees in evil-smelling mud, and without the faintest conception of where my camp was.

I struggled on till I had nearly reached the opposite side, which consisted of a sharply rising bluff, perhaps fifty feet in height, but here I met another obstacle, and that was the current of the stream which caused the swamp. There was a fast swirl of muddy water about ten yards across, and then the reeds again, and just beyond that, the hard, firm bank.

Holding my rifle over my head, I plunged through, half-swimming, half-floundering at the bottom, caught some papyrus the other side, and was soon out of the swamp on dry ground. At this moment, I heard the sound of an axe just above me, and as I reached the top, I saw the comforting sight of my green tent and the porters' small white ones within a few yards of me, and my cook crouching over the fire, busy with his cooking pots.

A most unpleasant disappointment, which I have twice met with, is to see an elephant standing broadside on, showing a nice sized tusk. One shoots and he falls over in the thick grass. One runs up to see what his tusks are really like at close quarters and to measure them, when, to one's bewilderment and dismay, one finds no tusks.

This is the first sensation, but in another moment one realises what it is. He is a one-tusker and as he first stood presenting his one tusk, one naturally concluded that the other is like it. When he falls, he falls on his one tusk, concealing it from view, whilst his tuskless side remains upwards.

I experienced an even more unpleasant surprise whilst shooting in Nyasaland. It was at the beginning of a new license, and so I had a whole year before me in which to get my two elephants. I left the station of Fort Manning and camped at a village twenty-five or thirty miles distant. The same night, elephants came into the plantations, to eat the maize, and I got up quite close to one. I could see his tusks shining white, but it was quite impossible to judge their size in the dark, and equally impossible to see by the starlight well enough to select a vital shot, so I returned to my tent.

Next morning I went out into the fields and found two

elephants on the extreme edge of the plantations, who had dallied behind for a last munch of the maize. They both had nice tusks, about fifty pounds, which in those days and in that locality, I considered very fair. As they stood pulling up the stalks by the roots, I fired twice, killing one and wounding the second.

I stopped a moment to make sure of the one on the ground, and then hurried after the wounded one. Neither my trackers nor myself had any doubts that we were on the right track, but it appeared afterwards that we had got on the wrong spoor. It led us into thick grass, it was quite fresh and a large footprint. We hurried on for about half an hour and there he was right enough, for we caught a glimpse of his massive stern moving through the grass in front.

We followed him, just keeping up with his leisurely stroll, which forced us to run at intervals not to lose ground. The track wound about in the grass and several times, when we got into a straighter bit, we caught another glimpse of the enormous hindquarters, but nothing more could be seen because of the denseness of the grass and the fact that he was walking away from us.

Suddenly, without any warning, he whipped round and with a loud trumpet galloped down on us with trunk raised above his head. Perhaps he was thirty yards distant when he turned. I seemed only just to have time to get my rifle to the shoulder and the safety catch turned over when he was ten yards off. In this thick grass, it is only possible to proceed on the path broken down by elephant or rhino, and so I stood my ground, not from any mistaken sense of bravery, but because it was impossible to do otherwise.

The elephant, having his trunk raised high, was exposing his chest, and so I fired with my mannlicher into its centre. He swerved at the shot, crashed into the grass, and fell on his fore knees a few yards to my right, whilst I pumped two or three shots into his shoulder to make certain that he did not rise again.

It had all happened so quickly and I had been so intent on the heart shot, that no thought of the tusks ever crossed my mind; if it did, had I not seen just before that they were a nice pair? It was only when I heard a wail from Matola, my orderly, standing behind me, of "Oh! Oh! a nyungwa," that I realised what had happened. I had shot a nyungwa, or tuskless bull, and, moreover, this was the second and last on my license so there was no more elephant shooting for me for a year in that protectorate.

While elephant hunting in the Lado in 1908, I climbed the high Madi escarpment and came out on to the plateau above. The cool mountain air would have been only too delightful, after the mosquito-infested Nile bank, if it were not that halfway up the ascent, a bad attack of fever came on. I struggled to the top and then lay down under a tree till my tent was pitched. After several days of ague, high fever, and semi-deliriousness, I was so weak that I could not stand without support.

The country had then a very bad reputation. After the Belgians had given up Dufile, several porters sent through to Loka by this way had been murdered, and so the country since then had been given a wide berth. The inhabitants of the villages left no doubt about their hostile intentions, as they turned out with muskets and spears and threatened to shoot my porters if they came near them. We were badly in need of food for the men, and I did not know what to do, as I was unable to move. We had no weapons except my own two rifles.

My Swahili cook Husseni, a stout fellow, took my rifle and went to the nearest village and after a palaver managed to induce the chief and one or two men to come back to camp and brought them into my tent. I rated them soundly for their inhospitality to strangers and taking advantage of me being sick in this way. I told them that they would not dare to have behaved like this if I was well, and that I was friendly with both the Congo and the Uganda governments, so if anything happened to us they would be sure to hear of it from one or the other. Husseni then displayed our wares and told them that these would be theirs if food was produced.

This had the effect of making them produce a limited

supply of flour. A day or two afterwards, I was able to sit at the door of my tent and enjoy the cool air and beautiful scenery of the mountains. The country, just at that spot, is the prettiest I have seen anywhere in the Lado, and I always cherished a pleasant recollection of it, in spite of the rather adverse circumstances under which I had seen it. After two days' convalescence, want of food compelled us to move. As the country ahead was reported full of people, and devoid of elephant, I returned by the way we had come.

Two years later, I arrived in the same spot, up the same pass, to take over this country for the Sudan government. The same chief came to me, and professed his affections for the old and everlasting adhesion to the new government. It was evident that he did not recognise me, as I had had a large beard the last time I was there.

I told him that I had heard that they were very bad people and hostile to strangers, and that several people had been murdered in their country. He protested volubly saying that his people were the most innocent and friendly in the world, they loved strangers, and welcomed everybody to their country. It must have been some other people I had been told about. It was quite true that some of the Madi were bad people but his were exemplary.

I then said, "You were not so very hospitable to me when I came here two years ago, and I was sick." We had a good laugh over it, and since then he has been most docile, and given no trouble to us.

During my first visit to the Lado Enclave in 1908, I was trekking down the Nile between Wadelai and Dufile and came to a group of Madi villages, called Alivejo. On my arrival, I noticed that the people were sulky and hostile. No one rose at my approach and no chief came to greet me. The natives I addressed would not reply, but just sat and glared at us. I was sitting under a tree waiting for the tail end of my caravan to come in, when some one said, "There are two white men." I looked up, and saw in the far distance two figures evidently wearing helmets, and one of them with a white umbrella, whilst behind them were several naked savages.

I did not take much interest, thinking that they were two elephant poachers from the other bank. Suddenly my cook said, "Why it is our white man," meaning my travelling companion, Captain Hart, whom we had not seen since we entered the enclave, as we had separated to hunt and failed to meet again. I picked up my glasses and recognised Hart as the second figure, and wondered who his companion with the white umbrella could be. On further investigation, he proved to be a native whom Hart had rewarded with helmet, shirt, and umbrella for services rendered.

We had lunch together under the tree, and had much to recount to each other of our adventures up to date.

Hart was camped at the other side of the swamp. He had been up to the Lugware country and had more ivory than his limited porters could carry, whilst for the same reason I was hopelessly tied to the river and my canoe.

We decided that we must make a depôt and leave our ivory in it, and this village seemed a suitable locality, excepting for the very hostile attitude of the natives. Hart returned in the afternoon, and promised to be back again with his camp next morning, taking some of my porters to carry his extra loads.

I then set to work to try and ingratiate myself with the natives. I first sent for the chief and he came very reluctantly, a tall, sulky man. I talked to him for a while and then he asked in a very surly way why I did not give him presents. I replied that he knew perfectly well that it was the custom for him to bring a present first to give the stranger, and until he did this, I considered that he was evilly disposed towards us.

He went off and returned later with a very meagre gourd of flour and said that they had no food here but had to buy it from the opposite bank. I then asked him if he had any objection to my building a hut on some rising ground behind his village. He replied that he supposed the white men could do as they liked. I said that if he was going to be unfriendly, I should certainly do as I liked. I had only asked in consideration for him and his people, as I did not wish to put my hut on a spot which he might subsequently want to till and to cultivate.

I then showed him the site I wanted and asked him if he intended cultivating there or contemplated using it for any other purpose during the next few months. He grudgingly admitted that he did not, so I produced calico and presents and told him that this was in payment for the right of building so near his village.

During our conversation, a great wailing and lamentation arose at a large village near the water's edge. I inquired the cause and was told that they had been out in canoes hunting hippo, the meat of which they sold for flour on the opposite bank, and that to-day a hippo had upset the canoe of the chief of that village and killed him.

Early next morning I moved my camp to the higher ground behind the village. The wailing was still continuing, so I asked if they had not buried the chief yet, to which they replied that he was not yet dead. I asked if I could see him, rather a risky experiment, for if the man was moribund and died directly after my ministrations, the people would hardly have become less hostile to us.

I was taken down to the village and found the chief, supported by a number of women, in the centre of a stockaded enclosure, whilst round him was a great crowd, wailing and lamenting for him. His arm was tied up with a rough splint made of reeds, but nothing soft in the way of dressing or padding had been used, as these people had no cloth or clothes of any kind and could devise nothing else. I undid the splint and found that his arm was lacerated by enormous gashes from the hippo's teeth, the bone was broken, and the lower arm was only attached to the shoulder by two pieces of flesh. It was a ghastly wound and I had little hopes of his recovery.

The native is extraordinary, however, in his recuperative powers and, if given a chance, heals most rapidly. The reason most of their injuries develop into large, festering sores is that they get filled with dirt and are treated by being plastered with mud. The swarms of flies that settle on the wounds also tend to make them unhealthy. I squirted out the wounds with strong antiseptic and dressed and set the arm as well as I could. During the rest of my stay in the village, I dressed him twice a day and gave him sleeping draughts at night. When I left, to my relief, he was not yet dead; on the contrary, he appeared much better.

After attending to the chief, I was asked to look at another wounded man. I found a sulky looking person, sitting on the opposite side of the zariba nursing a great gash in his thigh. I dressed this likewise, asking how it happened, and was told that he had done it himself with an arrow, owing to his bitterness about the accident that had happened to his brother. He was suffering, however, I believe, more from jealousy than bitterness when I saw him, as his brother was surrounded by a sympathising crowd, whilst he was left to sulk alone.

Presently Hart turned up, and we set to work building a hut surrounded by a strong stockade. From this time onwards, the people seemed much more friendly, and even the sulky chief paid us visits frequently.

When the stockade and hut were finished, we buried the ivory and left our spare trade goods in the hut. We had a very goodly stock of these; in fact, small things like salt went such a long way that our expenditure was very much less than we anticipated. However, in food stores we had skimped ourselves, and now we had practically nothing left.

Hart good naturedly undertook the dull and uninteresting task of trekking down to Nimule and laying in a fresh stock, whilst I went up into the Lugware country, where he was to meet me later. We left a Swahili, whom we had picked up at Koba, in charge of the depôt, giving him a rifle and several of the porters to keep him company.

Having made all our arrangements, we trekked off. It was a little over two months before I again visited our base camp. I arrived by canoe, and as I drew near, I saw a little crowd of natives at the landing stage, one of them waving his arm at us in a peculiar way. I did not know whether it was intended to be menacing or friendly. As we approached, he became more violent, performing all kinds of evolutions with his arm, but in what appeared to be a very stiff and awkward way.

It was only as we drew in to the bank that I recognised who it was; it was the moribund chief with his arm completely healed up. Although it was stiff and bent, owing to my very primitive setting, he could move it about and swing it round his head and wave it in the air, and it was his facility in this respect that he was demonstrating with great pride.

He appeared really pleased to see me, and said frankly that he would not now be alive if it had not been for me. He told us that all was well with our belongings, and an immense crowd escorted me up to the zariba, from which the Swahili presently came to greet me. Very different was it to my first arrival in this village.

I hoped that a sense of obligation at his recovery would show some tangible form in the way of a presentation of a sheep or even a chicken, but the depth of his gratitude never extended so far. However, just at this camp we were not so hard pressed for want of meat as elsewhere, as it was one of the few places we struck in which game was in any way plentiful. There was a large herd of kob which seemed never to leave the neighbourhood, and one could generally secure a waterbuck in the early morning. It was largely this that had influenced us in choosing it as a depôt, as the meat of waterbuck could be exchanged on the opposite bank for flour for the porters.

CHAPTER IX

ABOUT LION

THE first time that I had anything to do with a lion in its wild state was in Somaliland in 1899, when I came on the spoor of a male and female. There is something very thrilling in this first contact with an animal one has been taught to hold in awe and respect from childhood.

The Somalis say that a lion makes you jump three times. The first is when you suddenly hear him roar, whether at night or in the daytime; but more particularly in the dark he gives you a start. The second is when walking along you meet his spoor. You may be looking for it, but it always comes as a slight shock when you find it. The third and last is the time when you first sight him. They say that even a bold man is thus frightened three times by a lion, but after the sudden shock of seeing him is over, he is no longer afraid.

The first time I ever set eyes on a lion, I did not experience this sensation, because I did not know what it was. He suddenly got up in thick grass and went off grunting. I had a momentary glimpse of something red, and thought that it was a bush pig. I fairly kicked myself when I realised too late what I had missed.

In Nyasaland there are periodical epidemics of man-eating during the rainy season. The grass is long then, and the lion, finding it difficult to approach game unheard, make raids on the villages when impelled by hunger. They are often very bold in their attacks on villages, and yet very wary in the way they avoid being killed by the European sportsman. The country is so thick that it is almost impossible to find them in the daytime, whilst, however hard one tries to forestall them at night, they generally manage to evade one by visiting some other village to that in which one has stationed oneself.

The most certain way to get them would be to obtain immediate news of any cattle or natives killed, and to track them up whilst still on the body. In this, however, the possible victims themselves are the greatest obstacles to success. So superstitious are the natives about the lion, that seldom is it possible to get *khabar* until too late. The news is almost invariably held over for a day or two, on some excuse or other, so as to give the lion a chance. No native wants you to hunt a lion on the information he gives. In the back of his mind he has a fear that the lion would get to know who had given him away, and revenge himself in some manner. In East Africa it is quite different; the natives are ready and willing to bring in news and lion are, moreover, much easier to find.

The lion generally chooses an absolutely black night

for a raid on a village. As I have said, it is almost always during the rains that he takes to man eating, when the sky is generally cloudy, and the nights dark. I have several times been in a village when a lion has passed quite close, no doubt reconnoitring, and on one occasion when a hut was broken open, but it was invariably too dark to see or get a shot. The latter incident I have described in "The Game of East Africa."

In 1904 I was in Fort Manning in Nyasaland. We twice heard a lion roaring near, and he passed fairly close to the station. There was great excitement and we turned out with rifles, but could not see him as it was dark. I thought afterwards that these were reconnoitring visits to learn the lay of the land. Some ten days after the last of these visits, I was having my bath, when suddenly I heard a great commotion in the fort, the sound of many voices, and the blowing of bugles. My house was about a couple of hundred yards away, so hastily donning some clothes and snatching up a rifle, I ran down to the fort with Mr. D. D. Lyell who was stopping with me. All sorts of ideas flitted through my head as I ran. An attack, a mutiny, a fire, what could it be?

When we arrived, there was such an excited babble of talk, that one could not discover for some time what it was. I dragged a sergeant aside and asked him what had happened, and he said there was a lion, pointing to the gate of the fort. I had come in by a small gate at the back and I now noticed that the main gate had been shut. I had never seen it shut before. I asked where the lion was and several people pointed at the gate, so I said, "Open it, then, and let us have a look at him." The gate was opened and of course there was no lion. Lyell and I ran out, but we saw nothing, so then I started to find the originator of the story.

Presently, the hospital assistant appeared and said that he was responsible for the story. He would not like to say whether it was a lion or not, but some great beast had sprung at him twice, as he had been walking down to the stream. He had shouted and run for the fort, the guard had then called out and blown the bugle, and that was all he knew.

He took us to the spot and there, true enough, was the spoor of the lion and the marks of his spring, as he had torn up the turf, evidently having his claws out ready for action. I believe the fact that the hospital assistant was wearing boots saved his life, as when he turned to run it must have been the unwonted sound which made the lion, accustomed to bare feet, stop to consider, else why should he have paused? The man was one hundred and fifty to two hundred yards from the fort, and easy to catch in a bound or two. He must have paused a second at the sound of the boots, and the next moment he heard the guard shouting, and then finally went off.

We followed the spoor with a lamp as far as we could that night, a pure waste of time, but we were very keen in those days. Next day we spent in tracking him, and learnt that he had followed in the tracks of the cattle and was making his way over to the zariba, when he met the hospital assistant.

We had the cattle driven out the same way that day and on their return tied up one and sat over him, but without result. The lion came back all right, but this time he inspected our garden, and walked over the vegetable beds. We sat up then in the garden, but he was too cunning for us, for he visited another part of the station. Altogether he came three nights running, but we never got a glimpse of him, nor were we able to follow him up to his lying-up place by day.

The same year I was hunting in North Eastern Rhodesia. Whilst camped one dark night on a steep bank above the Loangwa River, I woke up with a start to hear lion roaring close by. I hurriedly groped about in the dark for the matches, but before I could find them, I heard a scratching noise at the flies of the tent. I seized my rifle, which was beside me, and pointing at the sound called out, "Who is that?" There was no reply, but the scratching sound continued. I called out again, but there was still no answer, so I decided to shoot. At the last moment, I thought perhaps it was only a hyæna, and how foolish I would look shooting at one when there were lion about. Anyhow, I decided to wait a little longer.

The creature, whatever it was, began crawling under the flies, and this time I really was going to shoot, when I heard the voice of one of my boys call out, "Mkango bwana, Mkango" (a lion, master, a lion).

What induced the boy to come under the flies instead of in at the door, and why he did not answer, I cannot make out, unless it was fear of attracting the attention of a lion possibly behind him. Anyhow, it is easy to imagine how thankful I was that I had paused before firing.

I went out of the tent and we waited in silence for some time, and then we heard them go down to drink from the river close below the camp. After drinking they stood there. It was a party of three, and they uttered roar after roar, which sounded really magnificent, echoing backwards and forwards between the steep banks of the river. However, they were rather too close to be pleasant, and we were very thankful when we heard them climbing the bank and going off to a safer distance. They hunted for some time in the vicinity, and then we heard their roars die away in the distance.

A few days later, I heard a lion roaring continuously at 8 A.M. I have noticed several times the bush lion roaring at this time and even at 9 o'clock, but do not

GAMRA OASIS. BORANA COUNTRY

The stockade in the centre of the pool was erected by Abyssinian hunters for protection whilst awaiting lion, buffalo, and other game coming to drink at night.

THE WHITE RHINO

Showing the square lip which distinguishes this species from the black.

ever remember hearing the plain lion so late, although I have often heard him well after sunrise.

At a village near Fort Mangoche, also in Nyasaland, a man was sitting one night at the door of his hut drumming, whilst his wife was cooking food inside. The hut was an isolated one, being several hundred yards from the rest of the village.

Suddenly the woman heard the man call out, "a lion has got me." She took a burning fagot from the fire, ran out, and smacked the lion in the face. The astonished animal let go, and she dragged her husband into the hut and hastily put up the poles which form the door. The man died a few minutes after, and the woman sat there with the dead body.

Presently the lion returned and scratched gently on the door. This he repeated several times till it got on the woman's nerves. At last she could stand it no longer, so she took another fagot from the fire, unbarred the door, and fled to the village, leaving the dead man. The lion then walked into the hut and took him.

These native doorways consist of a couple of stout stakes sunk into the earth on either side, and between these a number of poles are slid to close the door. It forms a strong barricade, stronger than the lion can break through. He generally gets into a hut by breaking a hole through the wall or jumping on the roof and burrowing down through the thatching. Whilst I was at Fort Manning, a well-known man-eater came and scratched at one of these doorways. The owner of the hut seized his spear and, thrusting it between the poles, was lucky enough to stab the lion to the heart.

Simba station on the Uganda railway used to be a famous place for lion. I was looking for some near there, when I saw a herd of zebra run forward towards a reedy watercourse, snort, and run back again. Their conduct was so peculiar that I watched them for some time. They were all staring at something in the bed of the stream, and snorting at it. A few would run forward and then rejoin the herd, whilst at other times the whole herd would move forward and then back again. So engrossed were they with this game of Bo Peep, that they did not notice me till I got close up to them; then they turned and bolted. At the same time, two lion got up out of the stream bed and fled in the opposite direction.

It was at Simba that I was mauled by a lion. In the dry weather they used to come and drink from a small pool, formed under the water-tank by the drippings and overflow. This was a tank raised on a high iron frame for supplying the engines with water. I stationed myself here one night, sitting astride a girder. After a while, a lioness came strolling down the line and commenced drinking at the pool about six or seven feet below me. It was difficult to shoot, as she was directly underneath me. Whilst I was trying to move into a firing position, she must have heard me, as she gave one bound of about four yards to one side, and then stood listening. I then fired and she raced about two hundred yards up the line, and fell dead across the track.

I was just thinking of descending when I heard a rustle in the grass and presently two lion came out on to the track, just opposite the dead body. They began scratching at and pawing it, then they lay down beside it and whined, and then got up and scratched again. It is difficult to say how long this lasted; perhaps it was half an hour. Then they stood up and began to roar alternately. This they continued for about half an hour, and then they began slowly to approach the water-tank.

The leading one came on, swinging his head from side to side, his head covering his chest. When he got close, I fired at him. I found out afterwards that the shot just caught the corner of his jaw, breaking part of the bone of the lower one, and then glanced off into the shoulder. He collapsed into the water trough just below the tank. The second one stopped on hearing the shot, and then advanced again, not a bit discon-certed, to see what was the matter. I gave him a shot and he waltzed round and then rushed into the grass, where he was found dead next morning, about a hun-dred yards from the line. By this time, the one in the water trough had picked himself out, and I had just time to give him another shot as he left the track, after which I heard him collapse in the grass close to the line.

As the moon had now gone in, it was difficult to see. I went up to the station and got my orderly to bring a lamp. I passed the spot at which the last lion had fallen, being able to see nothing in the grass, and went to the lioness. I then returned and could just make out something lying in the grass. The pointsman, a boy, and a few other station hands had gathered in a little group on the line by the water-tank, whilst the spot at which the lion was lying was perhaps fifty yards on.

In the dark, the body, which was just discernible, appeared a long way below the line. I imagined that I was standing on an embankment. As a matter of fact, I afterwards discovered that the track was only a foot above the ground level. I thought I would just have a look over the edge and if the lion sprung I should be able to stop him, especially as he had to spring upwards.

I approached the edge and immediately the inert mass assumed life, and with a roar sprang on me with one bound. The orderly, who was a few yards behind me, not the gallant Matola I have spoken of before, immediately retired precipitately. As the lion sprang, I fired into his chest and he landed on me, his right paw over my left shoulder, and he seized my left arm in his teeth. As my left arm was advanced in the firing position, it was the first thing he met.

The weight of his spring knocked me down, and I

next found myself lying on my back my left arm being worried, and my rifle still in my left hand underneath his body. I scrambled round with my left arm still in his mouth until I was kneeling alongside of him, and started pummelling him with my right fist on the back of the neck. He gave me a final shake and then quickly turned round, and disappeared in the grass a little nearer to the station than I was.

I reloaded and covered him but could not see him clearly enough to fire. I then passed the spot at which he was lying, keeping my rifle pointed towards him. I could not see him in the grass, and thinking him well left alone continued towards the station, meeting the admiring audience who had witnessed the scene just past the water-tank.

Afterwards, when I found that I had not the use of my wrist, owing to a nerve being practically severed, it gave me great hope to remember that I had been able to reload and come into the firing position again without difficulty.

I found that I was drenched with blood and my coat and breeches torn with teeth and claws. I retired to the waiting-room, where I got the station master to syringe out my wounds with strong potassium permanganate. There were eight big holes in my arm, and I afterwards discovered three claw marks on my back, presumably made when his paw passed over my shoulder.

I sat up in the waiting-room for about six hours, when the Nairobi train came in, the guard having been wired to bring some dressings from Makindu. Having bandaged up my arm, he escorted me to the train. This was about five in the morning and all the passengers were asleep in their berths. I reached a carriage all right, but just as I got to the steps my legs gave way, as I was very weak from loss of blood. The guard had to help me in, and I must have looked a very disreputable object. The lamps were shaded and the carriage nearly in darkness. The two passengers in the carriage, being suddenly awakened from slumber and seeing this disreputable object staggering in, helped by the guard, evidently thought that it was some one in the last stage of drunkenness and, calling out that there was no room, tried to push me out. When it was explained to them what had happened, they were of course as kind as they could be.

The shaky journey up to Nairobi, after my wounds had stiffened, was very painful. The pain in this case was probably due more to the severed nerve than anything else, because a big wound is, as a rule, less painful than a small cut.

At Nairobi, I was taken to the hospital where I was very kindly treated. After a few days my arm swelled to enormous proportions and assumed every colour of the rainbow, but owing to the assiduous attention of the nurses it was just saved. It was seven months, however, before I could use my wrist, and about two years before I could feel really steady with it when shooting, although I shot my next lion after this event some nine months later. I was anxious to see how I should feel facing a lion again, as I was afraid that I might have lost my nerve; but I seem to be all right, and have bagged seven since.

To finish with the lion that mauled me. I gave very definite instructions to my orderly before leaving, that no one was to go near the spot next day until he had been to the top of the tank. From this place he could get a good view without danger, and was to fire at the lion to see if it was dead. I repeated these instructions three times, as he was rather a dense person.

In the morning a procession went out. Being natives they did just the opposite to what Europeans would do; the smallest of the party, my boy, led, while the soldier with the rifle came last. The boy tripped up to the lion, who was still alive and lying in the same place, and got clawed. Apparently, the orderly, who belonged to the same tribe, did nothing to help him, but the boy eventually managed to crawl away. The next train was then stopped alongside the line and the hard-dying lion was despatched from the guard's van.

I have generally found a lion fairly easily killed, when compared to hartebeest and other game, but any animal once wounded, otherwise than in a vital spot, is much more difficult to finish than an unwounded one. No doubt if I had had a big bore, I should have stopped him, but I was shooting with a mannlicher.

I think I have never seen anything funnier than two belated lions I met near the Ndurugu, British East Africa, returning home with their stomachs dragging on the ground. A herd of kongoni was following them and running after them to look at them. I never saw anything look so sheepish and ashamed as those two lion. Both were much too full to be comfortable, and were subject to the stare of a whole inquisitive herd in broad daylight. They looked intensely deprecating and self-conscious, as if they wished to say, "It wasn't us at all that killed one of you last night; we are just taking a walk and wouldn't do any harm to any one. I wish you wouldn't stare so, it makes us feel uncomfortable."

In 1907 I was sketching south of Embu. I was returning to camp one day when some native guides from the Embei, whom I had sent back to camp, met me and said that they had seen a lion sitting under a tree. We went to the spot, a nullah with a steep slope on the near side; and they pointed out the top of a tree, which could just be seen above the side, as the spot under which they had seen the lion.

My Dorobo hunter and I crept to the edge of the nullah and saw two lioness lying near the base of a tree, at the bottom of the nullah on the opposite side. There was a thick tree growing close to the foot of our slope, and we climbed down the side sheltered by this. Then we crept along the bottom of the nullah, sheltered by the palms growing beside the watercourse, till we reached a point opposite the tree and about fifty yards from it. There was nothing to be seen, and I was just crawling along a little farther, on hands and knees, when a lioness suddenly came out from behind a clump of palms and lay down facing me.

I did not dare move because there were only a few little clumps of grass, which did not cover me, and the least movement would betray me. I waited perfectly still, on all fours, for some time, when she suddenly got up and disappeared behind the palms. I then very slowly and carefully sat down and got into firing position. I waited an interminable time and at last thought that she must have gone off under cover of the palms and reeds.

I did not like to move, in case she could see through the palms, which were close to where she had disappeared, and so nearer to her eye than mine. Finally she came out again suddenly and lay down in the same place as before.

I took careful aim and pulled the trigger and saw her roll over. There was a short pause, and then two more lion, both maneless, but one probably a male, trotted out and looked at the lioness. I had a shot at the nearest, and then, to my embarrassment, four more rushed out; the one I had hit dashed past, crossed the watercourse to our side, and then went off. I fired again at another, and she rushed for a pool on my left, and fell headlong into it. By this time the others had split up and gone off in different directions, with a chorus of grunting and growling. I retrieved the two, but the one which had my second shot got away and I could not find him.

After this I went back and told the Embei guides, who were very nice but not very brave people, to go back to camp and fetch porters for the skins. One of them said that he could not possibly go alone with all these lions about. It was explained that all the lions had gone off in the opposite direction, and after a little while he was prevailed on to go. Almost immediately he came tearing back and said that he had met four lions in the way who would not let him pass. I hurried to the spot and found not a vestige of spoor, so was forced to the conclusion that the Embei was drawing on his imagination. This, seven in all, was the largest number of full grown lion I have met together.

When I returned to Embu, I heard that two lions had been seen in broad daylight within a hundred yards of the soldiers' lines, and Captain Gordon, who was stationed there, had seen one at 6 P.M. We sat up for him without success.

Two days later, Gordon saw one of them cross the road towards the lines at the same spot as before, but this time it was at dusk and he missed him in the uncertain light. The day after, he was alleged to have again been seen at the same spot, but he was never bagged and we never could make out what it was that attracted him to this spot so often. He had certainly been round that night, as the next day at dawn I found some tracks of blood, as if he had clawed a bush pig and it had escaped him.

After this, I was looking for lions north of Nyeri and had seen two, but had not obtained any, when I camped beside a small swamp. I was listening from my tent one night to the porters talking round their fire and heard one of them spin a yarn about a former visit to this very spot. He said that he was with a white man who went out and met nine lions just here; he shot two, and then one rushed at him and bit off his hand.

Then the lions went off, and he returned to his tent. Presently he called the head man and gave him a letter which he was to present in Nairobi; it was for the pay of the porters. Soon afterwards they heard a report from his tent and went in and found that he had shot himself, as he was ashamed to live with only one hand. They took the body and carried it to Fort Hall, where it was put in a box and sent to England. This last touch, giving the story a happy ending, I think rather a fine effort.

Next day I called the porter to ask him more about

the story, as it had interested me, but he pretended that he did not know to what I referred and said that he had never heard of any such story.

I asked the district commissioner at Fort Hall and other people, who had been some time in the neighbourhood, if they had ever heard anything of the sort. They were all certain that no such event had happened since they had been there, nor in the history of Fort Hall, which was only ten years old then. I am forced to the conclusion that this rather pathetic little story is only a specimen of the wonderful powers of imagination of the native.

I was returning from a trip a little way down the Tana and came back by el Doinyo Sapuk and camped at Lion Rocks near the Athi. This is such a well-known place for lion and, moreover, so near civilisation, that I never hoped to get one there. I arrived at about 4 P.M. and shot a kongoni for bait in case there should be any about. Next morning at dawn, I heard a lion roaring quite close to camp, so I scrambled into my clothes and rushed out. I was just in time to see a red-maned lion making off at the other side of the Athi, and heard the roaring again from farther down the river.

I then went to the kongoni and found that it had been eaten, all but the fore quarters, and there was the spoor of three round it; one of a male went towards the river and must have been that of the one I saw, while that of two lioness went down the river and it was them I must have heard roaring.

I followed the stream and found the remains of a zebra which had been killed the night before and completely devoured, all but skull and shin bones, before they came to the kongoni. Then I caught sight of a lioness in the distance, but could not get up to her and lost her spoor on the rocks.

In the evening, I killed two impala, one eight hundred yards from camp, and one in a little gully with a perpendicular wall of rock each side. I imagined myself in the morning climbing up the back of the rocks and appearing at the edge to find the lion on the impala just below. It comforted me to think what a nice near and safe shot it would be, as they would be unable to scale the wall of rock and yet would only be about fifteen yards or so from me.

On my return to camp just after sunset, I was passing a little boss of rock, with cactus on the top, about a hundred yards or more from me, when my eye suddenly caught something on the top. I looked closely and saw perfectly motionless what I took to be a lion's head. I could not be certain, so took out my glasses and looked up. It had disappeared, so it *was* a lion's head. I sat down and sighted my rifle on the spot, in case it should reappear; but it was dusk and I could not see the sights well, so, after a little while, I returned to camp, which was a few hundred yards away.

This rock was just above one of the impala I had shot. I had not been in camp more than half an hour when I heard the lion roaring, as he came down from the rock to the impala, no doubt calling his companions. He must have been watching with some interest my shooting and leaving the impala there.

Before it was quite light next morning, I visited the first impala and found it completely demolished. I then made my way to the second, that lying in the gulley. I came to the foot of one rocky side and heard a low growl from the top of the rock. It was just light enough to see now, so I climbed up. I reached the top and put my head over and saw the heads of several lioness. As I was getting into a position from which I could fire, my field-glasses swung against the rock, and made a slight sound.

The lioness dodged down, and I crept up behind a little bush on the top. I saw a black-maned lion, who had left earlier, going out across the plain, and a lioness sitting up, who did not give me a shot. Then I heard a scrunching noise from behind the bush, and then a red-maned lion flew out and disappeared over the edge of the rocky wall. I had just time to give him a flying shot in the flank as he went.

All the rest were now out of sight amongst the rocks. The only one I could see was the black-maned one trekking straight out across the plain several hundred yards away. I put a shot in front of him which, when it struck the ground, made him turn and come back towards the rocks, a piece of luck I had hardly hoped for.

Then getting down from the rock I rounded a corner and saw the wounded, red-maned lion sitting up, but he disappeared round some rocks before I could fire. The black-maned one was now coming back across my front. I took a running shot as he passed, and he answered to the shot and tore, grunting all the time, towards a thick clump of bush into which he disappeared.

There were now two wounded lion to retrieve. I reconnoitred the bush carefully and heard one growling from the inside. I could see nothing and walked round and round. At last I got my cook to fire a shot at random into the bush, whilst I stood ready to receive him if he came out.

Nothing happened, but suddenly a lioness appeared from one side and tore across to some caves near. I fired as she ran; she answered to the shot and disappeared into the caves. That now made three to recover.

Leaving two men to watch the bush from a distance, I went, for a change of air, to look for the red-maned one. We found the spoor and followed it till it got lost on some rocks, and then went to look at the place at which the lioness had disappeared. It was a long, winding cave which did not look inviting, with a wounded lioness inside somewhere and all sorts of winds and turns. It seemed as if one was going to lose them all.

I then returned to the bush and approached it carefully. It was only a small and clumpy bush, about five yards across, and every moment I expected an infuriated lion to rush out. At last I got right up to it and peered through it. It seemed only possible that I should see either a live or a dead lion, as we had seen him go in there, and he could not have come out without being observed. However, in hunting one always meets with the unexpected. I saw no lion, but the mouth of a cave completely blocked by the bush. I got under the bush but could see no distance into the cave as it was darkened by the undergrowth. The next thing to do was to cut it down so as to be able to look in.

Whilst some porters undertook this job, I went again to search for the red-maned lion. We struck the spoor beyond the place at which we had lost it, and it took us into a thickly bushed watercourse. Presently, I heard something moving, and the lion broke out on the opposite side of the watercourse and started going up the hill. I fired as well as I could, but could not see well, as I was closely pressed in on all sides by bushes. I hit him, and he rushed back into the bushes and I heard him breaking his way through towards me roaring lustily at intervals.

I hastily retreated, as I could not see a foot where I was standing. There was a wall of rock just outside the bush patch, and I climbed to the top of this. The bushes were too thick to see through, so we started throwing stones at where we thought he was. At last we located him, and every time a stone hit him he growled, but he would not move and we never got a sight of him. At last a big stone hit him, and he moved down into the bed of the watercourse, where he was immune from the stone throwing.

I then went in again after him with my gun bearer, Tengeneza. I reached the spot at which he had been lying and found a lot of blood, and then cautiously approached the watercourse. The bank was thickly lined by bushes. I parted these and looking through saw him just below me in the bed of the stream. He tried to spring out at me but only got half-way up the bank, and slipped back, and I finished him there in the hollow. We found afterwards that a leg had been broken, otherwise it would have been an easy matter to have sprung up the bank to where I stood, about four feet above him.

We now returned to the cave and found that the bush had been cleared away from the entrance. We could see about four or five yards inside and after that all was darkness. We threw stones in but nothing happened. The cave was just high enough to stand in at the entrance but rapidly shelved so that to get any distance one must crouch. There were loose boulders on the floor over which to crawl, and it looked so dark and uninviting, that I was only seeking for an excuse to get away.

About six porters, my gun bearer, and cook, Husseni, were waiting to see what I would do. Suddenly, a brilliant idea struck me. I pulled out my watch and said, "Good gracious, it is already eleven o'clock; we have wasted the whole morning. We must trek on at once." So saying, I moved to go away.

My cook, who is either a perfect fool or else an extraordinarily stout fellow, said to Tengeneza, "Come along. Let us go in that we may ease our minds once and for all whether this lion is alive or dead."

Tengeneza demurred, but Husseni approached the cave. This was too much for me so I said, "Look here, Husseni, just you leave that lion alone. It is my lion and not yours." Then I told one of the porters to rush back to camp and tell the head man to pack up ready to start and then I went into the cave, secretly cursing Husseni for being a madman.

There was only room for one, comfortably, so I led, followed by Husseni. After advancing a little way, one's eyes got accustomed to the dark and I said, "Do you see that in front? Do you think it is a boulder?" Husseni peered round my shoulder, "I don't know, master." "Anyhow, I am going to have a shot at it," I said; which I did. Nothing happened, and the reverberation in the cave was too great to hear what my shot hit. There was darkness to each side, and the lion might be on either side or lying on a ledge. The thing in front I decided was a boulder.

To make certain, I advanced again and put the muzzle of my rifle against it. It was soft and it was only then that I knew that it was indeed the lion, and that he was dead, which was rather lucky as he had been growling from inside not so long before. I felt him and found that I was at the head end, so I told Husseni to crawl over the boulders to one side, and that he would find his tail somewhere and then we could pull him out.

Husseni fumbled away in the dark for some time and then said, "Bwana, I cannot find his tail." "Feel about for it," I said, "and if you cannot find it take hold of a leg." We slowly dragged him out over the stones, and when we got him to the mouth of the cave, we found out why Husseni had been unable to find his tail. He was a magnificent black-maned lion, but he had no tail. It had rotted off. I do not know if it had been caught in a trap or bitten off or what had happened to it, but there was only the smallest little stump left.

That was two out of the three. I next went into the big cave to look for the lioness. It was a rambling kind of cave with all sorts of turns and passages. I only reconnoitred as far as I could see well. There was an opening in the roof which let in a certain amount of light, but when I passed this, there was nothing but darkness.   I thought I would just let that lioness be and content myself with the two lions for that day, so returned to camp, and then trekked off to the Athi River station.

CHAPTER X

NATIVE SERVANTS

As having a good or bad servant makes all the difference between being comfortable or uncomfortable, contented or discontented, he is a most important factor in African life and, indeed, in every other kind of life. One's boy is the spectacles through which one views African life. Sometimes he is a perfect treasure and then life seems well worth living; sometimes the very same boy is so hopeless that he is irritating beyond measure and one's whole horizon looks gloomy.

The usual African is a very uncertain individual and varies from time to time considerably. In Nyasaland one used to suffer from black days when nothing went right, whether the fault was entirely that of the natives, or whether one was partly to blame oneself, I do not know.

These black days would perhaps begin by finding one's askari (soldiers) had forgotten everything they had ever learnt. Every conceivable mistake they could make, they would, and one would find that they had invented a number of new mistakes that no one had ever thought of making before. A man on whom days of personal instruction in musketry had been spent would look at one blankly when requested to put his sight to fixed sights.

In despair one would ask a sergeant to tackle him, and the sergeant would carefully tell him that the five hundred yard sight was the two hundred and *vice versa*. Then on looking at the rifles on the tripod, they would be found pointing in every direction but the target, and the leaves of the backsights at every angle excepting vertical.

One would then go and see how another officer was getting on with his company and he would say, "I don't know what is the matter with them this morning; they are all as idiotic as they can be."

Having got the ordeal of parade over, one would retire to breakfast, thankful to leave them. Perhaps one would find no cloth laid, and on calling one's boy and asking where the breakfast was, he would look at one blankly till one said, "Food, quick."

There would be a long delay and wrangling of voices outside, and then perhaps the cook would appear and say that he heard he was wanted. One would be getting rather cross by this time and so would say that if breakfast did not appear in five minutes all the boys would get beaten. He would look in astonished amazement. He had never heard of such an outrageous demand as that any one should want breakfast in the morning.

So it would go on all through the day. The interpreter, by way of being a more or less educated native, would never put the questions one wanted, and would drive one to distraction by answering, "Yes" to a question such as, "What is his name?"

I dare say one's own irritability, after a certain time, helped towards misunderstanding, as one would get exasperated and perhaps not careful enough to give the lengthy explanations required to reach the native brain. Nevertheless, I have never met these absolutely black days in East Africa, Uganda, and other places. The natives there are happy-go-lucky, as most Africans are, and make the most extraordinary and uncalled-for mistakes. They do not, however, seem to suffer from that sudden and complete loss of all glimmerings of intelligence that the Central African appears subject to.

I have often pondered over this since and have come to the conclusion that the Central African, undoubtedly less intelligent than the northern Bantu, is more addicted to periods of blank unreceptiveness, when the mind is not working, and the individual is in a kind of state of coma. This state is induced by rest and having nothing to do, and so it was generally after a Sunday's rest, including feasting and drinking, or not having been sufficiently stirred up lately that these blank days occurred. A very noticeable thing with most Bantus is that work induces work, and leisure induces laziness of both mind and body.

One's boys always appear to their best advantage

under the most trying circumstances, so long as these circumstances are natural to them; there is nothing that upsets a native so much as new conditions. After a long and wearying march and a long period without food, it is really good to see the activity and care with which the camping arrangements are made, the celerity with which your dinner is prepared, and the thoughtfulness with which your little wants are looked after. Then, perhaps, before having rested or fed, one boy well be digging a trench round your tent, another washing your clothes; all will be busy at something, and one feels selfish to be sitting doing nothing while all this is being done for one.

Then take another day. Perhaps you start off hunting before dawn and get back after dark, hungry and utterly worn out. Your boys have had the whole day to rest and have not been worried at all. On such an occasion, one is seldom as well attended to as if they had been hard at work all day. One finds that the simplest and most ordinary duties have been forgotten. There is no clean water ready for drinking, insufficient firewood, although it only required a word to the porters to fetch it. The dinner has been skimped or forgotten, and there is no bath water or hot water for tea ready. The lamp is not lit and, in fact, nothing has been done since you left in the morning. With the prospect of an idle day before them, the boys have let their minds get into that state of coma from which it is difficult to arouse them.

It is rather difficult for a European to realise what such a state is, for his mind is always more or less active, whether consciously or unconsciously, even though he may appear to be doing nothing. I believe that the native is capable of assuming a state in which the mind is absolutely detached and not working, and when in such a state, he is only recalled by a start to his present surroundings.

The life of the head man of a village in Nyasaland, when not engaged in the strenuous pursuit of his official duties, is something like this. At sunrise he crawls out of his hut and sits outside. After a short time his wife crawls out and offers him some food. He eats this and then makes his way to a tree, perhaps a hundred yards from the village. Under this he sits in deep abstraction, till about noon a child brings him some food and water. After partaking of this, he moves a little so as to get the afternoon shade. He then sits in deep meditation till sunset, when he crawls into his hut and goes to sleep.

Sometimes he is joined by a few other old men under his tree. They hardly ever speak to each other, and if they say anything, it is to make some obvious remark as, "There is a dog," "Yes, it is a dog," "Oh," "Ah," and a further period of silence.

My cook, while at Fort Manning, married the daughter of a local chief. Soon afterwards the father came to visit his daughter, not so much from fatherly affection as with the idea of getting a present from the cook. I was on the verandah when he came. He sat down in the compound behind my house, and his daughter sat down about ten yards behind him with her back to him. I was doing some carpentering on the verandah and watched to see if they would say anything to each other, but they did not say a syllable.

Presently, I called the father to ask him some question about his village and he returned and said, "The white man says so and so." The daughter said, "Ah!" and they resumed their position with their backs to each other. I then went into the house to write, and when I came out again they were sitting in exactly the same position. An hour later the daughter got up and went into her house, whilst the father, having got some calico from his son-in-law, went off home.

The northern Bantus are much more lively and talkative than this, and really seem to take some interest in existence. I often think that unfamiliarity with a language and an inability to appreciate the limitations of a native's life make him appear much more stupid than he really is. If one comes to think of it, every one of the hundreds of objects with which a white man surrounds himself is foreign to the native and he has to learn their use. It must take some time for a raw boy to learn the purposes for which such articles are used, more especially as no native will ever ask another to tell him what he does not know, nor will any other native take the trouble to show or teach the new boy anything. He has to learn everything by observation.

Very strange are the mistakes made with the white man's belongings. Pictures are put upside down, a white canvas shoe is paired on the shelf with a brown leather boot, the table-cloth is arranged pattern downwards, and every conceivable mistake is made. A favourite saying of one of the old inhabitants of Nyasaland was, "that a native has only one way of doing a thing, and that is the wrong way," and it does seem as if he always manages to hit on the wrong way of doing a thing by an extraordinary fatality.

Take a tin of jam which has to be opened with a tin opener. To the native who cannot read the writing on the label and who never notices which side up a picture should be, the top and the bottom must look exactly alike. It is really immaterial which end is opened, but I have often remarked on the unerring instinct with which a native chooses the bottom to open.

I have often thought that when a thing was done wrong it impressed itself on one's mind, whereas the times it happened to be done right passed unobserved. With this thought in mind, I took statistics of a thing which could only be reasonably done in two ways. When my slippers were put out for me after my bath, as there was to the native eye no difference between the right and the left, there was a combination of two ways to arrange the slippers. Either the left slipper might be on the left of the right one or it might be on its right. It was, moreover, easy to make a note of one's observations by making a scratch on the wall. The theory of chance would lead one to expect that in the long run the two positions ought to come out about equal.

I forget the exact result of my statistics, but it was either eleven or thirteen times running that the slippers were put in the wrong position, viz., the left on the right of the right, and then I found them put right once.

I was so overcome that I ceased taking statistics at once for fear of spoiling the result. Of course it might really only be like a long run on the red at roulette, and I might have met afterwards an equally long run on the black, but I never noticed it.

I found that the Central African servant could seldom hold more than one idea in his head at the same time. For instance, if I told my boy after dinner to get me my pipe, tobacco, and matches, he would either bring none or only the last-named object, although one would naturally associate these articles together in one's mind. He did finally learn to bring them, or two of them together after a year's practice. I often amused myself by saying to him, "Get my pipe," and he would go and pick it up. Before he had given it to me, I would say, "and the tobacco." He would return and put the pipe down and take up the tobacco; then I would say, "and the matches," and he would hurriedly put down the tobacco and bring me the matches.

I was giving a dinner party in Zomba once and tried to spread myself over the feast. I took great trouble to explain all the dishes to the boys and the order in which they were to come. One of them was a savoury, and I had carefully explained that it came last. We got through the soup all right then in came the savoury. It was just being put in front of the guests, when I noticed it and hurriedly ordered its exit. After a long delay, we got the next course and then came the savoury again. Again I waived it away and we got on with another course, when the persevering savoury reappeared. One of the guests said, "What is this which keeps on coming in? I am going to have mine now, or else I may miss it," and so we set to and had the savoury and then went on with the rest of the dinner.

The Somali is a good servant. Of course he comes in a different category altogether from the Central African. I had an excellent one at Aden, who looked after all my things in the most careful and conscientious way. One day he came in with another servant and a policeman and explained that he was just going to prison for a couple of months, and so he had brought another servant to act for him whilst he was away, and to hand over all my things to him. He handed over and counted out everything down to the smallest detail and made the other servant responsible for them. It appeared that he was a well-known thief, but, like many good servants, he only stole other people's things and not his master's. When he came out of prison he came back to me smiling, and was very hurt that I did not reëngage him.

I have always taken great pains to learn the language of every country I have been in, or that was likely to be useful to me, and so at one time I took up the study of Somali. It is a very difficult language, but I myself believe that at one time I was fairly proficient. I could understand what the natives said, but I had great difficulty in making them understand what I said. There are several very extraordinary guttural sounds in the language. The ordinary European finds it hard enough to master some Arabic letters, such as *'ain* and the strong *h*. In Somali there appears to be a caricature of each of these letters. Whereas the Arabic *'ain* comes from the lower throat, often something resembling the noise induced by a sudden blow on the mark, the Somali *'ain* can only be compared to some of the noises reminiscent of a channel steamer.

No doubt, inability to pronounce these letters in the correct way made one somewhat difficult to understand, from the Somali point of view, but they did not occur by any means in all words, and one would have thought that one ought to be able to make oneself more or less intelligible after a time. However, if there was a slight error in a single and immaterial word, the Somali refused to understand the whole sentence, or anything one might say afterwards; which used to be the more annoying as one could understand when he made such remarks as, "What is the foreigner saying?" "I don't understand Hindustani or English," and so on.

When I went to Nyasaland after these experiences, I was filled with astonishment at the intelligence of the natives in understanding one. On my first arrival, I picked up a vocabulary and looked up "to want," and found "Kufuna"; then "knife," and found "Mpeni." Immediately the boy went off and fetched a knife, whereas after a year's study of Somali, the chances would be that I could not ask a raw Somali for the simplest object, and make him really understand me.

I have a sneaking admiration for the Somali. He is really indefeatable; he always comes out on top. He is the most extraordinary, arrogant, and conceited person in the world; he thinks he knows and can do everything, and it is impossible to convince him otherwise. He lives in the most hopeless country imaginable and there seems no possibility, at present, of ever being able to teach him that he is not a lord of creation, or at any rate the only part of the creation which he thinks worth anything, — that miserable bit of desert called Somaliland.

He often makes, as I have said, a very good servant, but I do not think he ever has any attachment for his master, although he is quite clever enough to simulate such a feeling if he thinks that it will inspire confidence and lead to extra wages. I believe the Somali, in the bottom of his heart, always despises the white man and imagines himself to be vastly superior in every way.

In the 1900 expedition, we left our baggage, servants, and a rear-guard in a zairba, whilst we made a long night march and attacked the Mullah's people next morning. In this engagement Captain Fredericks was killed.

When we returned to the zariba, I was much touched by Captain Fredericks' servant rushing up to me, wringing his hands, and showing every sign of, what I at first imagined to be, intense grief. He was an excellent servant and Fredericks had been a kind and indulgent master. The latter spoke Arabic, an accomplishment the Somalis look up to, and I thought that his servant was devoted to him.

"What shall I do? What shall I do?" he wailed. "My master is dead and I have not been paid my wages for the last two months!"

I told him that white men were not low thieves like Somalis and that he would of course get paid everything that was due to him. Down country, where there was no use for money, the servants and soldiers naturally did not draw any pay, but it was put by until their return to the coast. I doubt if anybody had any money to speak of. When, however, the servant had appreciated the fact that he would be paid in full when we reached the coast again, his grief subsided in the most wonderful way.

In spite of the Somali's obviously superior intelligence and ability, I would much rather have for servant the cheerful harum-scarum Bantu. He may smell and be forgetful, dirty, clumsy, and stupid, but he has certain doglike qualities which endear him to one.

The Swahili also often make excellent servants. They have all the cheerfulness and hardiness of the black, combined with a greater intelligence derived from the Arab. I had a Swahili cook, who was a perfect paragon in the bush, and as the greater part of my time with him was spent in trekking, he did me very well. Under very trying conditions he was at one time everything, cook, boy, head man of porters, everything rolled in one. Always cheerful, willing, and obedient and moreover intelligent, he was invaluable. However, he had one fault, he was an inveterate drunkard. He never helped himself to my spirits, but directly we arrived in a station, he managed to get drunk.

After several months exemplary conduct in the bush, we would roll up at a station. He would put up my tent, arrange the loads, and then disappear. No dinner would be forthcoming and nothing further would be heard or seen of him till twelve or one o'clock at night, when his return would be announced by a flow of the peculiarly disgusting oaths in which Swahili is so prolific. Usually polite and good-natured, at such times he would heap the most filthy abuse on porters, boys, or any native he could find.

Every time this happened, and it was only about once in three or four months that we touched at a station, I used to swear that I would give him a sound thrashing. He was always very penitent though, and when I remembered his faithful services, I could never bring myself to carry out my threat. When short of porters, I have seen him carry a tusk or a load through a long day's march, a thing a servant will never do, because it lowers him to the status of a porter. On arrival in camp, he would get up the tent, arrange my things, cook the food, dole out the porters' rations, bring in firewood, go off and buy supplies, nurse me when I was sick, and once, when I could not walk, he himself took one end of the pole of the improvised hammock and carried me for miles.

The native servant is always a potential thief. He may serve you honestly for years, except for minor pilfering, and then one day help himself to your belongings. As a rule, however, he only pilfers and this he cannot help doing. To try to put a stop to it, so long as he keeps it in bounds, is to make both your life and his a burden. I heard that a boy, who served me honestly and admirably on a long trek, returned to Mombasa after I left, with a good *chit* from me, engaged himself to another European and immediately absconded with two hundred rupees.

While on a little expedition one of my boys helped himself to money out of my box. I am very careless, and no doubt it was largely my fault for not keeping it locked up. If he had taken only half or three-quarters of what I had, I should never have been able to swear to the theft, although I might have suspected it, but when I found my bag of rupees empty, I knew that at least some must have been taken.

When I accused him of the theft, he immediately admitted it, and volunteered to work for me, for no pay, till he had made good his debt. He had also taken a note which he had asked a sergeant to cash, and it was the fact of the sergeant asking me if I had just given my boy a note which made me look at my box. As there was no way of spending money there, I asked what had become of it, and found that he had lost it all gambling with some Somalis.

He was duly but leniently punished, and then came back to me and asked to be reëngaged. This I should have liked to have done, as the chances are that he would have been honest with me in future, and I liked the youth. I argued that a known and discovered thief is just as good as an unknown and undiscovered one. However, as it would have been a bad example for the other boys to see him taken on again, I declined his services. A native does not feel any shame at being convicted and considers himself just as good after being punished as a native who has not yet been found out. I suppose he feels that he is not worse than anybody else but only more unfortunate in having been detected.

About the only servant I ever had whose honesty could be judged by European standards is a head man, Abdi Hassan, who trekked through Abyssinia with me and has also been with me in the Lado. However, he is a very exceptional man, his kindness to animals alone would distinguish him from any other native I have ever met. Only the other day, as we were trekking along, I heard him run up from behind to expostulate with a native, who was carrying two fowls head downwards, a practice so common in Africa that one often fails to notice it. I might add that the fowls were neither mine nor his, but the native's own, so he had no personal interest in the matter whatever. For an African, he is most wonderfully informed about current events. I do not know where he picks up his information, but he talks quite fluently about the royal family and asks questions about the French in Morocco.

The Northern African Bantu, as I have said, is much more intelligent than the Central African. They appear more observant and interested in one's belongings. They ask questions about anything of which they do not know the use. The Central African has not an enquiring mind, and it is seldom that he asks about anything he does not know.

The African is, on the whole, very thoughtful and seldom forgets anything he is told to do. That is to say, if you tell him to do anything next day or to remind you of something, he invariably does, although you yourself may have forgotten. On the other hand, he is quite likely to do something a hundred times in succession and forget absolutely about it the hundred and first time.

Many of his mistakes are attributable to not understanding and a fear of saying that he has not understood. If one does not make oneself clear, the boy invariably says "yes," and seldom asks you to explain more fully or says that he did not hear. This pretending to understand is sometimes very comic, and sometimes very annoying.

I was going down the Nile once, and we saw a steamer coming up. I was wondering if it was the post boat, when I heard some of the Sudanese talking about it and saying that it was the Compania boat. Not knowing what this was, I turned to a Swahili beside me and asked him what kind of boat it was. He turned and asked the Sudanese, who said it was the Compania, to which he replied, "Oh, of course, so it is." Then he turned to me and said, "Master, it is the Compania boat." "And what kind of boat is that?" I replied. "How do I know?" was the answer; "that is all they said it was."

Two other incidents connected with African servants and I will stop. In different parts of Africa I must have heard or myself asked the question from a boy, "What is this?" as a joint or stew is offered, some hundred times. The question generally originates from the fact that there are several kinds of meat in the larder, perhaps a leg of mutton and a bushbuck, whilst one's companion has shot a waterbuck or hartbeest. The invariable answer is, whether the boy is Uganda, Swahili, Yao, or whatever the tribe, "Meat."

Once I was travelling down-stream with my orderly Matola and another native in a very unstable canoe. Suddenly we rocked and the orderly who was standing up to pole was precipitated into the river, whilst the canoe half filled with water. The other native and I just managed to retain our places in the canoe, whilst the gallant Matola struck out lustily for the bank. Looking over his shoulder, he called out to me to see if my pocket-book was safe, as it was in the pocket of my coat, which I had taken off and hung over the end of the canoe. The purposes for which it was used must have been quite a mystery to him, but he knew that it was a thing I set great store by. It was the first thing he thought about on emerging from under water, whereas one would have thought the probability of crocodiles would have been sufficiently engrossing.

CHAPTER XI

THE Lugware had a very bad reputation as a hostile and warlike tribe. The Belgians told us that it was impossible to go to their country without a large escort of troops.

Hart was the first to come in contact with them, at the southeast end of their country, and found it a good elephant country, as no one had been shooting there. He was unable to proceed as he did not have enough porters and so returned to the Nile where he met me.

He had come across two funny old men at the villages he came to, who were distinguished from their fellows by wearing clothes. Even had it not been for this distinction, I should have had no difficulty in recognising them, when I saw them, from Hart's description. One wore a hat closely resembling a Chinese pagoda, whilst from their eccentric behaviour, he called them the two knockabout artists.

Under the auspices of these two gentlemen, I made my first essays in elephant shooting amongst the Lugware. They accompanied me from village to village and everywhere the people were as hospitable as their abject poverty permitted. Owing to frequent raids from all the surrounding tribes, who were better armed with muskets, their country had little to offer. Large tracts of it were absolutely denuded of stock and even chickens, while they said it was little use planting as the surrounding tribes came and burnt their villages and grain stores.

A purveyor of meat under these circumstances was a godsend to the people, and they came in from far and wide with news of elephant. After shooting a few days in the country of the knockabouts, I camped by a big river. The rains had already set in heavily and the streams were constantly impassable. Whilst camped here, I witnessed a lively scene. Many of the people from the other bank had flocked over for elephant meat. The stream was rushing down in full flood, and on each bank was a crowd of people watching their crossing. One after another they flopped in, holding spears or bows and arrows over their heads with one hand. Others had baskets of meat, and shouts of laughter greeted those who got into difficulties, or were swept down the stream. The women did not attempt to swim, but lay flat on the water whilst two men steered each one across.

I wanted to take a photograph of this merry, aquatic party, but directly I got out my camera one of my porters, who thought he knew all about the requirements of a picture, herded everybody out of the way. The only pictures he had seen me take were those of

dead elephant, before taking which any natives blocking the way had to be moved aside, and so he thought
that the driving away of natives was a *sine qua non*.
Seeing his action, an officious head man on the other
bank shouted out to everybody to clear out, the crowd
on both banks disappeared like lightning, those in the
water ducked or scuttled out of the way, and there
was nothing left to take but the empty river.

Slowly the people returned, but did not devote themselves to their water sports in the same whole-hearted
way as before and cast anxious glances from time to
time at my camera. So I put it away and prepared to
depart, when those on the opposite bank shouted at me
and a man came tumbling across the river to say that
the chief was bringing some milk for me.

This same chief was minus a finger, the raw stump of
which I dressed for him. He made desperate efforts
to get me milk such as I could drink, and it was only
on the third day that I finally got it pure by sending
my cook to superintend the milking. The first con-
signment that was brought was of very ancient date
and covered by a green fungus.

Two years later I visited this spot, after the enclave
had been taken over by the Sudan government. This
same chief recognised me at once, as was attested by his
waggling the stump of his finger at me. He said that
he was going to bring me some milk, and one of my
servants, who knew nothing about my former visit, as

then I only had natives with me from Uganda and East Africa, tried to explain to him how to obtain the milk clean. He was very indignant and said, "Do you think I don't know how the white man likes his milk, when he doctored my finger and I brought him milk every day?"

The natives with me had heard such stories about the Lugware and how it was impossible to go near them, that they were very astonished to find that I had been there before and was on friendly terms with all the chiefs.

Whilst in the country of the knockabouts, elephant spoor led me twice past spots at which I had recently killed elephant, a coincidence that I have noticed before.

I moved up the river and the knockabouts returned to their homes, he of the pagoda hat looking more eccentric than ever in a pair of my pajamas.

Whilst stopping at the next village, great consternation and alarm were caused by a native coming into camp and insisting on sleeping by the camp-fire. He was persuaded by the cook to go away but soon he returned saying that he had been home to feed and that now he had come back to sleep. My cook came and told me of this, and said that it was certain that he meditated some mischief, such as murdering us all while we were asleep or stealing a rifle. Would a man, the cook argued, leave his house, his wife, his children, and all his goods to come and sleep by a stranger's camp-fire unless he meditated some dark action? His house was but a stone's throw away and it would be easy for him to return home and come back in the morning.

I had the mysterious stranger brought to me. He was a pleasant looking and cheerfully disposed youth. As we only had a few words in common, the interview was not productive of much, but I gathered that he had brought a chicken earlier in the day as a present. Thinking that the cause of his not wanting to lose sight of us might be that he had not yet received anything in exchange, I made him a present, and asked him if he was going home. No; he was going to sleep by our fire.

As we were absolutely dependent on the good-will of the natives for food, and we always tried to establish as friendly relations as possible, I told Husseni to let him be, but to be careful about leaving anything about, whilst I put all my rifles under my bed.

We woke up in considerable trepidation next morning, but soon discovered that we were all alive and well, and the rifles all safe, whilst the genial stranger was still with us. He excused himself to get breakfast, and a few minutes later returned to accompany me out hunting. During the whole of our stay in the country, we found the much maligned Lugware most friendly and hospitable. They were, it is true, raw and utterly unsophisticated savages, but nevertheless they always made us feel welcome.

The river having gone down sufficiently, we crossed to the other side, and our friends came to the bank with us and bade us good-bye, and waved their hands at us as if we were never going to see them again, whereas we were going to camp just an hour away.

After choosing a site for camp, I went out hunting and shortly came on a spoor which joined some others. I was about to follow the newest, when a little Baganda porter called Maliko pointed out that the original and older spoor was of a bigger elephant and so I took that. When we got out into less hard country, we found that it was really a big elephant, and a lone one, for it never joined any others, so I rewarded Maliko with a vest on return to camp.

This elephant seemed to prefer to walk down wind and gave us a long hunt. At last, when the spoor began to show traces of being quite fresh and we were expecting every moment to overhaul him, the old fool marched down wind straight into the plantations of some villages and then hearing the people shouting got alarmed and stampeded off, so we had to begin the long track all over again.

At last we came out on a stream, and my porters urged me to go back, as the stream was too deep to wade and the elephant evidently did not intend to stop. I was not going to be diverted so easily, especially as I figured out enormous tusks, so undressed and crossed

ELEPHANTS SHOT IN THE LADO ENCLAVE

The tusks of the upper one scaled 94 and 86 pounds. The shooting of the lower
elephant is described in this chapter.

the stream, which after all was only up to the armpits but was going very fast.

Again the old elephant steered down wind and it seemed hopeless; however, we stolidly held the spoor till it crossed the wind again. Suddenly, coming round a corner, I got the start I had been preparing for for so long, as there he was, standing forty yards away. I thought that I would make certain of him, so exchanged the mannlicher for the big bore; not without some difficulty, however, as directly we saw him, the gallant Maliko retired with it.

I came up again and let loose both barrels. The elephant moved forward a bit and stood evidently badly shaken up. I must make certain of him and so turned for the mannlicher. The trusty Maliko was twenty or thirty yards in the rear. There was no time to be lost so I ran to him. Maliko misinterpreted this action, however, and came to the conclusion that I was hotly pursued by the elephant. The bush was thick and he could not see from where he was, so he turned and fled whilst I pursued him.

Finally I got the mannlicher and came back again and found my elephant patiently awaiting me. I fired four shots with the mannlicher, each of which misfired. I found afterwards that whilst crossing the river, water had got into the bolt and rusted it, a thing which had never happened with my old one, which I had had seven years, whilst this was a new one.

The mannlicher being useless, I must needs get my big bore again, and again Maliko retired before me. Finally I got the big bore and returned again to my old position. The elephant was still standing in the same place, only now he had turned away from me instead of being broadside. Probably he would have fallen anyhow in another few minutes, as he must have been very badly hit not to move. Anyhow, I would make certain of him, so I moved up close alongside and put a shot into the shoulder and he dropped.

The enormous tusks I had imagined from the size of the spoor were only forty pounds. The size of the spoor is generally a very fair test of age and, hence, size of tusk. Of the five elephant we shot in Uganda, my rule came out exactly. Here are the weights of tusks and sizes of spoor.

1. size of spoor, $19\frac{1}{2}''$ weight of two tusks, 114 lbs.
2. size of spoor, $20''$ weight of two tusks, 126 lbs.
3. size of spoor, $20\frac{3}{4}''$ weight of two tusks, $132\frac{1}{2}$ lbs.
4. size of spoor, $21''$ weight of two tusks, 136 lbs.
5. size of spoor, $22''$ weight of two tusks, $172\frac{1}{2}$ lbs.

However, there are often exceptions to this rule and this was one, as his spoor was twenty and a half inches and the weight of the two tusks seventy-nine pounds. I have noticed, though, that elephant have bigger feet in some countries than others. The relative sizes of tusk and foot are fairly uniform in one country, but cannot be compared so well with measurements from another.

The elephant had taken us round in a circle and so we were not so very far from our camp. We shortly struck a path which took us to a village and from there we got a guide to take us by the shortest way back to camp.

As we approached camp, we met all our friends from the other side of the river who had bidden us such a long and affectionate good-bye that morning. They were all unrestrainedly drunk, having got into this state at the expense of the villages this side.

The chief was waving an unfortunate fowl round his head, which he had brought me as a present. They rushed to greet us as if they had not seen us for years, and tears and protestations of undying friendship, interluded with hiccups, were showered on us.

I took down the bolt of my rifle and cleaned the firing pin and spring. It fired all right after this, but the spring had been weakened, and I was badly let down later with the same rifle. This was a new rifle bought from a gunmaker I imagined to be as good as any in England. I had not taken down the bolt of my old mannlicher for years and I now did so and found the spring and firing pin as good as ever.

A great feature of native information is its extraordinary inaccuracy. Some one hears from some one else that spoor has been seen, and he comes into camp and declares he has just seen elephant, and fills in picturesque details from his imagination. From long practice,

I have become inured to disappointments in this respect and never expect to find anything resembling what has been described to me. If a man rushes in breathless to say that two elephant are standing just behind my tent, I finish breakfast calmly and then prepare for a long day. I go out expecting to see anything or nothing. There is one thing I feel fairly certain about and that is, if we do see elephant it may be any number from one to five hundred, but that we most certainly will not meet with the exact number enumerated.

As I write now, I have just returned from a hunt after two males reported with tusks as long as a spear. I went out and actually did see elephant; they were six small tuskers, and I marvelled at the extraordinary accuracy of the information. There is not much difference between two and six. After I had left them and come back, a second native, not knowing that I had been out, came across them and rushed in to tell me that there were three and he had been watching them all day.

Whilst out near Hargeisa in Somaliland once, I came on a leopard. I forget if I fired and missed, or whether I did not get time for a shot. Anyhow, the leopard was only a second or so in sight and bounded off. Presently a Somali appeared and told me that he had driven the leopard from bush to bush by throwing stones at it, from a place about ten miles off so as to let me have a shot at it.

I apologised for not shooting it, and asked him if he would mind just driving it back again and I would be ready for it this time. This was of course an attempt to extort bakshish on the assumption that white men were the most inconceivable idiots.

The genial black's false information is, however, quite spontaneous. I believe he half or wholly believes it all himself, or at best he does it to please. Therefore, it is ridiculous getting annoyed with him for what he cannot help, and I always feel vexed with myself afterwards, if I have allowed myself to show any signs of bad temper. The Arabs realise that the black cannot help making these occasional howlers, and are often wonderfully long-suffering with them on this account. Instance the stories in the Arabian Nights of "the three apples," and also the slave who told one lie a year.

In the first, a senseless lie on the part of a slave causes a man to kill his wife on the charge of infidelity, and in the second, the slave causes all sorts of disasters. In both cases, the slaves went unpunished; they were not even whipped.

On the day after shooting the elephant just described, I got very irritable over some false information brought in, an irritability which might be natural in a novice but unpardonable in one who had had so much experience of the black. At 6.30 A.M., a youth dashed into my camp, as I was having a leisurely breakfast, to be followed by a quiet restful hunt near camp, and said that he had that moment seen three elephant with tusks as long as his arms outstretched.

This was the stock length for tusks in this country, just as in Uganda they are always the length of the narrator's spear, about eight feet out of the gums. I took no notice of the latter statement, but I really thought that he might have seen elephant or fresh spoor. I continued my breakfast, and asked if he had heard about them or really seen them. "Seen them?" He pointed to his eyes and said that moment he had just come from looking at them.

As it was 6.30 A.M., there had been scarcely an hour of daylight so far, so if he had seen elephant or spoor that day, the very farthest it could be was one hour away and the chances were that it was half that distance. So I set out after the youth and we walked two solid hours through villages northwards. Then we came to a small village and my guide sat down and had a long conversation with a man of the village.

Another man was produced. The youth cheerfully admitted, on being pressed, that it was not really himself, but this man, who had actually seen the elephant this morning. Of course this was manifestly impossible, as news could not have reached my camp by 6.30, but such is most native information and the point remained that there probably were or had been elephant in the neighbourhood, to make them think of coming to tell me.

I now set out with the new guide. This time we went through the bush. We walked for another solid two hours without seeing a trace of elephant new or old. I then got annoyed and sent him away. I continued with my porters and we actually did find the spoor of a solitary elephant. We followed it till 5.30 P.M., but it was still old spoor of the night before, and so we returned to camp, tired and cross. The annoying part was that where we finally left the spoor was the other side of camp and in the exact locality I had intended to hunt over that day. If I had pursued my original intention, we might have struck the spoor at eight o'clock in the morning at the place in which we left it at 5.30 that evening and so had the whole day before us to follow it on from there.

Having played out this locality, we moved on to Mount Gessi. Here I got on to the spoor of a herd, but the natives, in their eagerness for meat and desire to bring me back news, rushed out ahead of me and gave them their wind.

The people near Gessi were so pleasant that I decided to wait there a few days, or to make short expeditions and return again, especially as I was expecting Hart up shortly. There was a very intelligent boy here, the son of the chief, who arranged all my hunting in the vicinity, and spent his whole time at our camp sewing shirts out of the calico I gave him.

I shot two elephant under the mountain one day,

one a one-tusker. The second I had followed up wounded; when I found him standing and put a shot into him, he charged backwards into a thick patch of bush and finally sat down. I have never seen an elephant perform a similar evolution. He almost pranced like a rearing horse and moved some thirty yards or more stern first.

When he disappeared from sight in the bush, I could see nothing of him, although I reconnoitred carefully. Finally I followed into the bush, but it was so dense that I still could not see, till suddenly I came round a thick patch and found him with ears spread out, a few yards from me and still breathing. However, he was unable to rise and I finished him as he sat.

Whilst wandering over the hills, I passed the old site of a Belgian camp at Mount Wati. The old road had overgrown, but on the site of the station there was only short grass. Amongst this, I found, to my delight, some small button tomatoes. This was a great find, as not only had one no meat, but also the only vegetables I had been able to obtain for the last week or so were a few sweet potatoes, and very hard, dry beans.

I am not fond of elephant meat; in fact it is tough, strong, and distasteful to me, but I had to subsist on it occasionally. Two days after killing these two elephant, I began to be very hard up for provisions. I had not made any biltong of elephant meat as I might have done, I had grown to dislike it so. I had no milk, flour, sauce, or anything left. For three days I subsisted on beans and bovril. I managed to get a lamb about the size of a chicken but kept this for Hart's arrival. It is a boring diet, beans and coarse millet pulse for breakfast and ditto for dinner; moreover, it upsets the stomach.

It might be thought that the natives treated me badly in the way of produce; they really were very good but had nothing. A pumpkin was brought up for me from a village a day away. When very hungry, I bethought me of a village we had passed about ten or fifteen miles back, at which the chief had come out and presented me with a chicken. I sent a party back to this village with presents to try to obtain another. As I have said, the people had been robbed and looted by different expeditions and the surrounding tribes and had nothing, or what they had was hidden in the bush miles away.

When my people came to this village and asked for a chicken, the old chief said, "There is my village; go in and see what you can find. If you find any chicken there, take it and give it to the white man; but you will find nothing, for the one I gave him was the last one I had." Being natives they went and looked and found that the old man's words were true. I think that this is almost the most generous thing I have known of and the reader can imagine that one has had a soft spot in one's heart for the Lugware ever since.

Later, when I was in the service of the Sudan government, all the tribes round came to complain of the enormities committed by the Lugware,—how they killed and pillaged everybody and how I must not go near them without troops. I listened politely and then went up to their country. As I had imagined, they were not the aggressors. They had been shamefully robbed and looted by better armed tribes, but they are a fairly truculent people and any attempts made by them to regain what actually belonged to them, of stock and enslaved children, had been magnified into unprovoked and uncalled for assaults.

They are better off now, as they have had a little time in which to recover, but at that time they really were in a poverty-stricken condition.

On the bean diet I was really very bored till Hart suddenly rolled up, bringing fresh supplies from Nimule. I had had a shelter built at my camp, which afforded pleasant shade during the day. I returned from an expedition after elephant and found that Hart had arrived, and we feasted on such luxuries as bread, jam, tea, milk, and sardines and the lamb I had saved up. Next day Hart trekked on, whilst I returned to the following up of an elephant I had wounded.

CHAPTER XII

(Continued)

THIS elephant hunt began before Hart arrived back, but as it finished after he left again, I have kept it in one to make it more consecutive.

Whilst at the camp I had made at Gessi, a native came in to tell me about one lone elephant who lived by himself and never moved from a certain spot. I have so often heard about him that I begin to know him well, although I have never met him. I have heard about him in Uganda and in Nyasaland, but here he seems specially to thrive. He is so old that he can hardly move, his tusks touch the ground as he walks, he is always by himself, and stands about in the same place for months at a time.

I was taken down to a village three hours distant and from here we commenced our search. After wandering about for many hours we had come on no more recent tracks than some three days old. These had been seen the day before, and the rest of the story had been built up on this foundation.

We arrived back at the village at 3 P.M. and the chief brought out food for the porters with me. As we were sitting at this village some men came in from another and said that they had seen ten elephant close to their village.   On receipt of this news, we immediately started off again.

Now I think a hunter who has been going from sunrise to 3 P.M. on false news and then, whilst still three hours away from his camp, starts on new *khabar* at that time, either deserves some great reward, or ought to be restrained under lock and key.

We followed our new guide through a few villages, and then met two men who rushed sweating out of the bush and said, "There they are just there." We followed these new men for an hour and they led us to a place where elephant had been standing for their midday halt, but had evidently moved on some three hours ago.

Still undaunted, we proceeded till sunset and were then just about to abandon pursuit, when I heard something move in front.   I listened and heard the rustling of a big body pushing through the bushes.   I hurried on and found that one big bull had detached himself from the spoor of the remainder, and he it was that we had heard.   He had evidently got our wind and was moving on fast.   I raced down his track and it led us round in a semicircle till it joined the spoor of the others again.   Once more I heard a rustling ahead and so ran on.

Now an old bull very often cannot be bored to go

right away when he gets your wind, but he will stampede perhaps eight hundred yards and then stop, and
listen for you and try to get your wind. If he finds that
he is still being followed, he will do another stampede
and wait again. After a time he gets tired of this
game and either goes right off or gets seriously annoyed.

This is what this old bull had been doing; he had
hurried away from my wind two if not three times,
and now I was running after him again. I fancied
that I saw something moving in the bushes about fifty
yards away and next moment I was aware that an
elephant was crashing towards me. The bushes were
too dense to see through, he was coming from my left,
whilst in front of me was a more open space of about
twenty yards across and then thick bush again.

I hurriedly skipped across this space and turned
round just in time to see an elephant with magnificent
great tusks come out and stand on the exact spot on
which I had been stationed a moment before. On
arrival there, he missed the wind and stood moving his
trunk round nosing for a whiff. I had a splendid clear
broadside shot, and raised the mannlicher which had
played me false before. I had two beautiful misfires,
and then the third shot went off. It was badly aimed,
as I hardly expected it to fire, and it hit him too far
back.

Nevertheless, he dropped on his knees and I tried
another shot, which was also a misfire. I found after-

wards that the striker spring had broken and it was a wonder that it went off at all. The rifle was now successfully out of action till later I managed to fit it with a new spring at Nimule.

I then bethought me of the big bore. The last I had seen of it was in the hands of a porter, who was called the Kirongozi, or the guide, making tracks into the bush. I yelled loudly for him and ran to where I had last seen him. As I ran, I looked back and saw the elephant slowly pick himself up and begin a stately retirement. It was now nearly dark and by the time I had secured the big bore the elephant was nowhere to be seen. I raced down his track till I could not see to go any farther and then gave up, cursing the gunmaker and the Kirongozi indiscriminately.

The elephant had a truly beautiful pair of tusks, enormously thick and massive. It is very difficult to judge the weight when seen like that, but they must have been well over the hundred and as they were so thick they might easily have been one hundred and twenty or one hundred and thirty.

A long trek back in the dark did not improve my frame of mind, and when the cook served my dinner, I stated my views about the bravery of Baganda and Banyoro at some length, instancing Maliko and the Kirongozi as typical examples. My remarks were both unjust and unfair, as they were but porters, and were not paid for the work of gunbearers. My own gunbearer, Tengeneza, was with Hart, and he was as staunch a fellow as one could possibly wish to meet.

After some fifteen or sixteen hours' trek there was nothing better than beans for dinner mixed with red millet flour. Perhaps on a better meal I should have felt more generously disposed.

I decided to start early next morning and take my camp down to last night's village, and try to find the wounded big-tusker. Once a night has elapsed, however, it is a thankless task and hardly worth undertaking. The almost invariable procedure of a wounded elephant, when night comes on, is to make a series of winds and turns in thick grass and bush, which will perhaps take six hours walking or more to cover. Then having successfully bewildered any one who may follow, as they appear to imagine, they trek straight out of the district to an enormous distance. It is practically impossible to cover their night's walk during the hours of daylight next day.

To a late hour I heard the cook lecturing little Maliko and the Kirongozi about their enormities. Before daylight next day, we packed up and were ready to trek at sunrise. We were just about to move, when a native rushed in to say that he had that moment seen two bulls. Yes, he had seen them both with his own eyes. Apparently, a native never sees spoor when he is out by himself; he always sees the animal itself.

Two bulls in the hand appeared better than one in

the bush, so I left my porters with instructions to wait till two o'clock and, if I was not back by then, to pitch camp again in the same spot. The cook placed the big bore in Maliko's hands with final instructions on how to deport himself, and we started off.

A short trek down the pathway and we came to spoor of the night before. We followed this and I at once noticed that it was the track of one animal not of two. Just to chaff the native I said, "This is one. Where is the other?" The ready imagination of the savage was quite equal to the emergency. He had seen this elephant and he walked on till he met two other animals who had come from Mount Gessi. He was quite certain about this, although the mountain was seven or eight miles distant. Then the one had trekked on whilst the two were standing under a tree.

I began to look attentively at the spoor and then suddenly realised, of all wonderful strokes of luck, it was my wounded bull of yesterday. He had done his six hours of winding and twisting and turning in the thick country below, all of which we were saved, and this was his trek away. He was going along at a good pace and never stopped except once for a roll in a mud hole. About the other two reported, our guide was quite certain that they were standing under a tree close by; he had seen them there.

I thought that we might have a look before going on, as it was quite possible for other elephant to be about.

Photographs by R. A. Osborne.

BABY ELEPHANT WITH DEAD MOTHER

The young one was only discovered after it had been found necessary to shoot the female.

He pointed out the exact spot, and after taking elaborate precautions for wind, we approached only to find that the whole story was a myth and there was no spoor at all. I then hastened back and cut the spoor of my bull farther on. It was still my bull and I had no doubt about it, but the native pointed to it triumphantly and said that that was the spoor of the two other bulls he had seen and they must have moved on.

At last we came to a tree where he had stood for a moment and then moved on into some thick grass fifteen feet high. Remembering his behaviour of yesterday, I was really very diffident about following him through this stuff.

I must now leave the elephant, to remark on little Maliko. I was full of contempt for him before, but after this day I considered him the pluckiest person I have ever met. A man may do a rash or foolhardy thing without being in the least plucky. It is all a matter of temperament. If a man, while in a ghastly funk, performs a plucky action I consider him a real hero.

I remember once, when a boy, hearing a story of two soldiers going into battle together, one a fire-eater, and the other a well-known coward. As the first few shells came whizzing past, the former looked on the latter's pale face and said, "Hulloa, old fellow, how do you feel now, eh?" The latter replied, "If you felt like I do now, you would be running away."

Now little Maliko had received such a wigging from the cook that he felt heartily ashamed of himself. He followed close at my heels with the spare rifle and as we entered this thick stuff, his teeth were chattering and yet he valiantly stuck to me. Once or twice, I stopped suddenly to listen, and poor little Maliko started out of his skin, thinking that the elephant was at hand. I saw that he was about to run, and then he pulled himself together and stood his ground.

We got through this thick bit and both Maliko and myself breathed freer. Our respite was only for a moment though, as presently we came to a bottom of thick grass and reeds in which the track wound about and sometimes was nothing but a tunnel through the stalks of the grass which met overhead. I came round a corner suddenly on to a tree, under which the elephant had stood, and I felt glad that he had had the consideration to move on, as it would have been quite an awkward meeting at such close quarters.

Still we burrowed on through the reeds, little Maliko, shivering with fright, following close behind me. Suddenly, in one of the numerous windings, I was brought up sharp by a great black mass in front of me. There he was half-facing me exactly five yards away. This is the closest I have ever been to an African bull, unconscious of my presence, except that in the South Kensington Museum, and the closest I ever wish to be.

As I stood, one of his enormous tusks just came in the

way of the heart shot. If I had moved back a foot, the grass would have been in my way and I certainly was not going to move forward another inch. I had to do something. If I retired, I could never get in a position from which I could see him, so I decided to fire, aiming just to miss the tusk.

I cannot imagine now why I did not go for the head shot. Anyhow, I fired into his side just too far back for the heart; he plunged into the grass, and I took the precaution to reload before following. When I came out of the thick bed of reeds, I saw him crossing a broad, shallow valley. Before I was half-way across this, he was going up the opposite slope.

I followed at a run and caught him up in some bush country where I had occasional views of his stern. I fired into this and ran on reloading as I went. After I had repeated this operation several times, I was in the act of reloading, when I heard a scream of rage and he was charging back along his own track. I had no time to complete reloading before he was on top of me. I cowered behind a thorn bush about one and a half feet in height, at one side of the track, and he brushed past, his extended ear passing over my head.

He stopped about twenty yards beyond me, testing the wind. I reloaded and tried to move round for a shot, as his back was to me; but before I had got to a good position, he was gone and I never saw him again.

Maliko appeared after a time with the spare rifle, looking very scared. I noticed that the muzzle was plugged up with mud, showing that it had been dropped. It was lucky that I had not suddenly required it in this condition, as it probably would have burst. As a storm was breaking and it was well on in the afternoon, I returned to camp.

Next day numbers of natives went out to look for the elephant. They were to bring me in news which way he had gone and I was to take on my camp and try to find him. I have said that it is fairly hopeless trying to get a wounded elephant once a night has intervened. I have never yet done so but I am always just as optimistic. I believe that a wounded elephant after travelling forty miles or so reaches some place where he does not move about much till he has recovered.

I have often wounded an elephant and come up with him again the same day and then finished him, but never yet retrieved one that has got away wounded, once the night falls. I have, it is true, twice shot elephant late in the evening and not found them till afterwards, but that is a different thing, as in both cases they were lying dead quite near the spot at which I shot them and could not be considered to have got away.

It fills me with surprise how some men seem to get their elephant, year after year, by going out and shooting at elephant and then sending natives to retrieve them.

In a week or fortnight, the tusks roll up. In all my experience, I have never got an elephant that I did not actually down myself, on the same day, except the two alluded to above.

However, I determined that this big elephant should be an exception, and intended to follow the spoor just so long as we could hold it, even if it was a week or ten days.

News was brought in that he had crossed the big river, and so I took my camp on there and picked up the spoor, which was now old. I had an abscess on my leg, no doubt caused by the poverty of feeding of the last few weeks. It was intensely painful, till after two days walking it burst, which relieved the pain. I thought all would be well then, but on the third day my foot had swollen to such an extent that I was unable to get on my boot, and so I had to give up my big elephant and return to my camp, carried by my men.

On my return to the camp at Mount Gessi, I heard that our brother-officer, Captain Craigie Halkett, had been smashed up by an elephant near Wadelai. Afterwards I learnt that he had been charged in thick grass and that the elephant had stabbed him through the thigh with his tusk, and had then taken him up and thrown him away; he landed on his shoulder, which caused a big contusion. No medical assistance was available, and he lay in a critical condition till the steamer came, when he was taken to Butiaba and carried to Entebbe. Subsequently he completely recovered from this smash-up and is now as fit as ever.

After my abscess had healed up and the swelling gone down, I set off on the Dufile Road. This had become completely overgrown since the time of the Belgians and we lost the track for hours at a time. We reached the old Belgian station of Arenga, which had been burnt down by the natives, and I found some more tomatoes here, which pleased me greatly. The instinct of getting something unexpectedly for nothing is common to all mankind. As a friend of mine said, "Even a millionnaire is delighted to pick up sixpence in the street." It is something of the same spirit which prompts the poacher; whilst the pleasure the fisherman and shooter find in devouring the spoils of their chase is not lessened by the thought that they have not paid for them.

We obtained two guides to show us the way, and when we camped, a crowd of people surrounded us to watch the process of pitching the tents and comment thereon. As I was afraid that our two guides would get lost in the crowd and be unrecognisable later, I pointed them out, whilst I still knew who they were, to Husseni, so that they might be duly rewarded. Husseni, to make quite certain that the right men should get the presents, pounced on them and drew them out of the crowd, placing them on one side, till the loads of trade goods should be opened.

This action the crowd misinterpreted. They saw two of their number smelt out, or detected by some process, and dragged aside to meet their doom. There was no telling on whom the finger of fate would next fall, and so they all fled incontinently to a safe distance. When they perceived that the two suspects each received a present of salt and cloth, they returned, looking very foolish, no doubt imagining that if they had waited, others too might have been put on the proscribed list for punishment with salt and calico.

A day or two's march from Dufile, I met with a country of enormously tall grass. Here I came on the spoor of a herd and, following it, came up with them near enough to hear, but was unable to see anything. After manœuvring some time, I climbed a tree about sixty yards from where they were standing and saw only females and young. However, they moved on again before I had satisfied myself that there was not a bull in the herd.

I followed on again and presently heard the rumble of an elephant from one side. Thinking that it was one of the herd become detached, I circled round, for had I continued after the herd, I should have given him my wind. Suddenly I got a glimpse of the author of the rumble at about fifty yards' distance, a convenient elephant path, where the grass had been trampled down, just allowing me a glance at him down its vista.

He was a bull, but I put him down as quite a small one. However, as far as I could see, he was as good as anything in the herd, and as I was suffering from elephant hunger, not having shot one for some time, I let drive at him. It appeared afterwards that he did not belong to the herd but was a lone bull who happened to be passing from the opposite direction.

He disappeared into the grass and I followed his track, which went down wind. There was a copious blood spoor, but owing to his proceeding down wind and the thickness of the grass, which never enabled me to see more than a few yards, it was a most unpleasant business to follow. The day was sultry and there was not a breath of air, whilst the elephantine grass crushed in on all sides.

As I proceeded, one of my putties got loose. It became looser and looser till the end was trailing on the ground. Now to stop in the middle of an elephant track, with grass choking one on all sides, and to stoop over and undo, roll up, and retie one's puttie is a very unpleasant job. The sun overhead strikes one's back and neck, the blood runs to one's head, and the stalks of grass get in one's way and have a knack of getting tied up inside the puttie.

For this reason I went on and on, the puttie becoming looser and looser, hoping to meet with some ant-hill or tree on which to rest my foot while arranging it. At last there was a yard or so of puttie trailing behind me as I walked, and yet I was too lazy to stop and attend to it.

Presently I met a sapling alongside the path and it forked just about three feet above the ground. I put my foot up in the fork and started work on the puttie. I had just got it off and was commencing to roll it up, preparatory to retying it, when I heard from close by the very faint but unmistakable sound of an elephant's ear rubbing against his side. My foot was already in the tree fork, and it required little effort to raise myself up on it, but still I could see nothing. There was another fork a few feet up, and I raised myself into this and saw the elephant's head. He was facing me at thirty yards' distance, and the wind was blowing straight from me to him.

I let drive at his forehead from this position, but what with my efforts to hold on, I was unable to note what happened on my shot. All I could see was that he had disappeared. I approached a little nearer and could see nothing. I then found another elephant path at right angles and circled round on it but again saw nothing. Finally I plucked up courage and made straight for the spot at which I had seen him. I saw nothing till within a few yards and then got a glimpse of a black form on the ground. I came nearer and found him lying dead. To my surprise he was a very fine tusker. The grass in this locality was so enormous that it had quite dwarfed him, and being alone there was nothing else with which to compare him.

I examined the place carefully and came to the conclusion that if I had followed his spoor I might have seen him from a distance of ten yards; but this was doubtful and it would have been more probable that I should have had to come within five yards of him to get my first view. Of course I could not have had the faintest idea that he would have been there and it was only the very gentle ear-flap that warned me of his presence.

Now the moral of the story is this. If my puttie had not come down, or if I had been such a tidy and methodical person that it would have been more painful to me to walk along with a dragging puttie than to stoop in the sun to do it up, I should certainly not have had that warning. He had my wind and was evidently waiting for me. I should have walked up within ten or five yards of him without knowing that he was there, if he had not let me know before, but it is more probable that he would have charged at fifteen or twenty yards.

On my return to camp, I found that Husseni had bought a small Serval cat for me. He was sitting in the basket in which the chickens were carried on the march. Unfortunately, he died before he reached an age at which it would have been really dangerous for the chickens to have him as a fellow-passenger.

Husseni, ever zealous in trying to keep me well fed under very difficult circumstances, was in a great state of exhilaration. He said that he had just concluded an arrangement by which I could get two sheep, a luxury I had not tasted since the small lamb I got at Gessi. One of the villagers had brought an old broken musket to be mended, and Husseni had spent the greater part of the day in bargaining with him what he would pay for my services as gunsmith, and it was finally assessed at two sheep.

The musket was produced, a very old, rusty gas barrel of the tower-musket type, and, on first sight, I despaired of being able to do anything to it. However, on taking it to pieces and cleaning the parts and learning the mechanism, I saw that it was not in such bad order as it appeared. The chief thing wrong with it was that a pin was missing. Whilst the elephant was being cut up and the tusks extracted, I spent the time filing down an old screw into the proper shape to fit. Finally my efforts were crowned with success and on assembling the pieces I found that the hammer snapped all right.

The owner was very pleased at this, but he said the final test must be to see that it fired all right, and he produced cap and powder. Now the old gas pipe was so shaky and the barrel so rusty that I certainly was not going to take the risk of letting it off. I had only agreed to mend it, not to endanger my eyesight.

So I said of course I could let it off if I liked, as I was a white man and knew all about guns. The question was, could he let it off? If he fired, and it went off, then would he know that it was all right. So the musket was loaded and the owner shut both eyes and pulled the trigger. To my relief it went off and did not burst.

Then came the question of payment. He had promised two sheep, but native-like he tried to get out of paying. Husseni collared the gun and said that we should take it away with us if he did not pay. He then brought one sheep, which I had killed and began eating at once, so as to have no doubt about that. After a tremendous discussion with Husseni, he finally compounded for the second sheep by bringing four chickens, which were put in the basket with the Serval.

CHAPTER XIII

THE HAPPY BANTU

To understand the good-humoured, happy-go-lucky Bantu savage one must try to picture to oneself vividly the limitations under which he exists. Often one finds oneself unnecessarily incensed against him over a matter which is absolutely beyond his comprehension. I complained of the stupidity of some porters one day to a friend, who replied, "It is a good thing for us that they are so stupid, for if they had any intelligence they would never agree to hunk our loads round the country for us."

Once I was making desperate efforts to get some native porters to place a number of bales in an approximately straight line, so that I could count and check them. The chief difficulty I laboured under was that there was no word for "straight" in their language. When I came to think it out, those natives had never in their lives seen a straight line or anything straight. Their huts are round, their trees crooked, they lived in a state of nature, and there is nothing that I know of in nature that is straight except the horizon at sea.

The same thing applies to balance, level, and almost everything that we have to do with in our life. It used to be exasperating work hoisting the heavy spars for the building of beacons, and the natives employed were professional porters and by no means so dense as the raw savage. One used to arrange the men under the spar with forked poles to push the end upwards. On each side would be one or two to steady it from swaying to right or left. It seemed useless to explain to them that if the whole lot got to one side as the pole was going up, it would be impossible to keep control of it in the air. That in order to get it up, it must be pushed from underneath or by an equal number of men both sides.

A moment after it started, there would be twenty men lustily pushing it from one side and one unfortunate individual supporting it from the other, too stupid and too happy-go-lucky to realise the danger he was in of being flattened out by the falling spar.

What could such people know of leverage or dynamics? How were they to know that, if they pushed straight up against the force of gravity, they could use

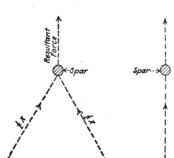

the greatest power and, moreover, there was no leverage from their forked poles against them? It was impossible to explain to them that if the spar was to go upwards, they must conform to one of the two diagrams.

But that a diagram such as the next was bound to end in disaster.

Again, practically every article, artifice, and art known to the European is absolutely foreign to the savage. He cannot possibly understand the use and purpose of the simplest thing till he has been taught, and not even then in many cases. Often when I am reading or writing, a boy comes and moves the lamp away; perhaps he thinks it is in my way or he may want to put a cup of coffee in its place or use it to look for something. He has not the faintest idea that the presence of the lamp is essential to the reading or writing.

Practically every night when my boy brings a large plate of meat and gravy for my dogs and holds it out for inspection, he spills most of the gravy, says, "Oh ! Oh !" and in his desperate attempts to restore the level, spills some more. It reminds me of trying to work with a very delicate spirit level, and making a mistake at first as to which side the bubble has disappeared.

The improvidence of the savage is wonderful. He

is an optimist of the highest order. Never does he learn by experience. Cheerfully will he eat all his remaining food, perhaps sharing it with others, quite oblivious of the fact that there are several days' journey in front of him and no possibility of obtaining more until the journey's end. His sharing his food is not real generosity; he sees that he has got enough and to spare for the meal, and never thinks of the morrow. It is too much trouble to tell the others to go away, so he just lets them eat with him.

On a trek in North Eastern Rhodesia, I watched my porters, day after day, cutting the strips of bark with which their loads were tied up, to save the trouble of unknotting them. This happened nearly every day for a month; on arrival in camp they whipped out a knife and cut the last strips. Every morning they had to sally forth and cut and prepare new strips before we could proceed. They never learnt any better, not even at the end of the trek; they are probably still doing it.

Affection between husband and wife, parent and off-spring, as we know it, is practically non-existent in many of the savage peoples, whilst the mother's love for the child is much the same as that of an animal. I have noticed this to be especially the case farther south, where the people are not so intelligent as the Bantu of the north. The black mother is an excellent mother whilst the child is very young, like most animals.

Directly the child begins to grow up, she has no further use for it, and it has to look after itself, like the offspring of any other animal.

Where the native shines is in his home, the bush. He can generally beat the white man in bushcraft, endurance under the trying conditions of a tropical climate, and at going through thick country he is often wonderful. To show himself at his best, however, he must be in his own locality; if he is transplanted, even a short distance, he deteriorates. The white man, who is a keen hunter, is generally much more in touch with the native and in sympathy with him than the one who does not care for sport. It is easy to see why this should be so. The latter meets the native over matters of discipline, taxes, labour, and many other things which are of the white man's invention and making, and so difficult for the native to understand. The hunter meets the savage on common grounds and on matters with which the latter is, in a primitive way, more conversant than he himself is.

I have never met the bushman, so cannot speak of him, but of all the African savages I have met, I have never found anybody as skilled in bushcraft as I had been led to expect. In some parts they are very poor, in others passable. If they are of any use at all, they are of course better than the average white man. It could hardly be otherwise, considering they have been bred and born for generations in the bush to which a white man is a stranger.

One's first ideas of the savage as a warrior, tracker, and bushman are generally founded on boys' tales of West Indians. The disillusionment is disappointing when it is found that he is neither lynx-eyed, stealthy, cunning, quick-witted, or quick of hearing, and that he is a wonderfully bad marksman with the poor weapons he has. Practically the only things in which he is really remarkable are his powers of enduring the rays of the fierce sun and the way he has of getting through thick country at a rapid pace, especially when escaping from anything.

The African has seldom good long sight; most Europeans could beat him at long ranges in open country, provided they knew what they were looking for. Of course if they had never seen such an animal as a giraffe in their lives, the chances would be in favour of the native seeing it first.

At short distances in thick bush the native is generally better than the white man, and sometimes much better. This is only natural as the white man is absolutely unused to marching for hours with his range of vision confined to a radius of within a yard of his nose, with occasionally longer views between vistas of broken-down grass or thick bush.

I find that, as a rule, I can keep level or ahead of the native in detecting game so long as I am on the *qui vive* and fresh. That is to say, in the early hours of the morning I should probably see game twice, to once that any of the natives with me would see anything. Directly the sun gets well up, I go off and then the native defeats me abjectly.

The native often comes in for much abuse, owing to his vagueness about time and distance. It is very annoying to the traveller, but it cannot be helped. He has never had a watch, he has no words for times of the day except morning, evening, and sometimes noon; and evening is the only time really very material to him. He generally knows if there is time to reach a certain place or village before it gets dark.

As to distance, it really does not concern him much if he takes a few days more or less to reach a place. Time is no object to him. The same applies to season. He would probably remember if a certain event happened during the rains or during the harvest season, but practically never how many years ago it was. He would be equally vague about the number of months that have elapsed since an event. He generally errs on the lesser side; he will say it was two months, when it was ten, but never say ten, when it was really two.

As a rule, he only has the words "far" and "near" to describe distances; they may be qualified by the tone of the voice or by the word "very." The usual European, on hearing that a place is near, would expect to find it within the next few hundred yards. If it was as near as this, the native would not say "near" or "very near," but he would say it is "here."

Places other than villages and streams are often grazing grounds, or tracts of country between two rivers which bear a name. So the traveller, after being told that he has reached the spot for which he has been making, may have to walk on another two hours to his camping ground, much to his indignation. He will keep on saying, "But you said we had arrived at Shokoli." The natives assure him that this is so. "Then where is the water to camp at?" "Just here," the natives will reply, and they will trudge on again in the sun for another half hour and then he will begin to get annoyed.

A lot can be done with these "nears" and "fars," if you know the natives' way of thinking well. If you have been walking along for several hours and pass a village and ask a native there, how far it is to your destination, he will cheerfully tell you that it is "very near."

He is not going to do the march with you in the heat of the sun. If he wanted to go there, he would start early in the morning and do the journey in two or three hours. The chances are then that the place will be seven to ten miles distant. If he says, "Oh, very near," in a tone of surprise or contempt, it is probably only four to six miles.

Now ask him to come with you and show you the

way. If it is only a few miles he will readily consent. If it is ten miles he will probably demur a bit and then admit that it is not so "very near."

The "near" of a man in the village will probably be a "far" or "very far" of one of your porters, who has been marching with you. If your porters, after doing three or four hours' march, say that it is "near," it will probably be only a few miles.

With a "far" you must realise whether the native means far for one day's journey or for more. "Far" generally means a long day's trek and a "very far" is too long to do in the day. However, if you are setting out from a place to travel to another, the same "far" may be "near," meaning that it is only two short days, which the native will call one day as he only counts the night's slept *en route*. In estimate of days, the native estimate is, therefore, always one day short.

The Somali "near" is generally a fairly long one as they are accustomed to travel such distances for water. The Somali will say, "Oh, near," in a tone indicating that it is nothing and point to a tree or bush in sight and say, "That tree or bush." At first one imagines that the tree or bush indicates the site of the place and is inclined to agree that it is fairly near. After having passed the bush and marched on some twenty or thirty miles, one begins to wonder what the tree or bush had to do with it.

In open pathless wastes like most of Somaliland, the native marches fairly straight on a bearing, till he reaches the spot he is making for. The tree or bush was to give the direction of the place, and if one takes a compass bearing on it, from the point at which it is indicated, one will find that the guide keeps fairly true to this bearing.

In the Awemba country, distances are measured by the "Mtundu." You are told how many Mtundu it is to the place you wish to reach. Now a Mtundu is the space between two streams. As the greater part of the country is a gentle rolling country covered with wood and long grass, it is seldom that any view is obtained, and if it was, it would be generally impossible to locate the position of the next stream. So a Mtundu may be one or may be ten miles, and, if anything, you are worse off than with "near" and "far." Also the uncomforting thought occurs, after crossing a small dip, that perhaps this does not count as a Mtundu, which is generally the case. The Mtundu must not be taken too lightly, and it saves disappointment to avoid counting any but *bona fide* unquestionable ones.

There are no professions amongst the happy Bantu, except occasionally there are families of blacksmiths and hunters. As a rule, however, everybody is supposed to be competent to do everything there is to do, a difference only being made in the sexes. There are things which are considered men's work and others which are women's work. There is, however, no village mat maker, potter, ornament maker and so on, with rare exceptions. That is to say, they are as ignorant of specialisation as they are of division of labour. If a man wants a mat, he makes it for himself; if he wants an earring he makes it likewise.

This is perhaps the reason why the native, as a rule, thinks that no special knowledge is required to perform any work the white man has to offer him. If anybody else has filled the post, he thinks that he can do so equally well. When a native comes to ask for work, he, as often as not, says that he will do anything that is required of him. He is equally ready to offer himself as a carpenter, gardener, transport driver, in fact anything. If he is asked if he has had any former experience of any of these professions, a question which will surprise him, he will admit that he has had none, but perhaps say that he knows all the white man's work well, because he was once cook's boy.

If a chief was asked to select a man for a job, it would never occur to him to choose any one especially qualified to fill the post. If it was something that would be popular, he would choose a friend of his; if the reverse, he would choose a small boy or the least likely person to dare to grumble.

So if a guide was required for a rather tedious journey, he would call up probably a small boy and tell him he had got to go. It would never occur to him to find out first if the boy knew the way or had ever been to the locality before. If some one was required to carry a load, he would pounce on the first cripple he met.

I was starting in a steamer to go up the Nile a short way, and then intended to land and march. Some porters had been requisitioned from a neighbouring chief and were to go up with me in the steamer. There was some delay about getting off, and just as I thought everything was ready, I saw the sergeant, who was accompanying me, cross the gangway carrying a man in his arms. I imagined that it was a sick man being brought for medicine or dressing and was rather annoyed that our journey should be delayed. I waited patiently for him to be brought up to me on the upper deck, but no one came and presently the sergeant reported that all was ready to start.

I asked him who it was that he had carried on board. "Was it not one of master's porters from chief so-and-so?" he replied. I went down to inspect the man and found that he was a paralytic cripple who could not walk. He had been selected by his chief as a porter for me, and it had never struck the sergeant that a man, who must himself be carried, would be rather useless as a porter, in fact somewhat of an encumbrance on a long journey.

Division of labour is practically unknown amongst the African savage. They have been forced into living in communities, probably partly from fear of attack, but it is seldom that even two sections of a tribe will act together in case of such attack. In every-day life every one acts for himself; practically nothing is done for the common weal. Even in attack or defence, there is no cohesion; each man does as he likes, but the knowledge that there are others makes him feel bolder.

It is very difficult, practically impossible, to make any large body of savages work in cohesion. I have often seen twenty natives make the most futile efforts to lift a log of wood off the ground, that two ablebodied Englishmen could lift with ease. This is partly because they are, as a rule, weak in the arms and partly because none of them make any effort. Each one sees that the log is too heavy for him to lift by himself and so thinks it an impossible feat to be asked to accomplish. If after great exertions the log is lifted, they generally make the most awful groans and put it down again. Probably also each one thinks that with so many others at work, it is not necessary for him to be more than a spectator.

I was watching a party of natives, the other day, raising one end of a tree which was going to be used as a beam of a house. With awful groans they got the end about four feet off the ground and then were gradually letting it down again, inch by inch. I thought it must be heavier than it looked, so gave a hoist to the end, and up it went above my head, leaving all their hands groping for it. It could not have required more than an eighty-pound or one hundred-pound shove to send it up, and there were ten men, each one of whom would have thought nothing of picking up a fifty-pound load and walking off ten miles with it, quite unable to lift it up. Moreover, I cannot devise any way of making them put a due proportion of work into a united effort, unless one was to treat them as one treats a sluggard in a team of oxen.

Some people would say this was laziness, but it is not; the same men would patiently toil all day long at lifting up twenty-pound stones to a platform. It is sheer inability to understand that a few men working together can accomplish much more than one singly.

To continue with the raising of the beam. You get one end up, with the end on the top of the wall to prevent it slipping back, and you tie a rope to it which is given to ten men to hold. You then start hoisting the other end and look up to see what the ten men are doing. Half of them have let go altogether, one is sitting down to pick his toes and is holding the end of the rope under his chin, the remaining men are lightly holding it with one hand and engaging in conversation. Any moment the beam may slip off and come rattling down on the heads and toes of those below. They do not understand the responsibility of their position; that is all.

The native is not, as a rule, a reliable and trustworthy person, either as a witness or as a newsmonger. There is generally some one thing true in the native statement. It is a nucleus of fact around which a nebula of fiction has formed. For instance, a man rushes in and says that there is a solitary big male Puku, with enormous horns, just behind my tent. On going out, I see nothing, but on proceeding a short way, two hornless females are pointed out in the distance. The nucleus of fact here is Puku; he said Puku and there really were some.

A Dorobo hunter says suddenly, as we are walking along, "There goes a lion." I look up and see a hyæna. The nucleus is, "There goes."

A native rushes in perspiring at every pore and says that he has this moment seen ten bull elephants passing close by. One walks out fifteen miles and is shown the five-day-old spoor of one elephant. The nucleus of truth in this is, "elephant passing."

It seems a point of honour with a native never to correct another or to teach him anything. You get a new and raw boy. Your old boy will almost immediately detail him to lay the table whilst he himself takes a rest. When you survey the wonderful ingenuity he has used in putting everything in the wrong place, you call your old boy and ask him what has happened to the table to-day. He will not understand you till you carefully point out that everything is in the wrong place, and then he will say that the new boy is a very ignorant and worthless youth, forgetting that he himself was just as ignorant at one time over these matters.

You then tell him to show the new boy how to lay the table, so he calls him, abuses him soundly, and tells him to lay it properly. The latter is naturally nonplussed, and after making various attempts, is told to go away whilst the old boy arranges the table.

The next few days the old boy will lay the table, whilst the new boy sits in the kitchen, then he will be deputed to lay the table again, with the same results. When you complain again, you will hear that he is so lacking in intelligence that it is really impossible to teach him anything.

You leave a village and find elephant spoor close to the village. Various people have different views as to its age; some say that it is fresh and some old. You follow the spoor and make minute observations and at last decide that it was of the day before. Then you suddenly remember that a native from the village has been following you all the while and that he is sure to know if elephant came into his fields the night before. He has followed you and watched your observations and listened to the trackers' conversation as to the age of the spoor and never made a remark, and yet he must have known for certain from the first. If you had followed the old spoor all day long, he would never have volunteered a statement. You now ask him whether

these elephant came back to any other part of the
fields last night and he says, "No."

"Did you notice this spoor yesterday?"

"Yes."

"When did they come here?"

"The night before last, early in the morning."

The African native is very tolerant. He never says
"You liar," but only grunts assent to the most impossible story or statement which he must know is an
absolute fabrication. I have often heard some boy
laying down the law and talking the most awful bal-
derdash about game to my two old trackers in Nyasaland, whilst the latter would sit at his feet as earnest
listeners. They must have known what pure rot he
was talking, and it must have been apparent to all that
he had no experience at all, whilst they had been doing
nothing but hunt for thirty or forty years. Yet neither
they nor any other listener would ever say, "Shut up,
you young fool," or words to that effect.

Perhaps one of a group of porters will make a buzzing
or some other irritating sound, and continue for hours
amusing himself by keeping it up after everybody else
has turned in. Never does anybody say, "chuck it"
or "stow it." They often get very angry with each
other over very trivial matters, and then there is nothing
rude they do not think of saying to each other, but
such matters as described above do not seem to annoy
them.

Practically everywhere I have travelled in tropical Africa, I have noticed a very crude but distinct kind of courtesy exercised towards the white man. Never is one molested by a crowd of urchins in one's camp. Now and then, a few small boys come and get in the way and gape at the camping arrangements, but if this is the case, an older man invariably comes forward and drives them away. Although always begging and asking for presents, they are in their way very hospitable people.

Once I was crossing the Minikazi, one of the numerous rivers that flow into the Bangweolo. The chief of the village on the opposite bank was engaged in ferrying his canoe backwards and forwards with my loads. After everything had crossed, I was ferried over and landed in the village, the poorest looking village I had ever set eyes on. The few hovels consisted of some poles with a little grass thrown over the top.

I produced some calico with which to pay the chief for his services, but he waived it aside, dashed into the village, and threw himself head foremost into one of the hovels, and a miserable specimen of a chicken hopped out through one of the many holes in the dwelling. It was finally caught, and the chief ran back and, throwing himself on the ground, presented the anæmic fowl to me. The laws of hospitality demanded that he should first make a present to the stranger before accepting my calico.

Very useful does the traveller find this almost universal law as, on arrival in a new village, he is practically certain of a chicken at least. In many places it may take him a couple of days' bargaining before he can buy another, or he may find it almost impossible to obtain anything else, but the first present is always forthcoming, however poor the people or however much they hate parting with their livestock.

In Uganda there are often telephone stations on the line of wire between two administrative posts. Such stations are in charge of a Mganda clerk, a title which is sometimes a courtesy one, when he can neither read nor write.

I stopped at one of these stations on the march once, as I was desirous of sending a message, but it was too late in the day to be heard. Owing to the sun or some cause or other, messages are only audible in the early morning or late evening. The "clerk" could talk Swahili to a certain extent, and so I asked him if he could deliver a message for me that evening, as I wanted to trek on. He cheerfully assented, but as he was certain to forget or mix up the message, I thought it would be better to write it down for him. I asked if he could read and he said, "Oh, yes."

"What language can you read?"

"Oh, any language."

"If I write in Swahili, will you be able to read it?"

"Oh, yes."

"Shall I write in Arabic characters or English?"

"Oh, it is all the same."

"You can read Swahili?"

"Yes."

So I wrote out my message in Swahili, and he looked at it and said that it was not the writing he was accustomed to. I then wrote out the same message in Roman characters, but still he could not read it. It was not the writing he knew.

"Well, what sort of writing do you know?" I asked.

"Oh, just writing."

" Can you show me the sort?"

He opened a box and produced a copy-book. The cover was adorned with what looked like endless *w*'s. I opened it at the first page. It was ruled paper, and on every line was an endless *w* or series of *w*'s joined to each other, stretching from end to end of each line.

I turned over the pages of this interesting Ms. Every page was the same one long succession of never-ending *w*'s. This, he said, was the writing he knew.

It struck me that perhaps it was some wonderful new adaptation of the Morse code; but no, they were all as alike as two pins. He had occupied, I presume, the long hours between a possible morning call and an unlikely evening call in the compilation of this document. He firmly believed that he had taught himself to write.

With this example of his optimism, I will leave the Happy African. I am afraid that I have painted his faults rather than his virtues, but I am none the less very fond of him. In spite of his obvious defects, I would not exchange him for any other native I know of to live with under similar conditions.

CHAPTER XIV

CURIOUS HUNTING INCIDENTS

IN 1908, whilst elephant hunting with Captain Hart in Uganda, we wounded a big bull on the Kafu River. We followed it the rest of the day without success, although we saw it once ahead from the top of an ant-hill. It was then decided that I should go after the wounded one next day, whilst Hart went off after fresh *khobar*.

I settled on a village ahead, in the direction in which the elephant had gone, and told my half of the camp to proceed there. We followed the spoor, passed this village, and later on passed another, so I sent a man back to tell them to come on and camp there. I followed the spoor till the afternoon, and it was then older than when we had started.

The natives with me tried to persuade me to return, as it was obviously useless following any more; but I insisted upon going on. The reason for this was that I had dreamed about elephant the night before, and always regard that as a favourable omen. My dream was that I shot some elephants whilst hunting in the Aberdare Range, and after the tusks had been cut out and brought into camp, they were laid out for my

226

inspection. They lay in pairs of different sizes, but what puzzled me was one odd tusk amongst them, a long, thin tusk without a fellow.

We followed on the old spoor till about an hour before sundown, when we came on a mud-hole and a lot of perfectly fresh spoor. As it was so late there was no time to hunt cautiously, so I rushed off down the spoor, through thick bush country, till I suddenly heard elephant just in front. A moment later, the bush ended and gave place to a large open grassy space and just below me in a dip were a few elephant. As there was no time to lose before sunset, I hurried across this open space, when I heard a noise behind and, looking round, saw three bulls come out of the bush I had left and walk leisurely across to join the others.

I was just about to move on again to the party whom I now saw were having a mud bath, when three more bulls came out of the bush, and then others, two or three at a time, emerged and marched across in stately procession until twenty-five bulls had collected at the mud bath.

The last of the procession was an elephant who at first sight appeared to have no tusks. He had his left side towards me, so his right tusk was out of sight. As he walked and his trunk swung forward, I saw his left tusk which was straight, long, and thin. It went straight downwards from his jaw, like the tooth of a walrus, and being discoloured with earth it was not noticeable against the background of trunk. When the trunk swung forward, it could be clearly seen.

It was the long thin tusk of my dream. However, as it was discoloured and malformed, I thought that it might be also diseased, so I resolved not to shoot it, although it looked the longest tusk present.

When all had collected at the mud-hole, I got nearer and began trying to decide which was the most shootable tusk, always a difficult task when there are many elephant, as one only sees a tusk or two at a time, and so one cannot compare them but must remember them. In this case, there appeared to be no really big male, and at last I decided on one with thick tusks and fired.

At my shot the whole herd turned and galloped back in a solid bunch, all jostling each other. It was not till they had passed close by that another shot offered at the big one. I took a rapid shot at him and then jumped on an ant-hill to see better as they disappeared. Out of all that herd only one offered the chance of a last shot and that was the deformed tusker. However, now I saw the right tusk. It looked immensely long and was not, moreover, deformed like the other, but had a natural curve, although much less than the average tusk.

I decided to risk it and let drive with my mannlicher and over he toppled. It was now sunset and we were many hours from camp, so it was impossible to follow up the wounded one, but he was found dead afterwards, the only elephant I have ever recovered which I have not myself followed till I finished or found him.

We then went to the fallen elephant. My water-bottle, field-glasses, etc., were hung on a branch of a tree close by, whilst I examined the elephant and cut off his tail. I have given a description of him in my "Game of East Africa."

After having taken the measurements I wanted, I began to think that it was time to get onto a path before night fell, so turned to my tracker, who had been waiting for me, and said, "Come along." He turned to a couple of local natives who had accompanied us and said, "Come along. The white man wants to go." But no one stirred, so I said somewhat impatiently, "Come along," again. Still no one came.

I had been going the whole day and food and shelter were still many hours away, if we could reach it that night, and, as is often the case when tired and hungry, I was very irritable. I cursed the tracker and told him to get my water-bottle and glasses at once. He turned round and cursed the two local natives and told them to get the water-bottle and field-glasses at once, but they only uttered murmurs of dissent.

I could not make out what had suddenly possessed everybody, and then I noticed that they were eyeing the equipment hung on the tree apprehensively.

Perhaps it was a sacred tree or one possessed of a devil. Anyhow, I could not be bored to wait, so I walked up to the tree, and the tracker then caught hold of me to pull me back and condescended to explain.

Whilst I had been measuring the elephant, a snake had crawled up and ensconced himself comfortably amongst the accoutrements and now remained in possession. "Is that all, you watery heart?" I said to the tracker, taking his long spear and dislodging the intruder. They then took up my belongings and we started our weary trek back, getting into camp at 12.30 A.M.

In British East Africa I was camped just above the Ruero, at a place where there were reeds at the edge of the stream. A lion was heard during the night, and in the morning some of the men came to tell me that there was a fierce beast in the reeds just below my camp, and that they were not able to draw water, as it growled at them whenever they came near. "What sort of a beast is it?" I asked. They were not certain but, anyhow, it was very savage, and "if it missed being a lion, perhaps it was a leopard."

A very savage beast, indeed, I thought, if it had not been scared away by all the vociferations of my noisy porters and if it was prepared to do battle to everybody who wanted water. Perhaps it was a lioness with cubs. Nasty thick reeds and an unknown animal out for blood, — it was with some trepidation that I made my preparations to take on this formidable opponent.

Before I could reach the spot, however, fresh news came in. The fierce beast had been seen and found to be one of the porters' boys who had run away, owing to some grievance, and hidden himself in the reeds, growling at everybody who came near.

In 1906, I was taking a quiet stroll with a friend one evening in Ngong forest near Nairobi. He went off, I think, after a bushbuck, leaving me in an open glade where he was to return for me. I was kneeling down drinking at a pool about 5.30 P.M., when I heard a slight noise and, looking up, saw something black pass along the opposite edge of the clearing and enter some bushes. I approached quietly to fifty yards of the spot at which it had entered and, by the movement of the bushes, saw that it was still there. I waited and two extraordinary pigs came out of the bushes and walked several yards in the open, and then disappeared into some other bushes where I heard them routing about in piglike fashion.

I was not able to see them again, nor did I ever see them afterwards, although I visited the spot and other glades round many times afterwards. However, I had a very clear view of them when they passed in the open, as they were not more than fifty yards distant, and I wrote down my impressions within an hour or two.

They were considerably smaller than adults of either wart hog or bush pig. No tusks were visible and they were true pigs in the shape of the head and body and not in any way like wart hogs. The body was a deep black and the face bright white. The chief point noticeable was this dead white of the face. I have never heard of any such pig being seen in Africa. If they were a new kind, some one else would have been sure to have observed them in a spot so near Nairobi. The only conjecture I can form about them is that they were some domestic pig run wild, but then they would have become an easy prey to leopard, which abound in the forest; perhaps they were some freak bush pigs.

I was returning to a camp on the Ndurugu in the dusk when I came close up to a kongoni. As lions were then roaring from several directions, I thought of shooting him for bait. I fired but hit him too far back. He stumbled and then went off and I ran after him till he came to a tree round which he cantered in a stately way like a circus horse, giving me time to come up to him. As I could not see my sights well, owing to the bad light, I came up quite close to him. He must then have described as many as six circles round the tree, the last only a few yards distant from it. I fired at him as he was making this last circle and he immediately left the tree and came straight towards me, when a bullet in the chest knocked him over.

A Young Ostrich

Koroli

Showing the shadeless flats of the Rudolph country.

I have known a wart hog when wounded to tear round in circles, but in that case it was hit in the head and no doubt the brain was affected.

I was returning to camp in the southern game reserve, British East Africa, after having been out sketching, and came on a female kongoni who performed similar manœuvres, but in this case it must have been stone blind. It was standing almost in my path, apparently looking at me, or at any rate in my direction. As we got closer and closer I began to wonder how close it was going to let me get.

When I was about fifteen yards from it, it started off, perhaps having heard me or my porters. However, instead of going straight away it described a circle of perhaps twenty-five or thirty yards' radius and came back towards where I was standing and seemed as if it would run me down. Although it was in the game reserve, I did not feel inclined to meet with the unromantic end of being run down by a hartebeest, and so swung up my rifle. It must have heard the movement or got my wind at this moment, as it swerved away and then described another circle, returning to the same spot. It repeated this manœuvre three times and each time it got to within about six yards I swung up my rifle and it swerved away. It then made more furious efforts than ever to get away and galloped faster and in ever-decreasing circles till at last it was pirouetting like a vedette's horse when an enemy is sighted. This made it so giddy that it staggered about for a little and then resumed larger circles, and I left it like that, still galloping round and round. I thought at the time what a very soft thing it would be for a lion to find.

Next morning, shortly after dawn, I saw a lioness coming from the direction in which I had last seen the kongoni; it was so full that its stomach was dragging along the ground. I watched her join four others, two lion and two lioness. I also saw two hyæna come from the same direction.

On some occasions animals appear to be absolutely blind and deaf for the time being. I have generally found wart hog fairly difficult to approach in the open plains. I was once sketching on the top of a little kopje on the Athi plains and whilst so engaged observed a wart sow and young one engaged in grubbing on the plain below. Having finished my work, I packed up my things and started down the side of the hill and across the plain towards camp, followed by a porter or two carrying my plane table and instruments. Our way took us almost directly past the place in which the wart hogs were grubbing. They showed no concern whatever at our approach, although the plain was perfectly open and there was not a vestige of cover.

When we got level with them, they were about a hundred and fifty yards distant, and they were still merrily grubbing away. I took out my camera and thought I would see just how near they would let me get. When I got to a hundred yards, I said to myself, "It is unlikely that they will let me get any nearer than this, so I will just take a snapshot now," which I did.

I then approached another twenty yards and said the same thing to myself again and took another photo.

I then walked slowly towards them another twenty yards and said, "It is quite impossible that they will let me get any nearer, so I will just take another photo from here," which I did.

I then walked up to about forty yards and said the same thing again and took another photo. After that I slowly approached another twenty yards and this time I had nothing to say to myself, so I just took another photo, and then began approaching very gingerly for I was so close I was afraid that they might run into me by accident.

When I was about fifteen yards distant, the young one trotted across me and I think got my wind. Anyhow it gave the alarm and they both scuttled off about twenty yards and then turned round and stared at me and finally made off. They were both, as far as I could see, in full possession of their senses and, according to the custom of animals feeding, they had often stopped work to look round for foes and had several times looked straight in my direction.

One day I was just entering on the long causeway by which the Fort Hall Road crosses the Thiririka swamp in British East Africa, when I saw four wart hog trot down the road on the opposite bank and enter on the causeway. I afterwards gathered that they had been disturbed by some passing natives and were trotting away from them.

I lay down in the middle of the road and they came trotting down the centre, till they were only a few yards distant, and I fired at the leading one. The other three immediately jumped off the causeway into the swamp, but the wounded one rushed straight towards me and it was only when I jabbed my rifle muzzle at him to keep him off, that he swerved to one side and passed me, dropping dead behind me.

In this case I was a stationary object and it is easy to believe that the animal did not see me until I prodded my rifle muzzle at him. In fact I have often had animals walk up to within a few yards of me, when I have been standing or sitting motionless, even though in full view. In the former case, however, I was a moving object and, moreover, moving over a perfectly flat, open plain, and so a most conspicuous object.

I have never heard of a case of a man being mauled by a wart hog, although I have been told of him ripping up the pony of a pigsticker. He does not appear to be nearly so plucky as the Indian boar; however, he could be just as dangerous if he chose and so I do not care to give him the chance. When he gets within a few yards, I think it is about time to give him a shot, although I have no proof that his intentions are not of the most friendly.

Once after shooting a wildebeest, I left my men to cut up the carcass and went off in search of a shady tree. I found one some hundred yards away and sat down under it. I had not been there very long, before I saw a big wart hog with fine tusks approaching. As he came nearer it became more and more evident that he also had selected this tree as a suitable place for a siesta.

I should like to be one of those very cold-blooded people who could wait, and see how long it would have been before he discovered me, and what he would do. Would he have lain down beside me or mistaken me for a tree and grubbed under me? In any case, there would have been little danger as, directly he smelt me, he would in all probability have turned and made off.

However, his tusks looked so long and gleaming and sharp that when he got to twenty yards I could wait no longer but fired into his chest. He turned and ran a distance I afterwards paced to be within a yard or two of two hundred. I found him lying hit through the heart with the blood spurting out in a jet, an instance of how the heart shot is not always instantaneous.

A day or two from Nyeri station British East Africa there is a hill famous for the number and irritability of its rhino. I was sketching there and in between times pottering about its bush-covered slopes. I found it a pleasant spot in which to stroll about and observe the animal life, as the thick clumps and patches of bush gave it all the difficulties and advantages of a bush country, as regards the game, whilst the spaces between the clumps were, as a rule, so open that there was little of that stooping, crawling, and pushing through obstructing branches which makes hunting in the thick bush so tiring.

Whilst silently manœuvring in this country one day, I suddenly came face to face with a great pig twice the height of the ordinary bush pig. I watched him move with head held low, sniffing the ground, till he disappeared in a clump of bushes and only then realised that this was the giant forest pig I had been so anxious to become acquainted with. I searched round quietly and carefully but he did not let me get another glimpse at him.

Whilst on that high, broad back of the Aberdare Range called "the Moors," something moving in a bottom near me caught my attention. On looking through my glasses I saw that it was a cat, but in colour it was jet black. I could not get a shot at it, and so was left in uncertainty as to what it really was. However, I heard later that a black Serval had been obtained in that locality, and so I have little doubt now that this also was a case of melanism in a Serval, possibly even the same specimen that was afterwards obtained.

The first ostrich egg I ever found was a solitary one, lying out in the open in the full glare of the sun's rays. I believe a solitary egg like this is often dropped before the hen has decided on where to make her nest. However, I thought that this was the beginning of what was going to be a nest, the first egg of a clutch and, therefore, quite fresh.

I religiously ate that egg in omelets for three days; telling myself how lucky I was to be able to get such a luxury far from any habitation.   It had a most unpleasant and strong taste, which I put down to being the natural flavour, without which no ostrich egg would be complete.   I now know that that egg was really bad and I fear to think how long it had been lying in the sun before I found it.

On another occasion, I found a similar lonely egg lying in the open.   I decided to take it in to some friends who kept an incubator for ostrich eggs. Unfortunately, however, it exploded with a loud report in my box on the homeward trek.

Whilst hunting in North Eastern Rhodesia one day, I wounded a reedbuck, out of a party of two males and some females.   I pursued it but could not get within shooting distance again and it was as good as lost, as once wounded and on the alert, it was not likely to give me a chance again of getting near.   I sat down and watched it crossing a wide "Dambo" or open grassy flat, deciding to let it go off and follow it up an hour or so later in the hopes of surprising it lying down in the grass.

When it reached the other side, perhaps five hundred to one thousand yards distant, it joined the party. The other buck, a younger one, looked at it and evidently noticing that it did not look quite up to the mark, thought it a good opportunity to take over the females. Accordingly, he set on him furiously, whilst the wounded buck stood up to him courageously.

The females went off leaving the two fighting viciously and I, seeing my chance, started running towards them. Presently, the young buck got the other down on his knees, and they went round and round in that position, the wounded one always facing his adversary. At last the young one got him prone on the ground and commenced goring him viciously. So busily engaged were they, that they did not notice my approach until I was about a few yards distant. I arrived just in time to "save the wounded one's life" by driving away his adversary and shooting him myself. Even then the lust of battle was so strong that the young one was loath to leave his victim, and stood watching from thirty or forty yards distant for a short time, affording me ample time to have shot him also, had I so wished.

A bushbuck is a plucky little animal and if badly wounded and cornered will often put up quite a good fight. Whilst sketching on the Ithanga Hills, I wounded a bushbuck badly and it retired into some thick bush. I followed with a native and found it unable to get away. For some reason or other, I was unwilling to expend another cartridge on it, as I was sketching perhaps I had not one; anyhow, we tried to collar it and it made vicious little charges first at me and then at the native, so that we had to take refuge behind trees.

Very ridiculous we must have looked, each peering out in consternation from behind one of two tree trunks about six feet apart and the bushbuck between us making up his mind whom he would go for next. Finally he decided on me, and as he rushed at me the native skilfully leaned out from his tree and caught him by a hind leg. He turned to go for the native and this gave me my opportunity and I seized his horns and threw him over.

On another occasion, I followed up a wounded bushbuck and came on him suddenly on the side of a steep hill. He sprang up to go off up the hill, and I put a shot into his hindquarters, at which he turned round and came half-rushing, half-stumbling down the hill and tripped me up. In this case the animal hardly knew what it was doing, and being badly wounded, probably decided that it would be easier to reach cover down than up hill.

CHAPTER XV

TWO SHORT TREKS AND TWO AFRICAN CHIEFS

IN 1907 I was sketching for the East African Survey. I found it necessary to climb the high peak of Nguzeru, or Kinangop, to continue my work. The only people who know these mountains are a few Kikuyu, who make a profession of hunting for honey and bringing it for sale or exchange to the villages on the eastern side.

I was fortunate in coming across two of these in the forest, whilst camped under the western side, and obtaining their services as guides. They knew the lower slopes well but their knowledge did not extend higher than the forest level, perhaps ten thousand feet, as their work did not take them to the bare upper slopes. A native is not, as a rule, inquisitive or enterprising; he is only driven by necessity and only does those things he is forced to do by circumstances, or notices those things that come into direct contact with him.

As an example of what I mean, I have been unable to hear of any native, amongst the crowded villages at the foot of Mount Kenya, who has been any appreciable distance up the mountain. There is a range of mountains near Nimule only five to six thousand feet high.

There are many people living close to the mountain on one side, but I have not yet been able to find one who has been to the top, or knows of any one who has. Of all the many thousands of insects which abound in tropical Africa, perhaps only a dozen or less have native names in any one part. These will be found to be flies that bite the native or his cattle or sting him or provide him with honey. With the others, he has no concern.

My guides showed me an elephant path, called the Njira Wanjohi, which crossed a high pass and led to the villages on the other side of the hill. It was used by the honey hunters of Wanjohi to reach this side of the hill.

As we walked along the narrow, winding path, often obstructed by fallen bamboos, it struck me how extremely awkward it would be suddenly to round a corner and come face to face with the leader of a herd of elephants coming in the opposite direction. For elephant move very silently, and in this part of the country, they are often very bad-tempered. It would be a matter of great difficulty to get out of the path and break into the thick undergrowth on either side.

Whilst thinking this, we heard a slight noise in front of us and the guide, who was walking just in front of me, stopped dead. In another moment a man appeared round a turn of the path a few yards distant, caught sight of us, and also stopped dead. He and the guide looked at one another for a few moments, like two dogs who are not quite certain if the other is going to fight or not, and then one said something, the other answered, and they went forward to meet one another. Behind this man came a string of men carrying the hollow logs used as beehives. It was the end of March and a new honey season was about to commence, so they were preparing for it by placing new hives ready.

We reached a little col still to the west of the range, at the source of a stream called the Turasha, and found a spot in which the undergrowth was low, and so cleared a place in which to camp. The ground was covered with rotting vegetation and offered little hold to the tent pegs. At the base of a steep slope was a spring, and a little pool of clear water, but just as I was stooping to drink from it, I saw that it was full of leeches.

Just after pitching camp, a bitter gale got up, and so I put on all the clothes I could find, shirts, pajamas, coats, indiscriminately one over the other, till I was so bulky that I could get on nothing more and then went to bed. However, the wind increased and I spent the greater part of the night hammering the pegs into new places as they became uprooted.

Next day I sent the porters on by the Njira Wanjohi to search for a sheltered spot, a little over the pass on the eastern side, in which to camp, whilst I climbed to the top of the peak to take observations. The last two thousand feet were bare, that is to say, there were patches of bare rock, coarse grass in isolated tufts, a giant sort of groundsel, and a few other mountain plants, but no thick or high vegetation.

At one place I found a long, flat ridge of rock littered with bones, evidently a spot to which vultures brought their prey for consumption, and from which they enjoyed the magnificent panorama of hills, forests, and beyond that plains spreading out below them. Elephant tracks led up to within a few hundred feet of the top, whilst a rhino track reached practically the summit, passing under the block of rock which formed the actual highest part.

From the distance, the mountain seemed to have a cairn perched on the summit. This in reality was a great block of rock about the size of a small house. From my camp I had been able to see with glasses that this rock was surmounted by a beacon or some object which looked like the basket or brush pole which I believe is sometimes used for trigonometrical work in West Africa. This puzzled me, as I had never heard of any survey party visiting the top; in fact I knew that no government survey had been there, as I had been given the points from which the top had been fixed.

When I got under the last block of rock, I saw that it consisted of a sort of black iron arrangement with flat hexagonal sides, shaped rather like a large stable lantern. This was on the top of a pole, and guyed down to the rock with four bars of iron.

After going round the mass of rock, we found a place

to climb up at the other end. On reaching the top of this end of the block, we were divided from the mass on which the beacon was, the actual highest part, by a neck of rock. This was perhaps wide enough to allow of the passage of a dog-cart, but the wind was so terrific that I felt compelled to crawl over this on hands and knees, although I have a very good head for heights. Two of the porters with me crawled across flat on their stomachs, but the other two refused to face it at all.

I then examined the beacon; the rock had been bored and the pole and the attachments for the guys had been cemented into it. On one side of the lantern-shaped iron box was a door opening with a catch. I opened this door wondering what it could contain, — the record of a former climber, a reward for the next climber, the will of an eccentric millionnaire, survey instruments ready to hand, almost every conceivable idea flitted across my mind except the right one.

I do not think that I have ever felt such a shock of surprise in my life. If ten rattlesnakes had come rushing out of the door, I should have been prepared to meet them, but what I actually saw was a small shrine and a picture of the Virgin Mary.

Remember I had never heard of anybody else having been to this summit, and if one had, the natural supposition was that it was an exploring or mountaineering party or a surveyor in the execution of his work.

Whoever else in the world would take the trouble to camp up in these cold heights and the fatigue of climbing this summit?

I afterwards found that it was the work of a mission in the Kikuyu country. They had very kindly left some bits of dry bamboo lying about; perhaps these had been used as ladders to mount the rock. With these my men made a fire in a crevice of rock at which to warm their hands.

I had to build a cairn of stones around each leg of the theodolite and plane table to keep them down. The wind was so violent that it blew my alidade off the table and the cold so great that I could only draw about one line, and then had to warm my hands at the fire before being able to draw another.

Mist was driving across the hill and objects only appeared at intervals, so work was extremely difficult. At noon the clouds closed down and we had to stop work and make for our new camp, which we found was in a more sheltered position. Also, it was on open grass with a firm hold for pegs and my porters had collected heaps of firewood.

Next day I felt like shirking the climb, the cold, and the awful wind. As so often happens, when one is prepared to dislike something very much, it turns out much better than expected. This day after I had reached the top, the sun came out, and the day proved most exceptional for the time of year. I could see all the points I wanted, even the summit of Kenya. Although it was blowing about four hurricanes, it was not so bitter as the day before and I completed my work.

The following day we went on down the side of the mountain through the bamboo forest, and the day after came to the village of Karori, a big Kikuyu chief. The country just about this village was delightful; it was at the edge of the forest and consisted of open spaces covered with short grass and large, shady trees. A little farther east the usual treeless country of the Kikuyu started, consisting of steep red hills and masses of cultivation.

Korori was one of the most real chiefs I have ever met. In his village he wears nothing but a cloak of hyrax skins trimmed with white beads. This he wore hanging from the shoulder usually, but when cold he gathered it round his naked body. The skin of the hyrax is looked on as a chief's perquisite in these parts and no one else is allowed to wear it.

He had three tin-roofed buildings in his village and there was a Swahili mason then engaged on the last.

The latter had been some time in the village and confided his impressions to my head man. He said that Korori held all his Kikuyu absolutely under his thumb, that he supplied all the arrow-heads used by the Dorobo hunters and that the tusks of every elephant killed or found dead on the Aberdares were brought in to him.

He also has a sugar-cane press out of which he derives considerable profit.

On my arrival he presented me with a very fat sheep for myself and a very lean one for my porters. As we had nearly come to an end of our rations, I was anxious to buy some more for my men. I told Korori and he immediately produced a bag of beans and refused to accept any payment for it. After a long discussion with him, he said that he could not accept any payment for anything that was to go into my own stomach, and if the beans were not enough for the men, he would make arrangements next day for me to buy the food I wanted from his people. He then brought a gourd of honey wine for me.

It is seldom that one can converse with any real interest with a native, but I found Korori most different to the usual savage. He is half-Dorobo and half-Kikuyu. He said that the white men and the Dorobo were all one at one time, and then the Dorobo became black. He was very insistent on this, and that the Kikuyu and the Masai and all other peoples were of different origin, but that the white man and the Dorobo were the same and both lived by hunting. I told him that this was in a way true, our ancestors were long ago Dorobo in that they lived by hunting. I then told him whatever I could think about prehistoric and cave men, and how at first they had not invented a way of making iron arrow-heads and so had to use stones.

Korori was most interested, in that it proved his pet theory. He then told me about the Kikuyu Wandorobo, and their ways of hunting and of the times when he was young and himself hunted.

On the next day he showed me over his house and stores, explained how the Wandorobo arrows were made, and in the afternoon came and drank coffee with me and smoked a cigar just as if he had done it all his life. I promised to send him a box of cheap cigars from Fort Hall.

The Swahili mason exchanged confidences with the head man again in the evening and said that Korori is a very big and rich man and has boxes of rupees in his house. He is also very generous and will frequently give twenty or thirty rupees to a strange native passing his village.

Whilst sitting talking to me, Korori pointed to a horse-fly busily biting his bare knee. "If I were a woman," he said, "I would drive it away, but being a man I just bear it." I noticed, however, that for some time afterwards he was furtively scratching his knee where it had bitten him.

After a pleasant stay of two days, sketching round his village, I paid off my two guides and said good-bye to Korori. He besought me to ask for anything I wanted and it was only with great difficulty that I escaped without having to take a captive vulture he had got. He supplied me with men as guides and to

collect porters' food *en route,* and I set off for Fort Hall.
The trek up and down a succession of steep, red hills
covered with cultivation is so monotonous and dull
that I will not describe it.

In 1908 I was at Lamu, and wishing to see something
of the mainland, decided to make a little trek, although
the rains were on, and it was a most unfavourable time,
as the low country was flooded. I left Lamu with two
other Europeans for Mkunumbi on a mashua, or small
open dhow. There was no wind, so progress was very
slow and it rained incessantly the whole time. We
arrived at our destination at sunset, having been wet
through since 8 A.M. The route was by winding
channels through the mangrove swamps.

Next day, leaving the other two, I trekked up to Witu;
it was raining the whole time excepting about the last
hour. At Witu the Sultan made me most comfortable.
He has a two-storied, tin-roofed house which I believe
was formerly inhabited by the commissioner after Witu
was taken over. I mention this because it is most
unusual to find a European- or Arab-built house in an
inland village. As a rule, even the biggest chief lives
in a mud hut like anybody else, although perhaps a
little larger than the average.

The Sultan of Witu is an old soldier, and like Korori
a most enlightened man. In his case, however, he
has seen much of Europeans and their ways, whilst

Korori seems to have developed his advanced ideas by himself.

He owns a large cocoanut plantation and is very well to do, chiefly on the proceeds, and he keeps his people well in hand. The population round Witu is very mixed. It consists for the most part of Watoro or runaway slaves. These people seem to have now formed a sort of type of their own, though originally they must have been drawn from the most varied elements, Yaos, Atonga, Makoa, Giriyama, Pakomo, and many others. These slaves escaped from their masters at the coast or island towns, prior to our occupation, and made colonies in the bush. Various expeditions were sent against them, but they soon grew strong enough to hold their own. There are also some Galla living in the neighbourhood.

Witu was the last stronghold of the Sultans of Pate. When that place declined, and finally became a dependency of Zanzibar, the throne was removed to Witu, and there the last Sultans of the line managed to retain their independence, till the place was taken by us, as a result of the murder of some German traders.

From Witu I proceeded to Kao on the Tana River. After some hours of wading through swamps, we reached a backwater. Here I was told to fire a shot, and after about half an hour's delay a canoe appeared and took me up a winding creek to the town of Kao, from which place other canoes were despatched to fetch the rest of my loads.

On the way to Kao we passed, at one place, myriads of little perch-like fish, which had got stranded in shallow water and pools, whilst women were busy collecting piles of them and carrying them off wrapped in their cotton robes.

Kao appeared, at this time of year, to be a low bank of mud, on which were situated about forty or more huts. On one side it was bounded by the Tana and on the other three by creeks and swamps. A good many cocoanut trees are grown round the place, but I am told that they do not prosper.

From Kao we made our way up the Tana by canoe. The canoe was propelled by two Wapokomo, one paddling in the stern, and the other standing in the bow with a long forked pole, with which he occasionally poled at the bottom of the river, but more often prodded the river-side vegetation and pushed against that. The paddler kept the canoe close in to the bank or, when the current was strong, paddled across to the other bank where the current was weaker.

To the poler, nothing seemed to come amiss; now he would prod at a mangrove root, now an overhanging branch, at another time he would collect a bunch of reeds with his fork and push against these.

The scenery was magnificent, as it generally is on rivers, but the weather was abominable and I was very glad to reach Mbelazoni, where I landed. From this place the old course of the Tana flows out at right angles to the main stream and joins the sea some thirty miles south of the present mouth. The river I have been calling the Tana so far is really the old Ozi River. The Tana was turned into it by cutting the Mbelazoni canal, a feat that was performed by Pakomo slave labour, by the command of one of the old Witu Sultans.

The old course of the river is silted up and it is only now when it is very high that any of its water reaches the sea by that channel. About and below Mbelazoni there are stretches of rice fields on the banks.

From this place I went at right angles to the present course of the river and reached the old mouth amongst sand-hills on the seashore, at a village belonging to one Hamed Igao. The change from the sodden, flooded country about the Tana to the dry sand-hills of the seashore, in the course of a few miles, was remarkable and exhilarating.

I had hoped to get news of elephant here, but it appeared that they had left the locality and, according to the local authorities, would not return till the Mkoma palms ripened. This coast ivory is very poor, but I had never shot one of these elephant or met them under these conditions, and was anxious to see what the shooting was like. The country they inhabit when there is thick thorn and bush not far from the shore.

I then returned to Mbelazoni and canoed back to Kao. The soil on the banks of the lower Tana is very rich but the climate is unhealthy. Cocoanuts are grown fairly plentifully, but for some reason or other, perhaps the richness of the soil, do not thrive as they do in the sand and coral rag soil of Lamu. From Kao to Witu the ground had become more flooded, and we had to wade waist deep for part of the way.

At Witu I had tea with the Sultan. I expected to be given tea in a tin mug but to my surprise china cups were set out, and then a cosey tea basket, of the picnic type, was brought up from down-stairs by a naked urchin, and on being opened a china teapot came forth. The urchin was then set to work to roll some cigarettes, the Sultan telling me that he had a special way of rolling, in which a screw of paper was left at the end, by which to light them.

After calling on a settler, I proceeded on my return journey to Mkunumbi. The Sultan was very aggrieved that I would not stop longer, and said that next time I came it must be to see and stop with him, not to rush through each time. After wading practically the whole way and getting drenched as usual, I reached Mkunumbi again, and thence returned to Lamu.

CHAPTER XVI

OFTEN when hunting in Nyasaland, North Eastern Rhodesia, and other tropical parts of Africa, I have thought that it would be too delightful if it were not for one thing, and that is the sun. The sun, with its concomitants of dryness, parched country, thirst, and the sick feeling it gives you after walking for long, just spoils everything.

If one wanted it to be perfect, one would also abolish the tall grass and the noxious insects and then it would be so delightful that one would never want to leave it. If the climate could be further altered to suit one's convenience, one would arrange not to have six months of parching dryness, and six months of slushy wetness, but only small rains, at intervals often enough to keep the country fresh and green.

The long grass which gives you a cold shower bath in the morning, and shuts in the heat during the middle of the day, which flicks you in the face, pokes you in the eye, conceals the path, trips you up and covers you, at certain seasons, with sharp, prickly seeds, is perhaps the most annoying factor in African travel. There is the seed which I call the thread and needle grass; it consists of a sharp head and long tail like a tadpole and it sews itself in and out of your shirt. There are barbed seeds, hooked seeds, sticky seeds, all sorts of seeds, which get down your neck, into your clothes, under your putties everywhere.

Apart from these drawbacks, however, wandering in the bush presents many charms. There are large stretches of wild, uninhabited country, full of game, to be explored, all sorts of waterholes, nullahs, nooks, and crannies to be ferreted out and investigated.

When I came to the highlands of East Africa, I found the country I had been trying to manufacture. The most perfect climate, cool and invigorating, no long grass, few noxious insects, no prolonged drought or swampy wet season, and plenty of game. The only fault I had to find with it was that it was too crowded with sportsmen. One can convert one's hunting into a real picnic in the highlands of East Africa, and it is a country which quite spoils one for a return to the feverish, hot, and unhealthy parts. It has one other drawback, however, besides its crowded state, and that is that it is a poor country for elephant.

Unfortunately, I have never in my life yet had time to have a leisurely, enjoyable trek with nothing to do but wander about and observe game; I have always been in a rush, and my treks are generally forced. Perhaps it is largely my own fault in trying to get too much done in the time available. If I have ten days' leave, I find the place I wish to get to is exactly five days there and five days back. If I have three months' leave it is six weeks there and six weeks back. At other times, when trekking, I have had survey or administrative work to do.

In spite of these drawbacks, from the sportsman's point of view, I have managed to spend many delightful times rambling about forest or bush. I can imagine no more deligthful way of spending a holiday, to one interested in animal life, than a comfortable and leisurely safari through East Africa. There one can find almost any climate one may desire, the extremes of heat and cold, damp and dryness, healthiness and unhealthiness, and anything intermediate between them. About the only kind of climate East Africa does not produce is that raw, rheumatic, damp weather for which our own island is so justly famed. The only thing against it, as I have said before, is that all the healthier parts are getting rapidly filled up with settlers and sportsmen and are becoming fuller every moment.

To enjoy a trek to its fullest, one must take an interest in small things as well as big. One cannot be always shooting big game; either one has shot enough of the species to hand, has enough meat in camp, or wants to find some less strenuous employment for an off day. Then if one takes an interest in plants, smaller mammals, insects, or any other form of life, one has them ready close at hand to study, many of them at one's very door, whilst the larger game must be sought for, sometimes, far away.

For those who wish to study the plain animals and not to shoot, I should imagine that a better place could not be found than the upper and middle pools of the Athi River. During the dryest part of the weather, these places contain the only water for many miles round, and the game come in swarms to drink. Nothing would be easier than to arrange a series of screens, or to dig a pit screened by brushwood, or to arrange a shelter in one of the thorn trees and watch and photo the game from there. As these pools are in the game reserve, special sanction would have to be obtained and the naturalist would probably have to prove that he was a *bona fide* naturalist, and not a sportsman in disguise.

In the upper pools there is practically only one pool of very dirty and bitter water during the dry weather. I visited these pools in February with Captain Cox, R.E., for the purpose of erecting a beacon for the survey in the neighbourhood. Before starting from our camp on the lower Athi, Cox shot a hartebeest, so that we should have a supply of meat when in the reserve. On arriving in the reserve, we found that our boys had left the kongoni at our camp, and the only fresh meat in the larder was a guinea fowl.

The boys were well cursed, with the result that bits of that wonderful bird appeared in different guises, strongly supported by potato and onions, sausages, eggs, and other makeweights, on three consecutive days.

We saw masses of game everywhere and it struck us that the heads were much finer than anything we had seen on the other side of the line. The safari put up two lions at the middle pools. We found the water here bitter, but obtained fresher out of a tributary to the Athi.

We then went on to the upper pools and found only one very discoloured and very bitter pool of water. Fortunately there had been a little shower of rain and going several miles farther up-stream we found some bare rocks on which a few shallow pools of water had formed. These just sufficed for us, but in another couple of days would have been dried up.

The African native generally walks fairly slowly, and when out sketching, if one goes at all fast, the men with the plane table and instruments are generally left a long way behind. Next day, as we were looking for a point, we found the men as usual far behind. Whilst commenting on this, they commenced running for all they were worth. Astonished at this unwonted zeal, we waited to witness the phenomenon and soon saw the reason; — a couple of rhino were trotting behind them.

They came up breathless but the rhino had now altered their course a little, and trotted past. They were not really chasing the men, as the latter tried to make out, but just happened to be trotting in that direction.

TOPI

WALLER'S GAZELLE

Whilst building a beacon under the south of Kenya there was an absolute epidemic of red-legged partridge round my camp. I do not know if they are always there in such numbers, or if it was an unusual occurrence. My porters set snares for them with hair nooses attached to withies, bent down like a bow and releasing with a catch.

A few grains of food were arranged one side of the noose. The bird put its head through to get the grain, and at the same time trod on a twig which let fly the bow. It was then borne up into the air.

During a day or two camped there, my men must have caught quite a hundred, whilst Kikuyu boys brought in others to sell at two for an anna.

At this place the natives told me of an animal, something like a Bongo from all accounts, but differently striped, which was said to live in the forest. I never obtained any more information about it, and in other places along the foot of the mountain the natives said that they knew nothing about such an animal. The native who was my informant described the horns as being twisted.

Whilst sketching on the top of a rocky hill near the junction of the Tana and Thika, I had a proof of the distance to which one can hear the low, grunting sound of the leopard. I was about two or three miles from my camp and I heard these grunts proceeding from that direction. I estimated that the leopard must be between me and the camp. However, when I returned and asked the men there from which direction the sounds had come, they were all agreed that they had proceeded from the other side of camp and that they were fairly distant. That is to say, I had heard the grunting clearly, although it must have been four miles distant, or perhaps more.

Although about as interesting to shoot as would be a sheep, the impala to my mind is the most graceful and prettiest of African game. It is generally found in wooded country on the banks of a big river or stream. Even in the countries of thicker vegetation, such wooded spots are free from long grass, and nothing could be more charming and picturesque than to see a herd of these antelope moving through the trees, with the lights and shades playing on their glossy coats.

They generally move on and on just in front of the sportsman and are usually very tame, never going far unless they have been much molested, but always just out of good sight, often baffling his effort to locate a good head from amongst their number. Their gracefully curved horns, greyhound-like proportions, and leaping movements are very pleasing to behold.

Their surroundings so recall an English park or wood, that I have often pictured to myself what an ornament they would be on any private land. They feed to a certain extent on pods and shoots, so perhaps it would be difficult to acclimatise them to new food, but it would be a very simple matter to round up a herd of these animals. If a zariba was built like a keddeh, on a small scale, it would be easy to drive a herd in. Once there, if fed and watered regularly, they would get as tame as some animals that I have seen who would take salt out of my hand.

The honey guide always appears to me such an interesting little bird. He is the only wild animal I can think of who has established an understanding with man, and in his case it seems to be a complete understanding, and with a man, too, who is noted for his want of sympathy with animals.

The arrangement between honey guide and human beings is based on mutual wants, and is evidently to the advantage of both. It is difficult, however, to understand how such an understanding ever commenced, unless we credit the bird in the first case with a considerable degree of intelligence. One can imagine the bird accidentally coming across honey hunters at work on a bees' nest, or just leaving a bees' nest, and learning that they were useful people to watch. Then one can imagine him after a time learning to follow about such a party and profit by their leavings.

The next step, however, is a long one. The bird knew that it was acquainted with many bees' nests which it was impossible for it to get at. It must have reasoned that the human beings were not acquainted with these nests, in fact that it was their business to look for and find nests, and that instead of being very superior beings they were, in this respect at any rate, rather stupid. The thought must have occurred to one bird at least that it might show these blind human beings the position of such nests to its own personal advantage.

To account for the bird in the first place conceiving this idea, we must credit it with an amount of intelligence and original reasoning powers quite apart from what is generally referred to as instinct, which very few would be prepared to admit is possible. I think that we are so imbued with our own importance and predominance in the scheme of life that we are apt to take too low a view of the original intelligence, apart from instinct, of some other forms of life.

Also the way in which we have got the whole of the animal kingdom ticketed and labelled in ascending order from the protoplasm to the highest form, man, is liable to give us, consciously or unconsciously, a false view of the relative intelligence of different orders. The lower in the scale, the lower the form and the lower the intelligence is a sort of conviction which we unconsciously adopt. If we look on animal life as a tree, it is easy to believe that any of the last branches may produce as good fruit as any other. Unfortunately, we imbibe knowledge from books and, by their nature, such information has to be propounded in two dimensions, and the tree business cannot go into two dimensions.

We have to have our knowledge of plants and animals served up with a beginning and an end, that is to say, in tables and lists and one subject after another.

Also, when we compare man's intelligence with that of the animal, we perhaps turn too much to those animals we know best and can understand, the dog, the horse, and the cow, and perhaps the last two are amongst the most foolish things in creation.

If we want to look for the next to man in intelligence, perhaps we should turn to the ant first, then to some kinds of birds, and then to the bee. Birds are a highly intelligent order; if one wants a good example, look at the Indian crow. With this bird the difficulty is not to believe that it has reasoning powers of a fairly high order, but it would be extremely difficult to convince oneself that some of its actions were caused by instinct. Such actions are purely extemporised for the occasion.

An Indian crow will make an absolute fool of a dog. One will attract his attention and make him rush at it to the full length of his chain and bark senselessly, whilst a second will hop quietly round behind him and help himself out of his platter.

So in the case of the honey guide, it is possible to believe that its reasoning powers led it in the first instance to the idea of showing man the bees' nests of which it knew.

Having got so far, the next step is more difficult to follow. So far the black man, for I suppose that it was a black man, intensely unobservant of anything that he cannot eat or drink, or that does not sting or bite him or otherwise minister to his comfort or discomfort, probably never noticed the quiet, little inconspicuous bird who has followed him from tree to tree, and sat watching him from afar till he had finished his work and gone his way. How then did he first become aware that the bird's twittering was an invitation to follow and how did he first realise what the bird wanted? I can imagine the scene; the bird, at first a little nervous, and then growing bolder, flying over the honey hunter's head. At last one would say, "A bird." The other after considerable cogitation would reply, "It is crying." Then with the air of having completely solved all the problems of the universe, they would proceed on their way.

Perhaps the bird continued time after time till he struck some one who was as great a genius for a black man as it was for a bird and that this one followed him to see what he wanted. However, even then it would not be apparent what the bird wanted, and after a short time the man might well have thought that he was being made a fool of.

I imagined when I heard of the honey bird that it flew from tree to tree in a straight line and finally sat just over the nest, chirping loudly. When I first came across it, and watched its zigzag, apparently aimless, flight from tree to tree and back again, and when on several occasions we were absolutely unable to find any bees' nests, I began to be sceptical about the honey guide's powers.

I argued that if you take any party of natives convinced of the bird's efficacy, and if when the bird appears, they all turn to looking for a bees' nest, encouraged by the bird's twitterings, the chances are that in many cases they will be rewarded by finding one. However, I have now no doubt whatever that the bird is actually a honey guide, although I suspect in it a vein of humour, or comradeship, which induces it sometimes to make a fool of one. "I have found honey often enough for you," I can imagine it saying, "now come along and find some for *me*. Twit, twit, twit. Would you like to go this way? or perhaps this is better?"

Apart from this, I have found honey so often by the help of the honey guide, and on many occasions so near where it first attracted our attention, that the matter is to my mind a certainty. You must not, however, expect him to go and sit over the nest; he leaves something to your own powers of observation and intelligence.

This has been my experience on perhaps a score of occasions. One is walking through the bush, perhaps returning from a shoot, when one hears twit, twit, twit, twit, and the little bird flies past and off to one side. One follows looking at all the big trees and ant-hills about, but hears the bird anxiously calling from ahead. One goes on a little, still looking carefully at every likely place, when one hears twit, twit, twit, from one side again. One goes there and hears the sound in front again and then dying down. Perhaps one goes on to this place but the bird does not encourage one any more, and one does not see or hear it. Looking carefully all round you find a nest, if you are clever. Perhaps you do not find a nest and perhaps you wander far away; in any case after you have been looking some time, the bird starts again and takes you off. I suppose it has assumed that either you cannot find this nest or that for some reason or other you do not want it, and it is taking you to another.

Till I did some hunting with some professional honey hunters, I was unaware what a blind fool I was in the matter of bees' nests, and I should not be surprised if I exasperated my first honey guides beyond measure. "There you are, can't you see it just in front of your nose? Don't you see the direction in which the bees are flying? Why don't you put your ear to the trunk?" must have been the thoughts that flitted through his little head.

I wrote an article to the *Field* which appeared in the issue of September 14, 1907, on the subject of the honey guide. In this I mentioned a case of five nests being found in two days, all close to the spot where the honey guide had attracted our attention, and this when we were trekking along a caravan route and were not anxious to stop our march. On one of these occasions we were not going to pay any attention to the bird, but it was so insistent, in fact it absolutely buttonholed us, that I had to follow it. I determined not to go far, but we found the nest within a stone's throw of the road.

The chances are that the habit of the honey guide is acquired from others, and is not what we call an "instinct." Perhaps it is carried on from one bird seeing another, or perhaps it has by now been done so often that it has developed into an instinct, although not so long ago it must have been acquired by reasoning powers.

My reasons for thinking the former are: first, that there appears to be a great deal of difference between individual birds; some seem very good guides, and some very erratic. Secondly, they cannot be dependent upon this form of sustenance alone, as in some places the times must be few when they can successfully buttonhole man to follow them, and so all the honey guides there have been cannot each have had sufficient individual repetitions of the experience to enable them to acquire the instinct.

CHAPTER XVII

I TRUST the reader is not bored with elephant. It is a subject I hate leaving. In former notes about them I gave it as my opinion that the biggest tuskers moved about in small parties of perhaps four or five together. I am inclined to think now that the very biggest will more often, or equally often, be found in male herds of perhaps about ten animals together, and such herds often contain quite small and young males.

In Nyasaland and North Eastern Rhodesia, there are a fair number of elephants, but the tusks seem to run much smaller than in Uganda and the Lado. There, sixty pounds or so was considered a very fair tusk, and the elephant carrying these were usually found in small groups. On the other hand, the females also were generally found in small groups, although occasionally they might be found in herds of twenty or so. I never saw or heard of anything like the great herds of several hundred which occur in Uganda, the Congo, and the southern Sudan.

I have always maintained that the size of the spoor is a very good general indication as to the size of the tusk. I do not mean to say that the rule is infallible, but by observing closely the spoor, the hunter will save himself a lot of trouble for nothing in following worthless tusks. If he followed nothing under twenty inches he would be fairly safe for a fifty-pounder, although bigger tuskers sometimes occur with smaller spoor and forty-pounders sometimes run to twenty-inch spoor. The rule applies better if all the animals in one country or district are compared together, rather than with elephant from another in which there may be a tendency to grow bigger or smaller feet. For instance, Uganda elephant are big-footed. However, by looking at the following tables he will be able to judge better for himself. I am afraid that they do not cover enough individuals to make them really trustworthy or valuable.

The Baganda as a rule, if they find fresh spoor, bring a stick showing the measurement, which is very satisfactory, as it prevents one dashing out after females or small males. They will also, if they find a dead elephant, bring in a stick the length of the part of the tusk protruding from the gums and a bit of bark the measurement of the girth of the tusks at the gums.

The height of an elephant is no indication of the size of the tusks or the size of the spoor. The measurements of the spoor below have been all taken off the dead animal's forefoot, so as to be uniform. The measurement is from front to rear, only *including the well-*

worn part of the foot and thus excluding about an inch of toe. Measurements on the ground would therefore read larger as a rule. My reading would correspond to the size of the faint impression on a hard surface, covered by a very thin layer of sand, just sufficient to show the impression. To be uniform with my measurements, about an inch should be deducted from a spoor measured in soft sand or mud, where the toe just shows, and one and a half to two inches in deep spoor marks, where the whole foot has sunk below the surface. Of course the hunter must judge for himself whether it be a clean spoor mark or whether the foot has slipped. In the latter case he must find where the second impression of the back of the foot comes.

As regards the heights at the shoulder I cannot guarantee them within an inch or so. An elephant will either fall on his side or in a sitting posture. If in the latter, it will be impossible to adequately judge his height at the shoulder.

If he falls on his side, the leg is seldom absolutely straight, and it will be found impossible to straighten it after death, whilst even the most intrepid hunter and ardent observer would hesitate to try to do this before. So after pulling the leg as nearly straight as possible, often a small allowance must be made for the actual position it would assume when straight. Next I have put in two uprights, one at the shoulder and one at the sole or assumed position of the sole. Then I have measured the distance between these two uprights from about five feet up their height. If these uprights are not absolutely vertical, an inch or so of error may easily creep in. What I want to say is that I have done my best to get a true measurement, but have only used rough-and-ready methods and so they may easily be a couple of inches out either way.

Another point is, and about this I am not certain, how near a lying-down measurement corresponds to a standing-up measurement. I believe a man is slightly longer when stretched out full length in bed than he is when standing upright. Perhaps an inch should be deducted on this account.

Only during the last few years have I been measuring elephants carefully, especially their tusks, with a view to observing the proportion of tusk outside the gums to that inside the head. Still later it occurred to me that a measurement on the outer curve of a tusk was not a satisfactory guide to the cubic capacity unless one knew how much it curved. A better guide would be a mean between the measurement of the outer curve and the inner curve, and so the tusks of the last few elephants I have shot I have measured in this way.

This again is no absolute guide unless one knows the size of the hollows, which would require very intricate measurement. I have tried to indicate these by putting in the column of remarks "old" or "young."

I have also shown the company he was found in by "herd elephant," which means that he was running with a big herd of females and young, "male herd," which means that he was with ten or more other males, "small party" which means that he was one of five or six, or else "lone," or "one of two," or more as the case may be.

Subject to clerical errors, I believe the measurements of tusks as under to be quite accurate.

TABLE OF RELATIVE MEASUREMENTS OF LENGTH OF SPOOR OF FOREFOOT, HEIGHT AT THE SHOULDER, AND WEIGHT OF TUSKS

No.	Spoor	Height at Shoulder	Weight of Tusks Lb.	Remarks
1	22″	11′ 2″	87½ & 85	
2	22″	10′ 8″	68 & 66	Approx. weight
3	21″	10′ 2½″	68 & 68	
4	21″	— —	55 & 50	
5	20¾″	— —	66½ & 66	
6	20½″	— —	53 & 52	
7	20½″	— —	40 & 39	
8	20¼″	10′ 9″	79 & 70	Broken tusk
9	20″	— —	40 & 39	
10	20″	11′ 4″	64 & 62	
11	19¾″	— —	124 & 112	
12	19½″	10′ 10″	61 & 53	Abnormal tusks
13	19½″	— —	50 & —	One tusker
14	19½″	— —	50 & 49	
15	19½″	— —	40 & 40	
16	19½″	— —	94 & 86	Tip broken
17	18½″	— —	40 & 40	
18	16″	— —	15 & 15	Female
19	15¾″	— —	15 & 14½	Female
20	15½″	— —	23 & 21	Female

As regards the girth of tusks, the measurement at the gums is generally a little less than the measurement just inside the gums, which can only be taken after the tusks are cut out. In very young elephant there is more likely to be a greater divergence, whilst in very old ones the two readings may nearly coincide. In some cases they do absolutely.

I have called a lone elephant one that was by himself when shot. Such an elephant might be going to join up with some others and, if found an hour or two later, would then have been in company. Again, sometimes an elephant remains by himself whilst recovering from a bad sore or a wound.

I have several times come across proofs of a single elephant having been alone for a day or so and, for that matter, he may have been much longer. For instance, a very old elephant I shot recently was by himself, and I had seen his spoor covering a period of three days, during which time there were no evidences of his having been with any others and I could find no old wound or sore on him. Whether there is such a thing as a really lone elephant who invariably lives, eats, and walks about by himself, I am inclined to doubt. I should think it more probable that some crusty old fellows go off and sulk for a bit and then join their friends again. There is one thing about a lone elephant, and it is that he is often very truculent and inclined to charge. Also, he does not, as a rule, go far, but rather, if he has been disturbed, waits to see if he is being followed and when a favourable opportunity occurs charges. This would be accounted for on the supposition that he was wounded or perhaps only out of sorts, and so does not wish to be disturbed, or is rather short-tempered and does not wish to go far.

As regards the measurements of the ear, the first two were taken at random and they were so near each other, although the heights of the elephant were very different, that I afterwards took another to see if the measurement was fairly constant. In the same way, the first two measurements of the tail were taken at random and they showed such an enormous difference that I took another to see how variable this measurement was.

Lately, there has been a discussion in the *Field* concerning the fold at the top of an elephant's ear. Some claim that it folds forwards and outwards in the same way as the fold of the human ear, and that the one set up in the British Museum is folded wrong. All I can say is that I must have seen some thousands of African elephants retreating from me with the flaps at the top of the ear folded inwards, or resting on the top of the head, and I have watched elephants flapping their ears from a close distance, under fifty yards, some hundreds of times and never remember seeing an outward fold. I admit that I have not

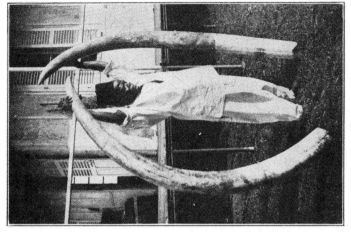

A Nice Pair of Tusks

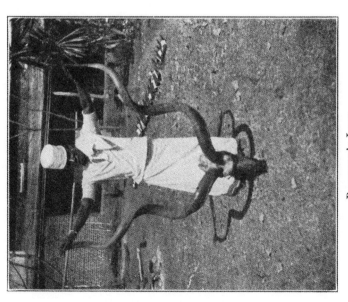

Beginner's Luck

My first and biggest kudu, measuring 63⅝ inches.

been on the lookout for such a fold, but I think that it would have struck me as an abnormal appearance.

Since seeing the discussion, I have observed elephant closely and have never seen an outward fold. Moreover, in the elephant I have shot since, I have observed that the top of the ear is so rigid and set that it would be impossible for it sometimes to fold one way and sometimes the other, although the loose flap might certainly be temporarily thrown over the rigid part, but if this happened it would soon slip back into its former position.

I have commented before on the silent way in which elephant walk. When seen moving in wooded country, the play of light and shadow on their backs produces an extraordinary illusion. Whilst watching what one imagines to be its broad back moving with the alternate shade and sun dancing on it, one suddenly realises that there is no elephant there. He has quietly shuffled off whilst the dancing lights and shadows have caught and arrested the eye. For his size, the elephant is as a rule most extraordinarily inconspicuous, whether moving or stationary. There may be a hundred elephant within a few hundred yards, and the nearest within fifty, resting in the shade, and one may be completely unaware of it till one hears an earflap or a gurgle.

The thickness of the country preferred by elephant,

of course, has much to do with it, but apart from this, they are often very hard to make out when standing stationary. I have often caught sight of a slight movement and thereby become aware of an elephant at a hundred yards or under, and then, although a great part of his body is visible, been unable to determine for some time which end is which.

I think when we realise how inconspicuous the elephant is and remember his size and that no one, that I know of, has ever claimed for him protective colouration, the folly of laying stress on the colouration of the larger mammals as being acquired for protective purposes is apparent.

As Mr. Selous says, there is no scheme of colouration one could devise that would not be inconspicuous under certain conditions. That is to say, that any colour or combination of colours and markings with which you could possibly bedeck an animal would be, in the forest or thick bush, difficult to see under certain conditions, especially if the animal was standing in the shade, when colour counts for nothing unless one is within a few yards. So under certain circumstances, all colours are protective, which amounts to practically the same as saying that an animal might have acquired any colour or any pattern it liked and yet be considered protectively coloured, which reduces the theory *ad absurdum*.

Wounded elephant often get very angry and vent

their rage on trees or inanimate objects. One of the district commissioners of Nimule told me that he wounded a big elephant near that place and on following it up found that it had gone for miles, pulling up and breaking down trees on the way, out of pure anger.

I remember firing at an elephant once who, when I hit him, rushed towards me, screaming with rage. When he got about a third of the distance to me, he met a tree and tore off the branches, screaming the while. Having done this he turned round and rejoined the herd.

Elephant get badly burnt sometimes by bush fires. It is the practice amongst the natives in certain parts to collect in great numbers and set fire to a large expanse of grass in a circle. Any elephant inside must break through the fire ring to get out and, in doing so, often gets singed. I am told they lose their head and rush backwards and forwards, whilst baby elephant often get burnt to death and are then eaten by the natives. I have never witnessed one of these performances but have met elephant with large sores on them which I believe are to be accounted for by burning in this way.

Elephant hate shouting and stamping of feet, and loud shouting and stamping in front of them will almost invariably turn a herd, even though apparently stampeding blindly in that direction.

CHAPTER XVIII

CURIOUS AFRICAN SAYINGS AND IDEAS

It is usually hard to make a native understand anything which is out of the way of his own simple life. If one is well acquainted with his methods of thought, or rather his lack of method in this respect, and tries to turn the corner instead of going straight ahead, one may often convey a definite idea to him which it would be impossible to do otherwise. Or if one descends to his line of argument, one may prove to his complete satisfaction a point by absolutely worthless logic.

A parallel occurs with us, where a smart repartee, having no logical value whatever and completely outside the point, will often discomfit an opponent and leave the maker with all the honours of war.

A thing that the ordinary native cannot understand is that the farther you go inland, the dearer will be articles imported, such as calico, etc. I have often heard natives complain bitterly that the shops of Nairobi are more expensive than those of Mombasa, and those of Entebbe than Nairobi, and so on.

Commenting on this to a shrewd trader in Nyasaland, he said that natives often complained to him that they could get calico at 4*d* a yard at Blantyre, about ten days' distance, whereas he charged them 5*d*. To have said, "All right, you go down to Blantyre and buy your calico" would not have convinced the native at all that it was not an exorbitant charge. He would think nothing of going down ten days to expend 8*d* on two yards of calico. Time is not money to the African.

"But lor' bless ee," said the trader, "there are always ways and means of explaining to the native. I say all right, you go and hunk me up a load of calico from Blantyre for nothing, and I will then sell you as many yards as you like for 4*d*." This argument was self-convincing.

There are in Swahili some wonderfully apt proverbs, a collection of which has been made by the Rev. W. E. Taylor. I have found that the quoting of a proverb often proves a point completely to the native satisfaction, especially amongst such a motley crew, as, for instance, caravan porters, who talk Swahili as a common language but are not really well versed in it. Often old Swahili words, which have completely gone out of use in the modern language, are retained in these proverbs. The very fact that they are unintelligible to him would make them even more convincing. They bear for him the magic of an unknown incantation.

A few examples of the proverbs are : —

"Do not show kindness to a dog, for he is insensible to kindness."

The pariah dog is, of course, the dog referred to. The meaning is that if you go out of your way to help an evil person, the chances are that he will return you evil for good.

"When you chance to meet your mother-in-law, it is then that you happen to be naked." A man perhaps in his village and working in the fields will throw off the greater part of his clothes, whilst he would wish to appear at his best when he meets his mother-in-law. The proverb means that it is just when one is least prepared that one is taken at a disadvantage. It would be applicable to a case in which visitors suddenly called when there was nothing in the pot or in the larder. Another one is, "The slowness of the tortoise takes him far afield." Meaning "Slow but sure."

As natives generally do things in the opposite way to the white man, so often do words and phrases bear to them exactly the opposite meaning to what one would suppose. I remember hearing a white man calling out to his boy several times, "Fasten up my tent," "No, fasten it up," and then in English, "Curse the boy; the more I tell him to fasten it up, the wider he opens it." He was using the word for "tie up," which the boy interpreted to mean tie back the door.

There is a proverb, "He who is not near when the

tree falls, the tree will not fall on him," which to the ordinary European would mean that one should stand clear of danger. The meaning really is that the lucky ones are those who are near, as they will have first pick of the fruit, it being the custom of the economically minded native, when he finds a fruit tree in the bush, to fell the whole tree in order to get the fruit. However, one Sultan of Zanzibar appeared to have noticed the *double entendre* as I have described it in the "Land of Zinj," for he sent this proverb as a message to a chief who had been refractory some time before. Imagining that he was pardoned and that he was about to have honours and presents showered on him, he hurried to Zanzibar and was put in prison, where he died.

Another proverb particularly applicable to the hunter is "He who has not a sharp knife will not obtain meat." When an animal is shot, there is a rush for the carcass and everybody begins helping himself to joints. Any one who had to stop to sharpen his knife would find, when he had finished, that the best part of the meat had already been appropriated.

The native is often insufferable in his begging. I believe he really respects you the more if you refuse him bluntly and point blank. However, it is very difficult to do so and it makes one feel extremely mean grudging a handful of salt or some trifle asked for. Abyssinia is perhaps the worst country to travel in in this respect. One is asked for a present by almost every one that one meets on the road, and yet they are a people who will, on occasion, show very real and genuine hospitality without looking for a return.

When approaching a spot at which I intended to camp once, I was accosted by two men who went through the usual polite inquiries after my health and the safety of my journey and followed me till I dismounted. I had heard one say to the other in a low voice, "We will go with the foreigner and ask him for some money."

The usual formula was to first expatiate on their poverty and my apparent riches and then ask for something. I determined to be first in the field this time, so before they had time to make the usual request, I dilated at length on my poverty, the expenses I had been put to, how I had lost all my camels, and how various other misfortunes had befallen me. Not knowing what was coming they expressed themselves as deeply sympathetic. I then went on to comment on their lordly and well-dressed appearance and finally asked if they would give me a dollar. With sickly smiles they shuffled off.

At different times I have had various natives to teach me to read and write Arabic, Amharic, and Swahili. At an early stage of this tuition, the same great thought has almost invariably occurred to all these stray teachers. With an air of great mystery, they produce a piece of paper and say that they have brought me something to read. It is a request for a present which it has occurred to them could be more delicately put in writing.

Different tribes have different ideas about what is brave and what is not, whilst others have not the least compunction in admitting that they are cowards. Although many are very plucky, their standards are very different to ours.

I remember hearing a discussion amongst some porters of different tribes about cowards and people being afraid, with instances given. At last one said, "Well, I do not call a man who runs away a coward; he may be a very brave man, but he just runs away. I call a man who cannot run away a coward. The other has heart and pluck." Then he gave us an instance in point, an incident from the fights against the Sudanese mutineers in Uganda. Two Sudanese were, he said, sitting up a tree with their rifles watching. They went to sleep or were not sufficiently on the lookout, and were surprised by a party. One leaped from the tree into a bush and got away, but the other was transfixed with fear and could not move. He had his rifle but he could not use it nor could he move or speak from fear.

In Abyssinia I met a venerable and pious Galla Haji. I was told he was making a pilgrimage to a distant shrine, having already made that to Makka. His silence and grave demeanour, whilst all the Abyssinians present asked me incessantly for all manner of presents, impressed me very much. Here, at least, was a man above such sordid, worldly things — one with his eyes ever fixed on the hereafter.

On leaving the place, I said that while everybody else had been constantly worrying me about what I was going to give them, he alone had not asked for anything, and therefore I hoped that he would accept some presents I had prepared for him. This speech was translated to him in Galla, as it appeared that he could speak no other language, which might have been the reason for his silence. He took the presents and through the same medium he replied, without thanking me for what he had received, that as he was going on a long journey, he thought that I ought to give him some money as well.

When I first became acquainted with the African, this want of thanks and immediate request for more, which so often follows a present given when the receiver had no right to expect anything, used to irritate me considerably. I soon found that I was judging the native by a western standard far too high to be applicable to him. When judged by an animal standard, the request became quite reasonable and explicable. Your dog is lying by your chair as good as gold whilst you are having dinner. Now give him something from the table which he has no reason to expect. Instead of taking it gratefully, offering profuse thanks, and going to lie down again, he will gobble it up and worry you through the rest of the meal asking for more. The thought which has occurred to him is probably, "Here is a decent sort of fellow who has just given me something; if I wait here and ask him he will probably give me some more."

So it is with the native. You have just given him something for nothing, and if this is your custom, there is no reason why you should not do it again. In any case he loses nothing by asking. The only thing to do is to tell him the story of the hyæna and the moonbeam, which is the African equivalent for the dog and the bone.

I heard some of my porters discussing one day the strength of the Abyssinians and the numbers of men and rifles they possessed. They were wondering if we would be able to take their country and were rather inclined to doubt it. My head man, Abdi, than whom few more loyal subjects of the British crown exist in Africa, interrupted their conversation. "Do not ask," he said, "if the British are able to take Abyssinia, but if they want to. I do not believe all these stories one hears of the strength of people. When it comes to the point, what do they do? Do you remember what we heard about the Nandi, and then when we went to their country they all ran away? Was it not said formerly that Zanzibar could not be taken except if the Kingi (king) himself came to take it with all his strength? Then what happened? I forget if it was a corporal or a sergeant-major who took it."

Another head man said that he had heard that it was written in a book (the suspicion of being extracted from a book gives any statement an air of truth and accuracy) that if one meets a snake and an Abyssinian together on the path, one should kill the Abyssinian first and the snake afterwards. It was also written of them that the elephant, the Abyssinian, and the locust were all the same, as to being without number.

I do not know why the elephant should be considered so numerous by the native. He has no head for figures and never follows a statement to its logical conclusion. He sees a great herd of elephant and thinks that they are without number, and, therefore, the same as locust, who are without number. He would not follow up the argument by thinking that a tract of country which would support one elephant in food would support a million or more locusts.

I am told that not many days from Mombasa there is a big snake called Mwanyika who inhabits a lake and eats fish, and men, and hippos, but he chiefly lives on hippo, of which he will eat a hundred a day. Such a bold statement is quite enough for the native. The suspicious-minded European begins at once to probe the statement. If the snake eats a hundred hippo, a day, allowing a certain amount for fish-days and human-being days, he will eat about twenty-five thousand hippos a year. To keep up this supply would busily engage, roughly, one hundred thousand hippo, breeding as fast as they could. Taking a map of East Africa, we fail to find a lake near Mombasa big enough to support this number of hippos; even Lake Victoria would not. One is therefore compelled to doubt the existence of Mwanyika, or at any rate to think that his appetite has been overrated.

A frequent statement I have heard made by natives is that lion are more numerous in the rains. Lion have forced themselves on his attention more at that time, so he says there are more. It never occurs to him to think where all the extra lions come from or go to. Anyhow, with the miraculous always at his disposal, he never has to follow an argument farther than one step and there it can end in a supernatural phenomenon. However, he does not even trouble to assign such an occurrence to a miracle. If asked where they have come from, he says, "How should I know?" and dismisses the matter from his mind.

Talking about the Somaliland Mullah, I was told that there was a prophecy that after the Mahdi seven prophets will arise. Of these the first one is the Mullah. After the seventh, there will be a general Tehad or holy war.

I cannot imagine a more horrible situation in which

to be than to find oneself in the power of an African, when he knows it. Fortunately, he is very easily bluffed and very superstitious. If he sees you alone, far from help, and in a position of which he is evidently master, some lurking suspicion must enter his mind that things cannot be quite as they seem; you must be counting on some force of which he is unaware. A native of another tribe, in a similar position, would be running away, which would inspire him with confidence. What more natural than to suppose that you have some powerful medicine or magic at your disposal and it is for this reason that you order him about so freely?

Even with the more educated African, bluff is a great factor. Coming down from Addis Ababa to Dirre Daua, I was much exasperated by the demands for presents from various persons who made a living out of blackmailing anybody who passed. I was at the end of my journey and also at an end of my resources, so I refused to give anything except adequate returns for any present brought me or service rendered. At Dirre Daua I had a tremendous business to get my things through the customs, I could not afford to give more than a few dollars bakshish, which I did, and finally got all my things on the train for nothing.

As the train moved off, I breathed freely, for I thought that it was all over, and no unexpected demands could now crop up between here and Aden, where I could cash a draft.

After travelling a few hours, we stopped and descended for lunch. I imagined that I had left Abyssinia behind forever, but it appeared that we were still in Abyssinian territory. Whilst eating my *déjeuner*, a man came in and asked me if the "Senegalese" in the train belonged to me. He referred to my Wanyamwezi porters but the Abyssinians call most natives they do not know Senegalese, as a Russian and French expedition once brought some into the country.

Imagining that he was the bearer of some interesting communication concerning them, such as that one of them had fallen out and broken his neck, or that they were having a fight, I immediately admitted having some men in the train. Instead of any such intelligence, however, he said that I would have to pay on them before they could be allowed to proceed any farther. "Oh, go away," I replied, and he went off.

Presently a small procession appeared; amongst others was the local Gerezmach or Fitorari. "These Senegalese," he began in Amharic, but I said, "Go away," again. "You will have to pay before they can go on." "Go away, I am eating," I said. "But you must pay, or they will not be allowed to proceed," he said.

When I had come in, I had coiled up my rhino-hide whip and hung it on a peg behind my chair. I now looked at the distinguished official, who wished to charge me export duty on my men returning to their own country, as if to appraise his value, and then turned very slowly, took down the whip, and lovingly uncoiled the lash. He did not wait to see what I was about to do with it, after it was uncoiled.

I finished my lunch slowly and deliberately but in reality in great trepidation as to what would happen next. I had threatened a high official with personal chastisement; it was his country and he was in command here. After lunch, I took my seat in the train and uttered a sigh of relief when it once more started and this time really took me and my empty purse and my "Senegalese" safely out of the country.

On the road to and from Dirre Daua, one meets constant streams of baggage mules carrying loads backwards and forwards from Addis Ababa, chiefly calico and ammunition on the upward journey and coffee and skins on the downward.

I can never think of the Dirre Daua road without recalling these long lines of sore-backed animals, and the constant whacks and objurgations of the mule drivers and the querulous requests that the beast will render information concerning its parentage which accompanies each whack. Strange to say, the mule always treats these anxious inquiries in contemptuous silence.

Once, after shooting an elephant, I heard the natives with me saying that it was a very lucky elephant and had fallen very well. I asked why and they said, "Oh, it has fallen looking towards our way home." I suppose to the native mind, somehow, it appeared that it was easier to carry the meat back if it was already "looking" in that direction.

The belief in the werewolf, under different disguises, is very common the world over, both amongst civilised and savage peoples. The Somali believes in a being called the Orgobi, who is a man-leopard; by day it is a man, and by night a leopard. It seizes people by night, the intimate knowledge of a kraal and its habitants being gained in the guise of a man by day.

The Somalis also believe that people can turn themselves into hyænas at night. A man alleged to be in possession of such a gift was brought for enlistment in the Somali irregulars in 1900. He explained that the gift was not a common one, and, as his services would be most valuable to the force in scouting at night, he required rather more than the ordinary pay; in fact he estimated his services at thirty rupees a month.

An agreement was accordingly made that he should be enlisted at this rate, in return for which he consented to turn himself into a hyæna, when required, and scout for the force in this guise.

Before the agreement was finally closed, it was explained to him that as this rate of pay was above the average, the government would like to ascertain for certain that he really was in the possession of the powers he claimed. He might be an impostor or he might have forgotten how to do it. Would he mind just turning into a hyæna in the corner, so that we could see that he was still in good practice? To this he replied that it was against his principles to change into a hyæna in public. He was used to going out into the night, to do it, but we need have no fear, he was well versed in the art and would not fail us.

The Somalis who had brought him thought that the European was unduly sceptical about the man's powers. "It will be a very good thing indeed for us," they said, "if we can get this man to accompany us, as he will gain much information for us as to the enemy's whereabouts."

Nothing could prevail on the man to give a proof of his powers, so at last an officer said to him, "Look here, here are thirty rupees and here is a chicote. If you turn into a hyæna now, the thirty rupees are yours. If you do not, you will have thirty chicote for being a liar and trying to deceive the government."

However, he was a clever rogue. He explained that he would be delighted to turn at once into a hyæna and gain the thirty rupees, but before he could effect the change it was necessary to eat certain herbs of the bush; he would go immediately and fetch the herbs and give an ocular demonstration of his powers. So saying he ran off to fetch his herbs and was never seen again; perhaps he changed into a hyæna and forgot how to change back. Allah knows.

CHAPTER XIX

In my "Game of East Africa," I gave some simple hints to add to one's comfort and convenience in camp and on trek. When I overflowed my chapter, I stopped, promising some more in the future, and here they are. As stated before, I do not claim to be the original inventor of such hints, but have picked up the majority from others. However, as they may be of use to someone else, I pass them on.

In a semi-civilised country, such as northern Abyssinia, in which thieves are plentiful and bold, greater precautions against theft are desirable than amongst the unsophisticated Central African. There is little to prevent an intelligent and enterprising thief from crawling up to your tent on a dark night and stealthily feeling under the flies. As the first things he would go for are your rifles, the last things you wish to lose, it is well to put these in a safe place. Resting on a camp table or chair in the centre of the tent is fairly safe, but perhaps the best place of all is to have them slung from the roof. There are generally hooks attached to the top of the tent, whose function has so far remained obscure to me, but they serve well for this purpose ; your revolver is, of course, in bed with you.

If you travel with the ordinary hurricane lamp, it can act as a night light, if turned low just before you go to sleep. It will remain burning all night with but little expenditure of oil. If there is an alarm or any noise, it can be turned up in a moment to enable you to investigate.

When a sudden storm of rain bursts at night, many conscientious men think that they have to rush out in pajamas and get wet through, slackening the ropes of their tent. If you lie comfortably tucked up in bed and say nothing about it, almost always some faithful native, who, living in a leaky hut all his life, is less averse and more inured to wettings than you are, will come and drive in your tent pegs as they get rooted out. However, in the case of the rain starting with a light shower, which afterwards develops into a down-pour, the faithful savage is generally not of much use, for he, like all other natives, thinks that tent ropes should be pulled as taut as possible before rain. Having made you safe, as he imagines, by straining every rope to its utmost, he will go off to his own shelter.

Then comes the downpour and you are unwilling to call to the faithful savage to return, but even now there is still an alternative to getting wet left to you. If you scratch a hole a few inches deep beside the foot of each pole and shift the end into it, you will have slightly slackened every rope in the tent and if the pegs are firm you will be fairly safe.

The sportsman, traveller, or collector usually has a lot of odd paraphernalia, such as rifles, cartridge bags, haversacks, camera, field-glasses, collecting apparatus, etc., being carried by various boys, guides, and men.

When he halts he wishes these collected in one place. The rifles will probably be rested against a tree trunk, until they are knocked over, to the detriment of the foresights, whilst the other things are hung up on odd branches or piled on the ground, which may be damp. It is very convenient to have a little bamboo tripod on the top of a convenient load. When you halt, this is immediately stood up and all the various articles are slung to it or rested against it. This insures that they will not be mislaid, as they may be if hung on various branches; or trodden on, as is likely to happen if they are on the ground. They are all gathered in one place and anything required can be easily found.

Yeast for baking bread may be made out of banana wine or other native spirits. If your cook is absent, drunk, or otherwise unavailable, and you want bread in a hurry, unless you are of a very ambitious nature, chupaties are the best things to make.

First, wash the top or side of a chop box and then make some dough. I suppose everybody knows how to make dough; but if you have not tried before, add the water by very small quantities at a time and always keep more flour in the basin than would appear to be required for the amount of water used. Having made your dough, sprinkle some flour on the top of the washed box, put a lump of dough on it, and, taking a bottle as rolling pin, roll it out, first sprinkling more flour on the top of the dough to prevent it sticking to the bottle. Knead it up and roll it out again several times, both from north

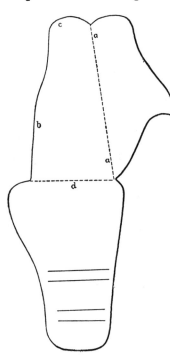

to south, and east to west, or else you get a long, thin strip rather than a round disk. The last two times you roll it out, put on a few drops of oil or fat before kneading it up again. Then roll it out for the last time and when you have acquired a disk more or less round and flat and about a quarter of an inch in thickness, put some oil or fat in a frying-pan and fry the chupaty, turning it over till both sides are brown. The only thing left to do now is to take it out and eat it. It is best hot.

A brother officer in an African battalion showed

me a simple and easy method of making a revolving holster, which has served me on more than one occasion. It can be made out of any old piece of skin or hide, so long as it is not too thick, such as a piece of bushbuck or impala skin. Of course a bit of tanned leather, if obtainable, is superior. The skin is cut in the shape of the first illustration.

The upper part is then folded at the dotted line *a* and sewn with a strip of leather or bit of boot-lace along the edges *bc*.

The top is now folded over a dotted line *d* and the end pushed through slits cut in the lower part. The holster is now complete and the waist-belt is passed between the upper and lower flaps where the arrow is shown.

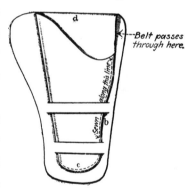

There is no sewing to be done or to come un-stitched except the short trip from *b* to *c* and even this could be fastened with a couple of metal clips if preferred.

In hot and damp climates it is not, as a rule, possible to hang meat until it is tender. Rubbing it over with pawpaw leaves is said to make it tender. A better way, and one which does well with the African chicken, is to parboil it for one hour and then hang it up for twenty-four hours, when it may be cooked and will be found to be quite tender.

The method usual amongst Africans of "blocking the paths" is very useful to indicate the road to a caravan or stragglers following behind. The ordinary African would never think of tampering with these signs; in fact I have often seen the branches I left in the way still there weeks afterwards.

However, if there is any reason to suppose that they will be altered, a better way of showing the road taken is to pick a well-leafed branch and, just after any fork in the road, to strip it of leaves as one walks along, as if one was peeling it for a riding switch. The trail of leaves will then indicate the path taken.

The value of Keating's powder to the traveller cannot be overestimated. Some sprinkled on the head and shoulders, or better still on a sheet of paper and blown off it into the air, will prevent flies from settling on one. Sprinkled on the window-sills and thresholds of doors, it will, in a great measure, keep out undesirable insects. Sprinkled in boxes it will keep out ants.

To soften a skin, as for use in the holster described above, soak it in water for an hour or so after skinning it and then rub it with a mixture of equal parts of powdered alum and rock salt.

If sulphuric acid can be obtained, a better way of dressing a skin is to scrape it as clean as possible and then immerse it for twenty-four hours in a barrel con-

ORYX

GIRAFFE

Standing on the right of picture.

taining sulphuric acid, salt, and water in the following proportions : —

> 10 oz. sulphuric acid
> 10 lb. salt
> 40 qt. water.

To clean and soften the hard native bean, they should be soaked in cold water for twenty-four hours and then taken out and boiling water poured over them, which will cause the outer skins to come off.

When one builds a hut or shelter, one is much worried after a short time by a snowlike fall of fine white powder. This is caused by wood-borers. It covers everything and sometimes induces a kind of hay fever. It can be mitigated to a certain extent by soaking the roofing poles in water, till they become well sodden, before using them, as after this they are not so readily attacked by wood-borers. There are certain kinds of hard woods which they hardly attack at all. These can be discovered by noticing in a native village any pole which has not been bored and asking its native name. I remember that in Nyasaland there was a kind of ebony called Mpani with a hard black core which the borers never attacked. I also made a list of several others, but the above was the most useful for roofing poles, as it was generally abundant.

As to food stores, one learns much about the relative value of different wares as one goes on, and I should like to give the result of my experience, only it would read more like an advertisement column than anything else. I try to get the greater part of them in tins and bottles that will be of service after they have been emptied of their original contents. Certain jam jars serve very well as tumblers or can be used again for butter or other things if they are provided with screw tops.

It is very convenient on trek to have a couple of wickerwork or basketwork-covered bottles provided with stoppers fitting with a lever catch. One can be used for carrying milk while a bottle of lime-juice or whiskey when opened can be poured into the second. Their advantage over an ordinary bottle is that they do not break readily and they can be opened easily, whereas a cork must be drawn or an ordinary stopper falls out when shaken up in transit. As the rubber washers about the stoppers perish quickly, it is as well to have a few spare ones.

Rectangular tins are more economical of space than round ones and, if they have serviceable lids, are more useful for packing things in afterwards. Some kinds of bottles are especially useful for collecting insects.

The general box of soup squares offers a great variety in the numbers of names and the different coloured papers in which the contents are wrapped up. They appear, however, to offer but one distinct variety of flavour and that can be only described as soup square.

Good packets of condensed soups, as used by the Congo government, may be had in France.

Meat extract or juice, to be used cold, is an excellent thing for waterless countries. When one is unable to eat and has not sufficient water to waste by boiling, so as to make tea or soup, some of this extract can be poured into one's limited allowance of cold water and drunk like that without further trouble. Even where water is available, a cold soup is very pleasant in the hot weather and this can be simply made out of meat juice with a little Worcester sauce and salt added.

All tinned stores should be taken out of their tins immediately on being opened. By doing so, they avoid getting a tinny flavour, whilst if such things as fish, etc., are left long in their opened tins there is always a chance of ptomaine poisoning. Tinned vegetables often are improved after they have been removed from the tin and kept twenty-four hours. If there is any uncertainty about any tinned food and one is too short to be able to throw it away, it should at least be cooked, which will be less risky than consuming it cold.

When I am likely to be out all day, I often get my cook to make some meat pasties for me. These are articles shaped like jam puffs but with meat in the place of jam. They can be put in the pocket and consumed as one walks along without more ado.

An excellent lantern, for marching at night, may be

made out of an empty gin bottle (gin because they are plain glass bottles). Take some cotton soaked in paraffine and wrap it neatly round the bottle about an inch from the bottom. Set a light to it and just before it burns out, when the glass under it will be thoroughly heated, plunge the bottle quickly into cold water. If the bottom is now gently tapped, it should break off cleanly at the place at which was the cotton wrapping.

Now take your bottomless bottle by the neck and slip a candle into it so that the end rests in the broad part of the neck. The lantern is then complete. It is sometimes a little difficult to light the candle, especially if it is short, without burning one's fingers, but a little ingenuity will overcome this. Once lit it will not blow out; I have walked for miles at night holding such a lantern by the neck.

By wrapping the cotton round the middle of a bottle and going through the same procedure, a tumbler or jam jar will result. The upper part or neck of a bottle may be similarly detached to form a funnel or tube. A useful fireplace, for use in a hut or tent, can be made out of an old kerosene oil tin. This with holes bored in its sides can be filled with red-hot embers from a fire outside and brought into a hut without danger of setting fire to it. When it burns down it can be replenished from the fire outside. If it is required for use in a wooden-floored room, without a fireplace, a piece of corrugated iron may be placed on the floor and the impromptu fireplace on the top of this.

A circumstance one often overlooks, in choosing camp kit or house effects for Africa, is the utter inability of the African to deal with a screw. He always tries to force it at the wrong angle and breaks or damages the thread. So if possible no articles, such as pepper pots, lamp burners, etc., which are likely to be intrusted to the African boy, should be provided with screws or screw caps.

On trek it is a useful thing to remember, when confronted by the problem of whether to march on farther or halt and when having only the information of a local guide to rely on, that in practically no case do the real considerations of water, etc., on the route affect the reply of the latter. If he says that there is no water in front it certainly means that he, the guide, does not wish to proceed that day. It does not of necessity mean that there is or is not water. If he says that there is an impassable river by a certain route it means that he, for reasons best known to himself, does not wish to take that route. There may be a big river or there may not. If one remembers this always, it saves one being annoyed the next day when one finds that one might easily have proceeded another hour or so, as wanted, and found a good site for camp.

In sending to a kraal for milk, if one thinks that there is any hope of being able to obtain clean milk, it is best to send two vessels, a big and a small, say a kettle or tea-pot for bringing the milk back and a small cup or basin for milking into. Failing the latter the native will milk into his dirty gourd and then pour it into your receptacle.

In crossing swamps and streams one often finds it very slippery and uneven going, owing to elephant foot-steps or muddy holes. To save oneself from falling, one clutches wildly at the surrounding reeds and rushes and afterwards finds a kind of down or fur on one's hands. These can be scraped off fairly well with a knife. See which way they are slanting, if any, and then scrape a knife over your hand against them and back the opposite way. Repeat this till most of them appear to have been extracted. I am told that there is only one really effective way of removing these miniature spines and that is to rub your hand in a black man's fuzzy hair.

An unpleasant feature of African life is the veldt sore. If one has been living on a poor diet, often the least scratch or prick turns into a sore which does not readily heal. I have tried many remedies for these but have only struck one really good one and that was one told me by a brother sportsman a few years ago. It is called Pazo, an ointment really produced for a very different purpose than that of curing veldt sores. This is generally very effective — quickly drying up the sore, especially when it is used in the early stages. A slower and perhaps surer way to heal these sores is to wash them well with warm water and then pour boiling water over a piece of lint, rinse it out quickly, and bandage it on as hot as can be borne. Do this night and morning and it gradually reduces the inflammation round the sore and allows it to heal.

Shorts are so comfortable and cool for wear in the bush, that I have, like many others, always worn them. At the end of a long day it makes a lot of difference having nothing dragging on one's knees, as with trousers or breeches, but being able to move in perfect freedom. However, now in my old age I am beginning to wonder if the disadvantage of having one's knees knocked about is really worth the advantages gained, especially in thick bush. Thorns tear one's knees and grass cuts them. One gets wary at avoiding thorny plants but one cannot always be watching the path. Insects bite one and flies settle on the scratches and cuts. Some of the thorns and grasses I believe to be poisonous in themselves. In any case the wearer of shorts has generally to put up with an interminable succession of sores, cuts, and bruises on the knee, many of which, with the help of flies and poisonous vegetation, develop into nasty places.

Some of these rank grasses are as sharp as razors and even the black man often cuts his fingers deeply by unwarily catching hold of them.

It is unnecessary to warn the hunter that he should

always have a box of matches with him and that he must take every care to keep it dry. The locally purchased matches are generally so bad and easily affected by damp that it is a good plan to have a reserve of some good English-made match in a small sealed box or waterproof envelope. This may be carried about for months or years and never used, but when the hunter gets left out in the bush on a damp night, and finds that his matches have been destroyed by crossing a river or pushing through wet grass, he will be thankful for the reserve.

CHAPTER XX

THE usual African punitive expedition is a poor enough show. It usually starts by some European being attacked or murdered, or constant raids being made by some tribe not in an administered area on some other tribe which is under the government. In both cases, the tribe to be attacked has, as a rule, not the slightest conception of the powers or resources of the government. In the former case, they perhaps think that the government is one white man, and if they kill him they will have finished with it forever.

In ninety-nine cases out of a hundred, directly an expedition reaches their country, the natives fly in every direction, scattering all over the country and hiding their stock in small herds. It then only remains to break up and catch what stock can be found and shoot down a few men running away till the "cease fire" is sounded. Perhaps some villages are burnt and then the column is withdrawn and messengers of peace are sent to tell the tribe that war is over, so long as they will submit to the government. If much cattle has been captured, some of it is usually given back after the natives have behaved themselves for a year or two.

Possibly one or two soldiers, who have wandered far away by themselves, perhaps on a private looting expedition, are killed or wounded but otherwise no casualties occur.

On the hundredth occasion, all starts as before, but either the strength or the courage of the enemy has been underrated or a small column becomes detached. Nothing is seen of the assailants except a few flying men. Suddenly, there is a rush in thick grass or bush and the little column gets massacred. The enemy are either very ignorant of the power of the rifle or else very sure of their ground before they will attack. In the first case, perhaps there is a severe fight and finally the natives are driven back. Of course such a situation is what every commander hopes for at the commencement of the expedition, as it gives his men an experience of the real thing and the enemy a lesson in the power of the rifle. Shooting down a few stray runaways and being unable to catch or deal with the real truculent men of the tribe will never have a satisfactory effect.

When proceeding with a column and baggage, with all the arrangements for food and porterage, it is practically impossible to surprise or catch the barefooted savage who, if he is no good at anything else, is always undefeatable in the art of running away through thick bush. I suppose that a moderately trained athlete would beat any native by points on a racing track, but put the two in thick bush and the latter would have it all his own way. To see a party of natives fly after a small wounded buck one would think that grass and bush were no obstacle.

So in the usual African warfare — I am not talking of the fanatical people of northern Africa — the show is hopelessly dull for the ninety-nine times and rather too exciting for the hundredth. However, if there is nothing to rejoice the heart of the soldier, the sportsman can often amuse himself, if he can escape from the crowd and get away by himself.

In January, 1908, I was building a survey beacon at the south of the Uasi Ngishu, when a runner came through with a telegram to say that I was to join an expedition going up into the Kisii country. By the time I got the message, the expedition was already leaving Nairobi. I decided that my best way would be to try to hit off the railway line about Lumbwa or Fort Ternan if a path could be found. A Dorobo with me said he knew of a path to Lumbwa, so after finishing the beacon, we started and by 5 P.M. found ourselves surrounded on all sides by thick forest. The Dorobo then said that he did not know of a way to Lumbwa; he had only thought he did. There were masses of forest and the mountain of Tinderet between us and Lumbwa and it was not much good attempting to cut through this if we could not find a path.

The country appeared more open westwards and I decided to steer for Muhoroni, so we started cutting our way through the belt of forest that separated us from the open country in that direction. We camped in the forest at sundown. Next day we cut our way out through the forest, and then I took my porters up hill and down dale, through the most noxiously entwined long grass, the whole day without a halt till after sundown, when we lay down.

Next day we reached Muhuroni in the afternoon. One would have thought that those two days of continual trek without halts and up and down steep hills without a path would have choked off any caravan of porters to be found. However, this was not so, as there were great heartburnings and jealousy over the selection of men who were to go on and those who were to return to Nairobi. Finally we got a train and boat to Kindu on the lake shore. The expedition had started a day or two before, and in the distant hills, one could see the fire and smoke of burning huts.

On my march up to meet the column, I was preceding my men, as is my custom, when topping a rise, I saw a Kisii warrior coming up from the bottom of the valley. I immediately signed to my men, who were as yet below the ridge, to stop, a sign which generally meant game and hence meat for them.

I then stalked my man, who was going slantwise across our path, from bush to bush, till I had got within twenty yards of him. At this moment, there was a report from behind. It appeared that one of my porters, armed with an old carbine which used to be the weapon of the night watchman in camp, had crept up to see what game I was after. He saw me crouching along apparently stalking something and then he saw the Kisii warrior quite close, so discharged his carbine into the air to frighten him away. This discharge had the effect desired by the porter, as the Kisii turned and ran like a hare down the hill and I after him.

At the bottom was a stream and into this he plunged. I ran to the bank and waited at the side but he did not emerge. I was soon joined by a few of my men, and I sent some to watch up-stream, and some down. I then reconnoitred the place at which he had disappeared and presently heard a faint sound like a hippo coming up to breathe, and on approaching the spot, the Kisii emerged from under a tuft of grass, where he had been hiding, and stood in midstream.

He had dropped his spear and shield in his flight and now a strange boy, who had attached himself to my party in order to get to Kisii Boma, rushed up with it, and thought he would get an easily earned reputation for bravery by stabbing him as he stood defenceless in the water. I knocked the butt aside and at the same time the Kisii took the end and snatched it out of his hand. Then he stood in the water in a frenzy of terror, waving the spear round his head with one hand and plucking up tufts of grass with the other and throwing them at me in token of peace.

By this time my men had collected on the bank in a little knot, and there was such a babble of noise, added to the Kisii's squeals of terror, that I could not make myself heard. I pushed my men aside and took a tuft of grass out of his hand which he appeared particularly anxious for me to have, and then taking him by the hand pulled him out of the water.

At this there was a general cry from my men of "Look out; he will kill our white man!"—natives always give credit to any unknown tribe for great ferocity and boldness — and a dozen hands seized on the spear. With all these bloodthirsty people about, the Kisii thought his only safety lay in my immediate proximity so, wet, dripping, and covered with mud as he was, he threw himself on my neck. At this moment my cook rushed forward and called out, "Look out; he has a knife in his belt!" and seized on the hilt and tried to draw it from its sheath.

The Kisii embraced me with one arm, plentifully bespattering me with mud, whilst with the other he tried to retain the knife in its sheath, convinced that it was required for his execution. The cook was equally determined to get it and thereby, as he thought, save my life, whilst I was only anxious to escape from the clammy embrace of my captive. We waltzed round in this position for some minutes, the Kisii keeping up an incessant howling and my men all talking at once, while I could only laugh at the ridiculous situation I was in, for what with the Kisii's clinging to me, and my own men trying to tug me away, I was having the worst time of anybody.

Finally we got the prisoner quieted down and a rope was put round his neck and we resumed our march. I have often made odd-and-end prisoners in this sort of way and there is one feature that is common to them all. Whereas at first they are terrified out of their wits, no sooner do they realise that they are not going to be killed in cold blood, than they assume the airs and graces of an honoured guest. So with our present prisoner. I gave him a load to carry to lessen the chance of his trying to run away and also to ease its former bearer to look after him.

He was a great stalwart fellow but after a few minutes he threw down the load, which was half a tent, and said that he could not possibly carry it, and he wanted to have the rope with which he was fastened undone at once.

The native is generally so innocuous and appears so brainless that one is apt to grow careless with him. It does not seem possible that he could ever do you any harm or show any great cunning and after a time one begins to be put off one's guard. As in the expeditions I was speaking of, after seeing nothing but flying natives time after time, one begins to grow sceptical as to the possibility of their ever pressing home an attack. I once galloped after two flying natives who were gun running. I caught up one whilst the other disappeared over the top of a little rocky ridge. I proceeded to the top with my first prisoner, but when I got to the summit I could not see the other anywhere, although there was a bare open plain on the other side. I rode along the ridge looking amongst the rocks and suddenly saw a little cave. Springing off my pony, I threw the reins to my prisoner and told him to hold them, but I just recollected myself in time and said, "No, I don't think," and held the bridle whilst I peered into the cave. When I looked to see if the native had appreciated the joke, his face was absolutely stolid. The astonishing part is that nine times out of ten, you would probably return from a protracted search of the cave and find your prisoner patiently sitting waiting for you. It is the tenth time for which you must look out.

I remember once spotting a deserter, and I told him to precede my pony back to the station. It was twenty-four miles and all went well for twenty of these. I then noticed that he was getting a little far ahead, so I called him back to keep pace with the pony's walk, but thought to myself that I was being over-fussy; he would not have the intelligence to gradually increase his distance or the audacity to run away. However, a few minutes after-wards, whilst going through some bush, he gave me the slip absolutely and disappeared in the most miraculous way. It is very dull work keeping one's attention fixed on a prisoner for many hours on end during a hot day.

Once in Somaliland we surprised a tribe at dawn and they commenced driving off their camels in all directions. I rode on and chased two mounted men who were driving off a herd of camels, and then went on and surprised two men on foot who were hurrying away. I took their spears and told them to come along with me. Presently, I saw a mounted man coming towards us, so I hid behind a large bush till he came near. Then I told my two prisoners to emerge and call to him, and tell him to dismount, which he innocently did. I then showed myself and said that he was my prisoner.

By this time, I had got six spears and another pony beside my own pony and rifle to look after, so I gave their spears back to the men and told them they must carry them for themselves as I could not be bored with them. The mounted man I told to lead his pony and then we set off back to find the column. On the way, I made a few more prisoners till we were quite a large party.

Everybody seemed so cheerful and happy to be a prisoner, that I was off my guard, and let the man leading the pony get on my off side. Suddenly he jumped on and started off. It is impossible to shoot at any one going away on one's off side, when mounted, unless one has a revolver or is left-handed. However, I did the next best thing to taking a shot at him by shooting my rifle from off my thigh in his direction. It had the desired effect, as he fell off his pony, and for some time thought he was dead. When he discovered that he had not been killed, I explained to him that I had only fired to frighten him that time and that next time I would really kill him, but I took good care to keep him on my near side for the rest of the way.

Finally I found the column, and I marched in surrounded by my escort of cheerful prisoners. To any one observing the procession approach, it must have appeared that I was the prisoner and that they were guarding me on every side.

We were just starting from camp one day in Somaliland in 1900; at that time we had no regular troops only Somali levies, when news was brought in by the scouts that a large body of horse and spearmen were approaching. We immediately hurried back to the site of our last night's bivouac, put out the barbed wire, and waited in an expectant attitude for some hours. Nothing happened, and then news came in that the Mullah's army had passed by.

I went out with Captain Fredericks, R.E., who was afterwards killed at Firdigin, to reconnoitre. To one side of our camp was a rocky ridge and this we ascended. The other side descended sharply in a series of terraces. We saw nothing till, just as we were about to return, I espied four horsemen in the distance coming along the foot of the ridge. We cautiously descended from terrace to terrace, till as they got level with us we were just above them. Suddenly, they all turned sharply into a steep-sided gulley in the hillside. This was an absolute *cul de sac;* the entrance was only a few yards wide, of which the greater part was a ravine cut by a watercourse and so the road passable for a pony was only about a yard wide. After going thirty or forty yards into the hillside, the gully ended in an abrupt wall.

It was evidently the intention of the men to hide their ponies in this gully, whilst one or two of them climbed up the hill to reconnoitre. We were very anxious to catch a prisoner so as to find out what the Mullah's force was going to do and where they were.

As the last horseman turned into the gully, I dropped his pony and it fell dead across the path, more or less blocking the exit. The others rushed up to the end of the gully and leaving their ponies commenced scrambling up the hillside like baboons. I ran round above them but by the time I saw them again they had nearly reached the top, dodging in and out of sight up a rift. I fired over their heads to try to stop them, without effect. I saw one man disappear at the top, crouching low and holding his shield over his back as he ran, fondly imagining that it was bullet-proof.

I called to Fredericks, who had been just round the corner and had now appeared at the spot from which I fired. He climbed down into the gully to seize the ponies, whilst I climbed round the top of the gully hoping that there was still a man in the rift whom I could intercept.

I climbed down the rift, which was full of crevices and holes, whilst Fredericks covered me with his rifle from the other side of the gully, where he could see better than I could in case a man sprang out of some unexpected place. However, I could find no trace of the men, except a whip dropped on a ledge. After reaching the bottom, we took the three ponies, one of which was a well-known white one called "Godir Hore" (fleeter than the Kudu), and returned to camp very pleased with ourselves. I rode the pony through the rest of the expedition alternately with my old camel and it afterwards earned the title of "fleeter than the snail."

On another occasion in Somaliland, I was rounding up some zaribas by night. There were three in the route of our march and I particularly wished to capture every man, woman, and child in these three, so as to prevent the possibility of any news of our approach being sent on to the tribe we hoped to surprise in our front.

Our guide took us to the neighbourhood of one of the zaribas and we were trying to find it in the dark when a strong whiff of cattle and goat came down wind to us. We followed this up wind and came on the kraal. By the way, if one is uncertain if one is on the path or not in a desert country at night, one can often satisfy oneself by picking up a handful of dust and smelling it. If it smells of camel or goat it is the path.

I had about twenty irregulars with me and we approached the village quietly. When we got near, a sergeant and I went forward to reconnoitre. We found two sentries at the door of the kraal about five yards apart fast asleep. I told the sergeant to wake one without any noise, whilst I went to the other, and pushing with my foot to wake him up at the same time pointed a murderous-looking great spear at his throat and told him not to make a noise.

I suppose if one was a black man it would be a fairly alarming experience to be aroused suddenly from sleep to find a white man standing over one with a great spear. Anyhow, this Somali seemed to think so. For a moment he was speechless with terror and then he covered his head up in his tobe and started screaming lustily. I kicked him and told him to be quiet but he only screamed the louder, and then seized my foot and began kissing and slobbering over it. I felt very like sticking him with the spear, as by now the alarm had been given.

By this time, the rest of the men had come up, so leaving him with them I ran into the village with the sergeant and we just arrived as they were coming out of their gurgis (camel mat huts). We explained quickly that we did not wish to hurt any one if they did not run away. It was a fairly big village and by the time we had despatched all the prisoners and stock to our bivouac under escort we had not many men left.

We then went on to the next kraal and repeated the same performance. When we had despatched these prisoners and stock, it was just dawn and there was only the sergeant left with me and still another kraal to tackle. However, this proved to be a very small one. It was just light as we approached it, so I directed the sergeant to surround the village from one side, whilst I did the same to the other.

While I was creeping round the wall of the zariba looking for the doorway, a man suddenly came out and walked into the bush. I followed him stealthily and when I was about five yards from him he suddenly heard me and whipped round, raising his spear into the awkward attitude above the shoulder that the Somalis adopt for stabbing. My spear was about four times as big as his, so levelling it I charged at him. I was longing to try that spear but I was baulked at the last moment, for he dropped on to his knees and cried for mercy. Subsequently, I broke the haft across the back of one of my own men at Firdigin who pretended that he was wounded so as to get under cover.

There were not many people in the village, so we rounded them up and brought them back. All the prisoners were left under escort with orders that they should be released on the next day, by which time we should have arrived at our destination. We proceeded on our way and succeeded in surprising the people we wished to.

The last little incident I will recall is of rather a different nature. I came to the branch of two ways in the Danakil country and was uncertain which was the best to take. Seeing a little village about half a mile away, I went to it with my head man to ask for information; meanwhile my caravan trekked on down one of the two ways.

There were about half a dozen men in the village and they were not very informative. They said that they did not know, and that both ways were the same, and one said that both were right and another that both were wrong. Whilst I was eliciting this useful information, my head man like a fool gave one of the men half a dollar and asked him to bring him some milk. When I turned to go, he told me that he could not get either the half-dollar back or the milk from them.

I asked where the half-dollar was, and they all denied having ever seen it. One man spoke rather thickly and my head man said, "I believe, master, that man has it in his mouth." It would have grieved me very much to have gone away and left them to think what a parcel of new chums we were, yet this appeared to be the only course to follow, as the Danakils are genial, cheery birds who would not think twice about sticking one with their big spears, so the use of violence was out of the question, unless I wanted to risk a fight and having to shoot some one.

However, with the native there are always ways and means, as my old trader friend said. I suggested that the man had the coin in his mouth and he shook his head and the others got quite heated about it. I felt rather annoyed but pretended to be vastly amused. I turned to the others and pointed over my shoulder and at my mouth by way of taking them into my confidence and saying, "Now you will see some fun."

Then I suddenly caught the man by the back of the neck, after the manner school-boys have of gripping each other and which must really be very painful to a scraggy-necked individual like a Danakil if one gets a good grip on him.

Like a conjuring trick the coin appeared out of his mouth and the man looked so discomfited that it compelled the others to laugh. I do not suppose that they knew that I was hurting him but imagined that it was only chagrin at losing his half-dollar which made him look so unhappy.

I had still my own to get back out of the man for trying to fool me, so I roared with laughter, poking him again and again in the ribs with the butt of my riding whip, as if I thought him the funniest and best fellow in the world, at the same time gripping him harder and harder by the neck. At last my merriment so overcame me, that I rocked about in an ecstasy of good-natured laughter, winking at the others, shaking him violently by the scruff of the neck, and digging him jocularly in the ribs with the hard butt of my whip. When I had half strangled him, I suddenly dropped him, and waving my arm to the others swiftly retired.

CHAPTER XXI

HUNTING THE BONGO

For long I had heard about the wariness of the East African bongo and had been anxious to try for it but it was some time before I had an opportunity. The first time that I came across its tracks was on Kinangop. From all appearances it seemed to be a very rare visitor there, probably occasionally wandering up from the forest to the south of the mountain, and all the tracks I had pointed out to me were old ones. Still, if I had no chance of hunting the bongo, I had an opportunity of getting familiar with its track, its haunts, and many of its habits.

Later I was sent to look for a suitable point for a beacon in the forests of the escarpment. It immediately struck me that this would be a most likely spot to find the bongo, and before I had reached the locality, I had learnt from Dorobo that it was indeed to be found there.

As it is a very wary animal, the next thing to do was to take every precaution, compatible with performing the work I had to do, that my porters did not disturb the animal, which would have spoilt my chances, as the slightest noise or disturbance would at once clear the neighbourhood of any bongo there were.

Fortune favoured me in this respect, as we found a goat path leading into the forest from the last villages and, after following it for a short time, came upon a large space which had been cleared by the natives to form plantations eventually. The trees had been felled and the undergrowth cleared and then it had been left waiting for the felled trees to dry so that they could be burnt; meanwhile no one came there.

I pitched camp in the centre of this spot, which was really inside the forest and yet my camp was some way from the edge of the trees. To the west was a belt of forest which separated us from the outer world, whilst to the east was the main forest and the prevailing wind came from this direction. As there was plenty of fire-wood to hand and a stream ran through the clearing, there was no inducement to the porters to penetrate the undergrowth and, moreover, from the lay of the land it seemed a very suitable place from which to search for the required point.

Having settled camp, I set out with a Dorobo to find the highest point in the vicinity, which was not at all apparent with the whole country covered with forest and mist, and incidentally to look for a bongo. We found plenty of spoor, some of it of the night before, on the banks of the stream some way into the forest.

To any one who does not know this particular forest

or a similar one, it may sound fairly easy work walking about in a forest, so it will be necessary to explain its exact nature before the difficulties of coming up to a bongo or even of proceeding any distance at all are apparent.

First imagine numbers of trees of all sizes, close together, with their branches so entwined that the sunlight only reaches the ground in a few patches here and there. Then imagine these interlaced from the ground upwards in a perfect network of lianas and creepers. On the ground there is an accumulation a foot deep of dead wood and twigs of all ages of decay, from the soft, rotten wood at the bottom to the brittle, crackling twigs on the top which betray your presence, walk you never so wisely. Then imagine numberless fallen trees scattered about in all directions, and finally fill up any interstices left, to the height of about six feet, with undergrowth, stinging nettles, convolvulus, and there you have the forest.

In parts there appears to be an absence of green undergrowth, except for shoots with which the floor is carpeted. Even in these parts, however, the gnarled stumps and branches, the lianas and creepers are so closely entwined, that there is not room to put your head through without pushing something aside.

The thickness of the green parts may be best illustrated by the following. Whilst pushing through such stuff I would suddenly bark my shins against a fallen tree concealed in the undergrowth. After climbing over this, one would perhaps push on for a couple of yards and meet with the same experience again, surmount this obstacle, and then bump up against another close by. Then one would proceed some way before meeting another series. After having this coincidence thrust home on me several times, I realised that the two or three trees met close together were but branches of the same fallen tree which was so entirely enveloped in undergrowth that it was invisible. Such, then, is the home of the bongo, who, as I have suggested before, is of a retiring nature and prefers seclusion.

Whilst making a search for the point required, I came on the fresh spoor of bongo of the night before. This animal appears only to move about, to any extent, at night, whilst by day it lies up listening for any sounds. It is practically impossible for anything to come near it without its hearing the rustling of leaves and snapping of twigs.

If the country in which it lives is so thick, the reader might ask, how does the bongo himself, who is as big as a cow, move through it? First he has had plenty of practice; next, he, when moving through bush, shapes himself like a wedge, his nose being the thin end, and lastly, he has plenty of weight behind him with which to break through and push aside obstacles and he does not himself mind making the crashing and crackling noises which would be fatal to his pursuer.

The bongo does not appear to jump obstacles like the bushbuck but pushes through or under them. A branch across the path which a bushbuck would jump, the bongo will crouch under. I take it that the bongo's attitude in moving is with the neck outstretched and near the ground, the nose right forward, the horns laid flat on the back, and the legs in a crouching position. If he comes to a netted mass of lianas he shoves his nose underneath them or through a gap near the ground and as he pushes forward the gap is enlarged by his spreading horns, whilst the thick lianas slip down them and over his flanks. Anywhere his horns can get through, the rest of his body can pass.

They generally go in family parties or two or three together. The females have horns and their method of procedure is, as far as I can see, just the same as that of the male. With the bushbuck the females are hornless and so they have to rely on crouching through or jumping over obstacles more than the male, who could push the undergrowth aside with his horns but does not do so, at least to the extent that the bongo does.

Well, to continue, having found a fresh bongo track, I argued that the worst thing that I could do would be to alarm the animal, as this would lose me my bongo that day, and also alarm the neighbourhood, prejudicing my chances in the future. If, however, I did not come up with it, no harm was done and I was equally likely to find other tracks the next day. So the thing to do was to go absolutely noiselessly, no matter how slowly, and if I only managed to cover a few hundred yards in the day, no matter, I would get another chance. The only thing I feared was a change of wind or a bad wind, in either of which cases I should have given up for the day. However, the wind was perfect, and so we, the Dorobo and myself, followed the spoor as gingerly as possible, I in front and the Dorobo behind.

There is one thing a Dorobo can do and no other native that I can think of, and that is to move noiselessly through thick bush. Every branch in the way I pushed very slowly and gently aside, and after slipping past, the Dorobo took it and placed it noiselessly in its original position. If I had not enough hands to deal with all the branches, he leaned forward and helped. The lianas we crawled through and under. As we proceeded like this, a shower of rain came on and the patter, patter on the myriads of leaves drowned all lesser sounds. It was the best thing that could have happened.

I was always peering ahead and listening for the slightest sound. Suddenly, from close by, came the sound I had been fearing to hear and yet hoping for, the sudden crashing of undergrowth. I rushed forward; one animal was crashing away ahead, whilst about fifteen yards in front, I saw the bushes moving and just caught a glimpse of something dashing across.

RETURNING HOME

I fired at once and at the same time heard another go off to my left. I then ran forward as fast as the undergrowth would permit and found a beautiful female bongo as large as a cow laid out dead. It was a very lucky shot, as I had to fire through bushes and grass and so could only guess where the heart was.

As there was no sunlight, I was unable to photograph it. I sent for some porters, but they were utterly unable to lift it, so finally we had to skin it and cut it up. As there was no sun for the next two days, all I got were some very misty pictures of the head with the skin spread out behind it.

Next night I had bongo-tail soup and bongo marrow, dishes I expect very few have eaten, whilst I made some excellent biltong of some of the meat which had streaks of fat in it.

Between the time that I shot the bongo and that at which the porters arrived, I made further investigations of the country and climbed a tree and in an interval, when the mist raised a little, decided on what must be the point.

The next day I set the porters to work to cut a path to the rise selected, and this done, we found that it would require an immense amount of clearing and trees felled, before one could see in the required directions. From now onwards I used to start every day at dawn to have a look round the forest, then join my porters on the hill at eight o'clock, work at cutting till 4 P.M., having my lunch brought up to me, and then take another turn in the forest till dark. The height was about eight thousand feet, the nights were very cold, whilst we practically never saw the sun for the fortnight we were there, and quite half the time the whole forest was enveloped in thick mist. The cool air and the lack of sun, after trekking about on the hot plains, made one feel as fit as possible and one never wanted to sit down and rest.

How my porters did not frighten the whole countryside with their noise and the woodcutting, I do not know, but, as I have said, there was a strong and constant breeze from the east. I used to reach the hill quickly by our path and from there take an old bongo track eastwards, which was fairly good going, and so get as far away as I could. I came across fresh bongo tracks again on several occasions and once came up within twenty yards of one, a male this time. However, I was only following them to learn their habits, as my license only allowed one to be shot, though I think if a tempting shot had offered, I could not have resisted it. As they are fairly common and so difficult to get, it would not endanger them in the slightest if a thousand were allowed on a license, as not more than two or three, if that, would be shot in the year all together.

The male I came up with had dug up a tree by the roots with its horns. I noticed this on several occasions, but in this case the marks were quite fresh. He had dug his horns under the roots in several places and then levered upwards till the root had broken; he had eaten some of the roots and some of the leaves and some of the bark of this tree, so that it had afforded him a variety of dishes.   He was with one other and we were betrayed by the wind as they had moved round before lying down.

Whilst returning from this hunt, I examined closely the leaf of one of the plants that grow thickly on the floor of the forest.   Some of these leaves were covered with a delicate pattern which resembled fine lace.   I found that it was caused by a small caterpillar which ate a carefully traced pattern round and round, starting from the outside.   He ate only the green part leaving a pattern of a network of veins.   Finally when he had gone round and round in diminishing circles till he had reached the centre, he there made himself a little place in which to transform.

The bongo's track generally sinks deep into the mass of twigs and rotting leaves which cover the ground. My way of walking with as little crackling of twigs as possible was to put my toe into the track of the animal I was following, and then bring the weight of the foot very gradually down.   Just where the bongo had stepped, the weight of the heavy animal had broken any twigs there were to be cracked.   However, unfortunately my foot was bigger than that of the bongo and so, unless one could proceed continually on one's toes, like a ballet dancer, one had perforce to put part of the foot outside the track.

The bongo eats bamboo leaves, as well as some of the small plants which spring up to the height of a couple of feet, and is also addicted very much to pith and rotten and decayed bark. It also eats charred wood from burnt trees.

Bongo forests are pierced by a network of old tracks and probably these are largely used in changing grazing grounds or travelling at night. They form about the only practical method of moving about the forest and even these involve a continuous crouching and crawling.

Whilst grazing they of course choose fresh ground to get fresh food. They often come to the edge of the forest or even at night a little way into plantations, which extended well into the forest. However, to lie up they choose thick undergrowth in the depths of the forest. If you see tracks in some of the more open parts, they may be followed quickly, as there is little fear that they will be lying up close by, but have only come to graze there at night.

The West African bongo appears, from all accounts, to be quite a dangerous animal, and cases have frequently occurred of natives being damaged or killed by them. I have been able to hear of no similar case with the East African bongo.

After a week of cutting, our space was cleared and for the next few days I had to be all day on the hill erecting the beacon. That finished, I had nothing to keep me and so trekked away at once to my next point, which was in the Kikuyu country.

I never had an opportunity of returning to these forests, but I met the bongo spoor again near the ravine of Kamasia. However, all I saw was old and I had no time to get out in search of them, as all my points were on clear, open hills, and so it only remained to build the beacons and move on.

CHAPTER XXII

ODD NOTES ON AFRICAN INSECTS

BEFORE proceeding with these few rough notes, I must state that I pretend to no scientific or theoretical knowledge whatever concerning the insect life of Africa. I am just a casual observer who interests himself in the life around him, when doing nothing else; I have neither the time nor the facility for making a study of them. Had one unlimited time at one's disposal, to be spent both in Africa collecting and in England determining one's specimens, the study of any one family of insects would afford more interest and novelty than the study of big game could ever do.

All big game animals must be known by now, with possibly one or two exceptions, whilst the habits of most of them have been described. Thousands of insects are awaiting discovery, and there are tens of thousands of which nothing is known concerning their life and habits. Their metamorphoses alone make the observation of one insect resemble that of several different kinds of larger animals.

The field is so wide and vast that it is like entering on new worlds, peopled with different inhabitants. It opens up new lines of thought and ideas concerning animal life as a whole. If the riddle of the origin, reasons for structure and colouration of living organisms is ever solved, the key is more likely to be found by the study of the myriads of so-called lower creatures, than amongst the larger and, generally speaking, more stupid animals.

From my point of view, that of the dilettante, they offer many attractions. There is the interest they give to what would otherwise be a dull march. They afford occupation during a halt or whilst camp is being pitched. Any odd five minutes in camp may be spent in an insect hunt. They are always ready at your door and even on your dinner table. For big game one has generally to lay oneself out for a hard day, one must go far afield, and an odd evening after a day's march is not of much use. Yet this time may be spent in a very successful hunt after insects, and if one is tired there is no need to go far; one can grope round in a few square yards for an hour at a time without exhausting its resources.

Again the arrangement and sorting out of specimens affords occupation for the evenings and rainy days, or as a rest from reading or writing. Lastly it enables one to look on the insect pests with more indulgent eyes. If your soup does get full of beetles, your tumbler of flies, and moths do try to extinguish your candle, there is always the chance of a new specimen being the offender.

Of the different orders of insects, there is one, many members of which have been lately observed to be especially malignant in their effects on mankind and animals. This is the order of Diptera or two-winged flies which contains many species able to spread and communicate disease to the higher animals. Formerly but little attention had been given to this order. Since the discovery that the mosquito was the carrier of malaria, and later the tsetse of sleeping sickness, the Diptera have received considerable study, especially that section of them which may be described as "biting flies."

Much has been discovered in the last few years, and yet the sum total of knowledge amassed represents but a small fraction of that which remains to be done. No doubt during the course of the next ten or twenty years, it will be found that many other diseases are spread by such insects.

The tsetse has probably received more attention than any other fly of late years. It is impossible for the ordinary layman to distinguish between the various species of this group, as very special knowledge and a microscope is required to determine any specimen. Even with the advantages of such knowledge and a microscope, experts themselves have often failed in detecting new species and have made mistakes in assuming an insect is one kind whereas it is subsequently found to be another.

However, with the naked eye, the difference can be told between the palpalis group and the morsitans group. I call the palpalis group those flies that were originally supposed alone to produce sleeping sickness. They are much darker than the others, and can be distinguished by the blackness of the hind legs, whilst the others have not this blackness, although some of them have black feet. In Glossina palpalis all the joints of the tarsi in the hind legs are black, whilst the foot is brown. It is liable to be confused with pallicera, as regards the legs, but the antennæ of the latter are orange-buff, instead of being dark as those of palpalis. Lately it has been discovered that other tsetse besides palpalis are able to carry the trypanosomes of sleeping sickness and, as investigations proceed, it would seem as if the different kinds are becoming more and more tarred with the same brush. If this is the case, a very accurate differentiation of species and subspecies has become less necessary to medical science than has been thought up till now. Nevertheless if tsetse is discovered in a new place, some should be caught and sent, carefully labelled as to date and place of capture, to the nearest sleeping-sickness commission or doctor.

There was a long correspondence in the *Field* between Sir Alfred Sharp, then governor of Nyasaland, and Mr. F. C. Selous concerning the habits of the common tsetse (Glossina morsitans) in which they disagreed entirely as to the habits of this insect. Mr. F. J.

Jackson, now governor of Uganda, pointed out to me that they were both right, although holding entirely divergent opinions, but that they were talking about different insects whose habits were not quite the same. Whereas Mr. Selous was talking about morsitans proper, Sir Alfred Sharp was talking about its Nyasaland representative. This differed so little in appearance that it had always been mistaken for the same insect, till it was discovered that it had a white foot and was then found to be a distinct species.

Countries may be tsetse-fly free, or inhabited by tsetse. In the former case, they are necessarily also free from sleeping sickness, or cattle sickness from tsetse. However, because tsetse have not been found by several observers, it does not follow that there are none, unless the observations extend over several years and are conducted by a number of observers.

There are bad seasons and good seasons for insects, and sometimes the insects in their preliminary stages of egg or chrysalis are liable to hold over a year and only emerge the year following. Some years there will be but few, and some years many, and when there are but a few, they are often liable to escape observation.

To quote instances familiar to the home reader, there are plagues of wasps some years, whilst in others there are but few to be seen. There are certain rare butter-flies caught periodically in the same locality, but, although they are much sought after by the collector,

sometimes several years elapse between captures.
Undoubtedly they are there all the time but they have
not been found.   Again, for several years running the
clouded yellow butterfly will not be seen or only occur
singly in the British Isles, and then one year they will
be most numerous.

The tsetse rather calls attention to itself than otherwise by biting the observer, but if there are only a few
about, it is quite possible that he may miss them.   Also
in some seasons they swarm in certain places whilst at
others but few are to be found.   The first time I crossed
the Kaya River in the Lado Enclave, I met tsetse of
the morsitans group in swarms.   For about six miles'
march up the Nile bank, I had to keep a branch of
leaves continually flapping about the back of my head
and neck as they settled in such quantities there.   I
went away with the impression that the river bank
at this point was always like that.   The next time I
passed not a single tsetse bit me, and I should never
have seen any if I had not been very much on the lookout for them.   I think I saw only two that time.

The worst place I have struck for them was the
Chambesi River, near Bangweolo.   Also the Mangazi
Valley in Portuguese territory not far from Fort Jame-
son was very thick with them.   However, it is quite
likely that at certain seasons or in certain years these
spots are almost devoid of them.   In any case, it does
not seem possible to state, even after visiting a spot

several times and carefully examining it, that there are no tsetse in that place. The most one can say is that one has observed none. If a number of observers make the same report, covering a period of several years, the chances are that the place is really fly-free. Yet I have heard men who have made one trek down a road or path, and never stopped to examine the water-courses, confidently assert that there were no tsetse on such-and-such a route.

If the country is inhabited by tsetse, they may be of the palpalis group or of the morsitans group or of both. Again either of these kinds may be infected or not infected, that is to say, some of them may be carrying trypanosomes and thus infection, or the country may be uninfected from the fact that no infected person or cattle have come there and been bitten, thereby infecting the fly.

So a country may be fly-free or inhabited by tsetse, and if the latter, it may be uninfected or infected with sleeping sickness and not cattle sickness (trypanosoma Brucei), or *vice versa*, or infected with both.

However, if a country is inhabited by the palpalis group and not by the morsitans, it does not follow that it is safe to send possibly infected cattle there, if you wish to keep disease out. It is not, I believe, definitely known yet whether palpalis, the sleeping-sickness fly, can carry the cattle-infecting trypanosome, whilst recent experiments would seem to prove that cattle can carry the sleeping-sickness trypanosome whilst remaining themselves quite unaffected by it.

Of other members of the order Diptera, there are the mosquitoes, certain of which carry malarial fever, and many other kinds, which are, so far as is at present known, innocuous, except for the annoyance they cause.

The malarial kinds (anopheles) may be recognised by the way they sit; their bodies stick out at an angle to the plane of the wall or object sat on, instead of being parallel to it.

Of other biting flies there are the seroots or hippo-flies, horse-flies and sand-flies. These are not at present known to convey disease except possibly accidentally. Although the seroot, for instance, cannot harbour the sleeping-sickness trypanosome in his proboscis, in the way that the tsetse does, it is quite possible that after biting a sleeping-sickness patient a few trypanosomes might be left on its proboscis and if it immediately bit some one else it might inoculate him with the sickness. That is to say, it could act as an accidental carrier of the trypanosome, but not as a host to it.

In the same way the ordinary house-fly and other common flies are able to carry and promulgate sickness, by settling first on one object and then on another. I believe they carry the germs chiefly on their feet. Enteric and ophthalmia are supposed to be largely carried by flies, whilst I believe veldt sores are mostly caused by flies settling on a small scratch or cut and inoculating it with germs. At any rate, if a cut or scratch is immediately covered up, so that flies do not get at it, it does not turn into a veldt sore.

Of other diseases carried by the lower forms of life, there is the guinea worm, the egg of which enters the system by drinking bad water, whilst spirillum, tick fever, and perhaps kala azar are conveyed by different ticks.

To return to the flies, there are several kinds which, themselves innocuous, have grubs which are nocuous to human beings or animals. Amongst these is a big fat-bodied fly which lays its eggs in huts and from these hatch the Congo floor maggot.

For the philosopher with plenty of time at his disposal, the order which offers the most interesting study is that of Hymenoptera, — bees, wasps, and ants. Their organisation and habits form an endless study, whilst the various forms and the neuter insects, which come from the same batches of eggs, will afford much food for reflection and thought to one interested in heredity and the origin of species.

In Africa there is a little pigmy bee, about the size of a small ant, which annoys the traveller very much by crawling over him. It seems absolutely without fear of mankind, as it is impossible to frighten it away. It does not sting, but if one sits near its nest, a swarm will buzz round and hundreds will settle on one and crawl about. As a wave of the hand will not send them off, it is necessary to brush them away as they settle, in which process hundreds must get killed, and yet those left continue to crawl over every human being who passes, with the utmost persistence. I do not know what they find so attractive about him. They make honey which is of a highly scented flavour, but owing to the small size of the bee, the total amount found is hardly worth taking. They generally live in the stumps of old trees.

There are numbers of different wasps and hornets, each with its own different ways and habits, many of which are very interesting. There is the mason wasp who builds a mud house, for preference on your bookshelf. Having completed her building, she, for it is the female, puts a caterpillar or grub inside and then lays her egg. When the young grub hatches, it feeds on the caterpillar till it is full grown.

Mr. H. King, entomologist to the Sudan government, pointed me out two wasps one of which I had often noticed dragging a big, black cricket about. Mr. King had discovered that this wasp stings the cricket in three places, thereby paralysing but not killing it. It then lays its eggs in the body and leaves it. The young grubs, when they emerge from the egg, feed on the cricket.

The other one he showed me was a wasp carrying

about a caterpillar in an aimless way, as if it did not know what to do with it. Round and round it went, settling here and there and returning again. The reason for this was that it was followed by a small fly which I did not notice till it was pointed out to me. This fly shadowed every movement of the wasp; when it sat on a blade of grass, it sat on an adjacent blade watching it; when it moved, it followed it.

It appeared that the wasp wanted to bury the caterpillar and lay its eggs in it. However, if it left the caterpillar for a moment, the fly would dart in and lay its eggs. If it was able to do this the grubs from the fly's eggs would feed, not on the caterpillar but on the grubs of the wasp. This was the reason that the wasp was so anxious to escape from the fly and the fly persevered in following its every movement.

Round certain ants' nests there is a cleared space. I at first wondered why no grass grew there when it was growing thickly round and seeds must be showered on the spot. One day whilst watching the workers stream in and out of a nest, I accidentally dropped some tobacco on this open courtyard. Soon afterwards a fatigue party emerged from the nest and set to work, busily clearing up the refuse I had so clumsily let fall on to their village square. I then dropped some grass seeds on the open space and these were also immediately cleared away. To the ant it must appear as if each breath of wind brings a shower of seeds as big or bigger than footballs which if not moved immediately take root and become trees as high as St. Paul's cathedral.

A well-known figure on the dinner table is an insect resembling a wasp with an enormous long, fat body, entirely out of proportion to the size of its wings. I am told that it is a flying ant and not a wasp. It is a clumsy fellow that flops on to the table and then wanders about dragging its long body after it, occasionally making a short flight up to the lamp with a loud buzzing sound and then falling back on to the table again. It is the most persistent thing; one may throw if off the table or out of the window a hundred times, but a moment later you hear a loud buzzing, and flop! on to the table it comes again.

Once, whilst pinning beetles in the verandah of my tent, after dinner, I was so annoyed by some of these fat-bodied ants that I moved my table inside and laced up the tent. No sooner had I set to work again, than buzz flop! and a great, clumsy fellow fell in front of me; he must have come in with me or crawled under the flies. I had a pair of forceps in my hand so I seized him with them and threw him through the ventilation hole in the top of the tent. As I heard him tobogganing down the side I congratulated myself on defeating him, as he would be unlikely to find this small hole again to effect an entry. I set to work again, but a few moments later he reappeared and I slung him out again

with the forceps.   I fear that I must have gripped him
very roughly this time, for when he made his next
appearance his cumbersome body was dragging behind
him, almost separated from the thorax.   Once more I
slung him out through the ventilation hole and went
on setting my beetles.   Presently a bodyless head and
thorax dropped on to the table in front of me.   Since
then I have never seriously tried to get the better of
one of these persistent creatures.

A procession one often meets with in the bush is
a long stream of black ants, which have just been raiding
a termite's nest.   Every member of the party is carrying a termite in his mandibles.   Sometimes one sees
the wounded being borne home in their midst, some of
them bristling with hostile termites, who have died
with their jaws firmly embedded in their black foes.
The victors do not disembarrass their friends' bodies of
these appendages, a circumstance which seems to
prove that, in addition to being blind, they are unable
to communicate all their ideas one to another.

A more interesting spectacle is the battle itself.   It
is generally the smaller black ants who are the bravest
and first go into the termite's nest to grapple with them.
The battle is usually subterranean but it may be
watched in the open by breaking off some of the inhabited part of a termite's nest in front of an invading
army.   Both ant and termite appear to be completely
blind and so there is much groping about in the dark

and the most comical mistakes occur. The black ant fences round till he runs up against a termite; it is his luck whether it is a big or small one. He takes a nip at it and the termite turns its head and appears to eject something (formic acid) at its enemy. If the black ant gets it full in the face from a big one, it completely paralyses him; he doubles up or staggers about as if drunk or ties himself in knots. After a time, longer or shorter, he recovers and is able to renew the attack, though often with less vigour or in a nervous manner.

In any case he is unable to stand up against the termite's acid ejections, but if he has the luck to get a good grip with his mandibles on the termite's stern it is always fatal to the latter. The termite cannot turn around far enough to disable his antagonist and is carried off without more ado. As the black ant is unable to tell which end is which, until he actually catches hold, he will often come up to the right end, that is the rear, and suddenly, hearing the termite move, will imagine that he is at the wrong end and dash round to the other side only to get a squirt of acid full in the face. Others, having located an easy victim in a small termite, will fence round for a grip, all unaware that there is an enormous, great fellow with open jaws just behind them feeling around for a grip.

Some, having become nervous after several rebuffs, will hastily jump out of the way of one of their own friends, only to land on the top of an enemy.

Others will be seen dashing round, up and down, in and out of a number of termites, only too anxious to meet one but unable to locate any. Once they have been repelled by a termite, they seem to lose track of its position and so it is only an accident if they renew the attack on the same one; it is just chance which they run up against next.

After the termite has squirted acid at several ants, his supply begins to give out or get less powerful; each black ant who attacks subsequently is less and less annoyed, until at last he falls an easy victim.

The smaller termites are unable to do anything but eject acid, but the larger kinds have powerful mandibles. They are very slow in their movements and find it difficult to get hold of the agile black ant, but if they ever get a fair grip, they never let go.

I have several times noticed a minute fly persistently following round an ant carrying a dead termite. I can only conclude that it is awaiting a suitable opportunity to slip in and lay its eggs in the body.

Of the seven orders of insects, that which contains by far the greatest number of species is the beetle. Their study is so great an undertaking that it is hardly possible for any one man to be an authority on more than about one or two out of the seventy odd families extant.

The poorest represented orders are the Neuroptera (dragon-flies) and Orthoptera (crickets, locusts, and earwigs). When walking through grass near the banks of a stream, the number of dragon-flies that will swarm round one is sometimes surprising. Some retire backwards before one, others follow behind, and others circle round keeping just above the top of the grass. The first time I noticed them darting at my boots, I thought that they fancied the look of them or the particular kind of boot polish I affected, which was at that time composed of hippo fat. However, I soon discovered that it was not my boots at all, but that my walking disturbed hundreds of small insects in the grass and that it was these the dragon-flies were waiting to catch.

Perhaps butterflies and, to a lesser extent, moths are the insects of which most is known; at any rate those are the collections which attract the greater number of people who take up insects. Africa produces numerous large and beautiful butterflies, especially amongst the high-flying kinds, which are difficult to catch.

Great numbers of caterpillars are met with whilst poking round in the bush. So little is known about the larval and pupal stages of the majority of insects, that it would be a great interest to breed these out and see what they turn into. To be a good draughtsman and be able to paint water-colour pictures of each kind and attach them to the perfect insect when it hatches out would certainly add much to science. If one is always on the move, however, it is impossible to breed out insects, as they require constant attention and changes of food.

The last order is that of Hemiptera (bugs and frog-hoppers). The bugs appear generally to live in large parties or hatch out in large parties together. They go through many metamorphoses and it is quite possible to mistake one insect, in several stages, for several different insects. They appear to wage war to a great extent on the grubs of beetles, and different kinds can often be seen walking about with a grub transfixed on the swordlike proboscis. They are unable to bite, like the beetles, but feed on their victims by sucking up their juices through this proboscis. The froghoppers are jolly little fellows and many of them are very pretty, unlike the brilliant but unhealthy looking colouration of the bugs. There is one kind with a forehead and horns exactly like a bison.

In collections of insects it is always the perfect insect that figures; very seldom are there examples of the preliminary transformations attached. Those of the greater majority of exotic insects are unknown and the difficulty of preservation adds to the want of knowledge about them. Moreover, they appear more uninteresting in comparison to the perfect insect. It is from these causes that there are perhaps a hundred or more collectors busy with the perfect insect to every one who interests himself with the larval and pupal stages.

For this reason insects have had to be mainly classified from their appearance during their last or flying stage. There is a certain amount of doubt amongst many families as to the order in which they should be included. All classification must be greatly arbitrary but a more general knowledge of the preliminary stages would most likely largely smooth the path of the classifier.

Further than this, it seems to me, knowing nothing about it by the way, that, were it possible, a classification based entirely on the characteristics of the egg and larva ought to be much more satisfactory than any other. Modern classification is not only an effort to tabulate our present knowledge and give names for the sake of convenience in reference, but it is, or should be in its highest form, an effort to reconstruct that tree up which each species has climbed and differentiated into different branches by means of accumulated variations. Thus if we say: The family Lamiidæ is divided into the genus Docadion, Lamia, etc., and that such and such species belong to the genus Lamia, it ought to be the same as saying that to the best of our belief these species sprung from a common ancestor whom we may call Lamia prototypicus. Further, that Lamia prototypicus, Dorcadion prototypicus, etc., sprung from an ancestor whom we might call Lamiidæ prototypicus, and so on back through the scale.

2A

However, as the different species probably broke off at various times from the generic type and some have differed more in a short time than others, the

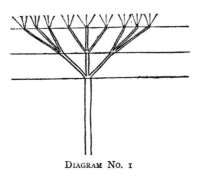

DIAGRAM NO. 1

drawing of a line and asserting that the genus starts from there is purely arbitrary. There is no symmetry in nature, and so a classification absolutely symmetrical is an ideal but not a practical possibility.

To return to the simile of the tree; if species diverged according to the first diagram, the work of the classifier would be made easier, and he could try to divide them into groups as shown by the transverse lines.

However, these species have diverged more on the lines of Diagram 2, which cannot be cut by any symmetrical lines. There is always the problem to face as to whether the line should not be drawn a little higher or a little lower, so as to include or exclude another branch or two, or in other words by putting the

DIAGRAM NO. 2

date of each prototype back a little further, you make it an ancestor of another branch or two; by taking it at a later date, you put another branch or two into a different family. So it is a practical impossibility for the classifier to attain his ideal, but that does not prevent him always having it in view. Now the larva may in a sense be considered as the fœtus of the perfect insect and, as such, it should show more clear signs of past relationship than does the perfect insect. If of three species springing into being at about the same date, from the same prototype, one had advanced and developed on its new lines very quickly, whilst the other two had progressed more slowly, the first one might be thought so different from the other two that it should be given a genus of its own. However, if the fœtus really goes through some of the past stages of the animal from which it springs, an examination of the larva should show how closely these three are related and so help the classifier to reconstruct past history.

Just as the examination of the fœti of mammals has enabled us to prove to greater satisfaction the relationship of certain animals, so should the examination of ova and larva help us to determine better the affinities between different insects. But how very insignificant is the data on which the classifier must rely, when trying to probe into the past. His task can never really be concluded. It is as if an antiquarian were given an old coin and a bit of pottery and told to reconstruct from them Roman history.

CHAPTER XXIII

As regards the larger game, the more I consider the subject and the more I see of them, the more am I forced to the conclusion that there is no such thing as protective colouration amongst them, except such as is purely accidental. Not only do the majority not appear in my eyes as protectively coloured, but their habits are such as to make the most perfect adaptations to their surroundings useless to them. The majority are very conspicuous, and they do not appear to rely on their colouration, but rather their fleetness of foot, ability to take cover, or the difficulty of the country they inhabit to escape capture.

As regards the smaller game and lesser mammals, with possibly a few exceptions, I do not believe that they have assumed their colours or markings in mimicry of any surrounding objects, although I admit that many of them may have been prevented from assuming more striking colours by the necessity or advisability of remaining inconspicuous.

With insect life, however, quite different conditions prevail. They do not, as a rule, roam over great areas full of different kinds of vegetation and a multitude of objects of all manner of shapes and colours. Their lives, especially in the first stages, are of a more sedentary and restricted nature. An insect may spend its whole life on one single, small plant. In many there is a specialisation so extraordinary that it prevents any variation of their existence; certain kinds can only live under certain particular combinations of circumstances. Thus there are many kinds of Ichneumons, each kind of which must lay its eggs in one special kind of caterpillar. If they are laid in any one of a thousand other kinds, the grubs are unable to live when hatched. Then, there are caterpillars who can only live on one particular kind of plant, out of the many thousands which have been provided by nature. I often wonder how this tremendous specialisation has arisen and why some species, more elastic in mode of living and omnivorous in tastes, is not better fitted to survive.

These very specialised modes of existence, however, enable a protective scheme of colouration to be of service to its possessor and, the more one sees of insect life, the more does one marvel at the wonderful adaptations to and mimicry of surrounding objects. It is more than coincidence that so many are so exactly like part of the plant they feed on, blight on the leaves, or other small objects. There must be some reason for this.

That these likenesses have been acquired for purposes

of protection appears a perfectly plausible and satisfactory reason, till one begins to examine them closely and try to put this theory to the proof. If the theory is sound, surely it cannot suffer by being put to the test. My complaint against the majority of the protectionist school is that they do not appear to subject their theory to the searching test of close outdoor scrutiny. Because it accounts so easily for these adaptations, therefore, it must perforce be true.

If an Englishman were to disguise himself as a German and travel in Germany, eating sausages, sauerkraut, and raw goose's breast, the natural conclusion would be that he did not wish to be recognised as an Englishman, and that he faced these horrors to avoid detection; in fact, that he was a spy. If, however, he was followed about and observed during all his travels and it was found that he never went near a fortress, that he took no interest in military matters, and proclaimed openly that he was an Englishman wherever he went, the reason for his disguise would remain a mystery.

This is what I feel about insects; the more I see of these wonderful adaptations, the more I wonder why and how?

Why should some insect be so marvellously like a twig or a leaf? "To enable it to escape from the birds," the protectionist will at once reply, but has this even been proved beyond a doubt? I am puzzled beyond words to imagine why it should have taken the trouble to become like that, yet I cannot believe that this explanation meets all cases, for reasons I will explain later.

How did they become like this? The Darwinian will reply, "Through natural selection and the survival of the fittest which in this case were, in the first instance, those accidental variations which were most like the object they now resemble." Common sense forbids me to strain Darwin's theory to its ultimate limits by imagining a slight variation from, say, a cock-chafer-like beetle, enabling its fortunate possessor to escape detection on the grounds that it is a leaf. Even if it is granted that it has a material advantage over its fellows when it has covered half its journey towards the leaf, such a journey will occupy perhaps a million generations, and during this time its chances of extinction are no less than that of its fellows.

I suppose that no thinking person, who has studied the subject, doubts Darwin's theory of the origin of species as to its main facts. That still remains firmly planted on the foundations of solid fact and argument Darwin himself laid for it. Many of the lines of thought, however, which this theory has suggested require to be elucidated and further explained. Darwin himself confessed that he was in doubt about the exact explanations of many minor points which, at first sight, did not appear quite clear. There has been a tendency to run away with some of these lines of thought without subjecting them to that conscientious inquiry and rigorous scrutiny which has made The Origin of Species so sacred in the eyes of the naturalist.

To return to the question *Why?* Many of the Mantis bear the most extraordinary resemblance to leaves, grass, and flowers. Such resemblance should undoubtedly be of service to them, as they are predatory in their habits and are accustomed to remain motionless for long periods at a time. When their prey comes within reach they seize it. It would seem, with their motionless habits, as if they were almost entirely dependent on their resemblance to a natural object, otherwise their prey would not come within their reach. But, on the other hand, many other kinds of Mantis do not bear such a remarkable resemblance to a natural object, yet these kinds are by no means the rarest. Therefore, it would seem as if the others have taken unnecessary trouble to mimic some object. I noticed a brown one the other night, settled on my pink lamp-shade; it was a good dead leaf or grass brown and would have been quite unnoticeable sitting on a blade of dead grass, but on my lamp-shade it showed up well. Yet it managed to catch its dinner whilst sitting there. If the struggle for existence amongst his kind was so severe that he must distort his body to appear like dead grass, how did he manage to get his food just as well or better, off my pink lamp-shade? However, perhaps this is not a fair example, as both the Mantis and the moth it caught were in a position which was not natural to them, viz., on my lamp-shade.

One of the most remarkable instances of mimicry I have yet seen was a certain Mantis about four inches long. Its head resembled a blue pea-flower and it was garnished with a topknot to resemble stamens. Its legs were thin stalks, adorned with buds and leaves at the joints, and also had flattened surfaces resembling green pods. It was altogether furnished with an immense amount of cumbersome appendages, extraneous to the parts of its body necessary for the natural functions of walking, eating, etc. It must have taken an enormous amount of trouble and gone to a great wastage of material to attain all these accessories, and yet I found it sitting *on the wrong plant.* It is often the case that one finds two insects of much the same habits, size, and kind, and whereas one is wearing a very good disguise, the other appears to have taken little thought or trouble about the matter. If the survival of the fittest has led to the disguising of the one, to enable it to continue its existence, what right has the other to be existing at all?

I was about to say that I have more often than not noticed that, whereas the disguised one is frequently of rare occurrence, the undisguised one is often very common. This might be considered, however, as an unfair statement, for it might be said that the one is probably less often detected, owing to its better disguise, and so is perhaps not so rare as it appears.

Some of the Phasmidæ (stick insects) show most wonderful adaptations. The gift of flight, which some of these possess, would seem not only to be practically useless but distinctly disadvantageous. They only seem to fly for a few feet, or yards, as the case may be, which renders them very visible, when otherwise they would have escaped detection. Surely they could have walked these few yards. Further, many insects, like the Mantis above, do not appear to know what their disguise is, or why should these insects be so fond of climbing up one's tent? I fancy that amongst the crowd of birds which collect round a bush fire are some which prey largely on these Phasmidæ as they fly before the flames, but this again is perhaps not a natural condition.

There is a certain Tenebrionidæ I have often noticed which is nothing more nor less than the half of a small dead seed pod, to the under side of which a body and legs are attached. To see it right side uppermost there is no doubt about it; it *is* the half of a seed pod out of which the seeds have fallen with the other half broken off. It lives at the bases of big trees, and amongst the dead leaves, twigs, and other débris it is almost impossible to detect. I have picked up many, having caught sight of them moving, especially after the ground has been cleared for my tent to be pitched.

"The ground being disturbed is an unnatural condition," the protectionist would say, "but under all ordinary conditions it is perfectly concealed and even if one or two are caught moving, the great bulk derive enormous benefit by the disguise." I grant this but I would disagree with the conclusion the protectionist would draw from the fact that this insect is the perfect resemblance of half a seed pod. He would say, "Therefore there is no reason to doubt that it has gained these characteristics for the purposes of self-protection, through accumulated variations more and more like the object mimicked."

But why was it not satisfied with any good general brown colour and non-committal shape and, if it liked, flattened body, when it would have been just as invisible if it lay still amongst a mass of débris? Why this extraordinary likeness to a seed pod which, now that I know its disguise, often enables me to find it?

When scratching round under a tree, if I see this particular kind of pod I always pick it up, knowing that it is not a pod but a Tenebrionidæ. Why is not its natural enemy as sharp as I am? Surely it is his bread and butter and he ought to know the peculiarities of his own food much better than I do the peculiarities of one amongst thousands of insects I only examine for amusement.

I am hoping one day to find the tree of the seed pod it so perfectly resembles, for there is no doubt that it is a seed pod and nothing else. I cannot help thinking that I have seen this kind of pod somewhere in another country before but cannot remember where, but this was before I had seen this beetle. Since I have met him, I have been on the lookout for the tree but have never found it yet.

Why then has it gone to the trouble of becoming like this particular kind of pod which does not exist, or at any rate must be excessively rare, in the places where I have found it? Of course in other countries the same beetle may be found and also the particular pod it resembles, but here in the Lado I have found the beetle only. If it can live just as well without being a perfect representation of any actual pod or leaf amongst which it lives, what was the object of this wonderful mimicry? Why could it not have been content to be just an ordinary brown beetle and kept quiet amongst the leaves? Why has it saddled itself with a pod two or three times its size which it must always carry about on its back?

It is not necessary for a creature so small as a beetle to be a perfect representation of anything, in order to be concealed whilst lying on the ground. Many beetles which are found sitting on leaves or blades of grass rely for escape on dropping to the ground like a plummet on anybody's approach. Although

GOOD–BYE

Young elephant wheeling round to go off.

such beetles are of the most varied shapes and colours, it is a fact that they are all difficult to find once they have dropped.

Red or white coloured beetles are of course easier to find than their fellows, but any generally dark coloured insect is excessively hard to find. Often have I searched for such a beetle, after seeing it drop, for a good half-hour without finding it, although I knew where it had fallen within a few feet. Perhaps the beetle had made off, but again I have often found it just as I was about to abandon the search. The same thing has often happened to me with dead beetles. Whilst setting some up in camp, frequently one drops to the ground and if the eye does not follow it quickly enough to see the exact spot, it often requires a long search to find it.

Even with his disguise our seed-pod beetle does not seem to be immune from detection by some sort of creature, it would seem, as I found one of which the edge of the pod had evidently been nibbled. Whatever it was that had tackled it had apparently given it up in disgust after nibbling down one side and so had done no harm except lightening the load on its back. Perhaps it was an animal who fed on this sort of pod and was disappointed to find that this one did not taste the same as usual. One must be careful in choosing one's disguise or one will only fall out of the frying-pan into the fire. It would never do to turn into a berry or one might find that one had a hundred times more enemies than before.

There is another way of looking at the question. If the beetle is too hard and nasty to eat, perhaps seed pods have mimicked the beetle so as to escape from the birds before they are quite ready to drop their seeds.

I have noticed a remarkable resemblance in colouration between certain bees and certain rose-chafers. The rose-chafer spends most of its time settled on a flower, with its head well buried inside, and then is very like a bee gathering honey, some rose-chafers being like some bees and some like others. Evidently a case of mimicry, the protectionist would say. The rose-chafer is mimicking a bee so that a bird will not take it for fear of its sting or, *vice versa*, that kind of bee is pretending to be a rose-chafer so as to escape the attention of the bee eater.

I am not saying that this is not the case, but before accepting such a statement I would like some definite proof that either the one or the other does actually profit by this resemblance. The pure statement that such is a case of protective mimicry would not satisfy me. If it was definitely proved that the chafer really mimicked the bee for purposes of protection, the next point that would arouse my curiosity would be, "Why is the bee coloured as it is?" Probably the protectionist would say that it was a case of warning colouration, to which I would reply that these bees are less injurious than the ordinary honey-bee; still it may be so.

However, when the laws of colouration are better understood, it is possible that one might find that similar habits, food conditions, and environment had caused these two insects, of very different orders, but similar tastes, to assume the same scheme of colouration.

It is quite possible that this may be so but to assert that this was the case without proof would be rash, as rash as to assert that these colours were purely caused by the exigencies of protection or mimicry.

To quote an instance of protective mimicry of another kind of insect actually given by the protectionist school, there is the peculiar resemblance between certain of the Danainæ and the Nymphalinæ. If the one really mimics the other, to what are the markings of the other due? However, this is a small question; the other must have been some colour or combination of colours. What defeats me is how did the mimicry start? How did a member of a different sub-family produce in the first instance a variety sufficiently like the mimicked species to be of any real service to it?

For a usual condition of a mimicking species is that it is different in colouration to the rest of its genus whilst it is also rarer in occurrence than the species mimicked.

This brings us back to the question *how?* again.

Amongst the tortoise beetles, there are some which are difficult to find, owing to their habit of sitting quite still and their resemblance in colour to the object they are usually sitting on. There are two small ones I have noticed very alike in every respect, except that the one is a shade of green resembling the colour of a blade of fresh grass whilst the other is coloured light brown like dead grass.

Assuming the origin of species according to Darwin, there seems to be little doubt that these two species have sprung from a common ancestor and that fairly recently. Now, if we are to believe that these insects have both assumed their colours for the purpose of protection and have sprung from a common ancestor, that ancestor must have had some colour either like the one (green) or the other (brown) and like neither.

Let us imagine him as either the one or the other or a neutral colour. Whatever colour you imagine him, it is a long step from green to brown. If it was one colour to start with, what possible use could it have been to him to assume his first variation of a slight tinge of the other, when the grass around him was either green or brown. When he was just half-way to his new colour, he would have been more conspicuous than he ever was before or would be since, because then he would be shown up to the maximum, whether he chose dead grass or green grass to sit on.

As a matter of fact, however, the brown variety is often met with on green leaves, where they seem to thrive equally as well as the green one, and so one feels rather sceptical about that strenuous struggle for existence which made it necessary for one of them to turn green.

I cannot help thinking that too much has been made of this fierce struggle for existence, especially when considering the perfect insect. There are some kinds of insects which are freely eaten by birds and other things, but the great majority, once they reach the perfect state, fall victims to old age or an inclement climate, or if they are devoured, it is often only after they have performed the functions of breeding and so this does not affect the continuation of the species.

It is in the preliminary stages that such thousands die off, to every one that passes through these stages to attain maturity. Therefore, it is in the first stages, and especially in the larval stage, that they are so urgently in need of protection, and it is just in this stage that one does not meet with such wonderful instances of adaptation. True, the caterpillars and grubs of many kinds are like the plants they feed on, but I have rarely met with those really wonderful instances of mimicry amongst larva that one does so constantly with the perfect insect. Many grubs are strikingly conspicuous and fall easy victims, whilst the majority seem to rely more on concealment than on a possible protective colouration.

The stick caterpillars would no doubt be quoted as wonderful instances of protective colouration and formation in the larval stage. Undoubtedly they are, but the whole is shaped much like any other caterpillar, there are no appendages such as imitation buds, leaves, etc., which serve no functional purpose and are often developed to such an extraordinary extent in so many insects in their perfect state.

No doubt the colouration of these geometers is protective, not only in appearance but also in actual fact. I do not deny for a moment that there are instances in which the insect derives protection or other advantage from its colouration. I will give one in point, but what I wish to insist on is that there are insects which, although coloured and shaped in wonderful mimicry of some object, appear to gain no advantage whatever from the circumstance. It is for this reason that I claim that the protective theory unaided will not explain observed facts.

The instance I would quote is that of a small, yellow spider which I noticed sitting concealed in the petals of a yellow flower. It was then in a position to seize small flies that unsuspectingly came to settle on this flower, attracted probably by its smell. What this spider does, though, when the flower fades, I am unaware. I am quite prepared to find it catching flies quite well on another plant.

Again, if it is to be believed that the perfect insect has assumed disguises to escape from the bird or other enemy, what are we to think of the intelligence of such an enemy who has not learned to recognise him under this disguise? With them it is their daily food and their life that is at stake. Surely the bird who fed on the beetle in its brown days, and watched it through all its changes till it arrived at its present green colour, must still be able to recognise it under its new disguise.

I put it to the reader, if he for generations had been subsistent on a green beetle for food or even on many kinds of beetles, would he not have grown extraordinarily cunning at finding such beetles? Would not his cunning have increased to meet his demands quicker than any beetle could have changed its form and colour? If he saw a green lump on a bit of grass, would he say to himself "green lump" and pass on? Would not he first carefully ascertain if it was really a green lump and not a beetle?

I am forced to admit, though, that many animals do seem remarkably stupid and dense at finding such food, but I have imagined in these cases that perhaps their heart was not in it, they were not really hungry or did not really want that sort of food, in other words, that the struggle for existence is not so keen as supposed, and that the late bird, even if it be a fool, manages to find a worm or two.

Original variations are so infinitely small that I cannot imagine that the first step in such an intricate and marvellous imitation as that of the Mantis I have described above could have been of any possible use to its possessor. The difference between this and an ordinary Mantis is, say, that of a million generations (a million million would really be more like it). An individual who had accidentally assumed a variation which took it a millionth part of the journey towards becoming a blue flower with seed pods would have practically no better chance to survive than any other. Supposing that it survived and produced progeny; the next accidental variation, for there must be a second and a third up to a million *accidental* variations before it reaches the end of its journey, might be in the same direction but might equally well be in any other direction. The odds are that it would not be in the same direction and, if it were in any other direction, it would nullify the part of the journey already accomplished.

A million variations all in the same direction and climbing towards the same goal are too great a stretch for the imagination if the word *accidental* is used. It is not a mathematical possibility. There must be some intelligence or law at work to produce such a result by such a means.

However, there is a point of view that Darwin has suggested, but which has been little dwelt on or amplified by his successors. That is, if the animal has developed from something very different, so in all probability has the vegetable. So, if a Mantis has changed from something very different to look like a blue flower with green seed pods, the chances are that when it undertook this change the blue flower was also something very different.

Put this back further to the ancestor of the original Mantis, and the ancestor of the original pea-flower and again put it back as far as you like. Go back to a time when there were practically no specialised animals or vegetables extant. Go back, if you like, beyond this and imagine a very low, primitive form of animal life bearing a resemblance, either accidental or again caused by some bygone occurrence, to some primitive form of vegetable life.

It is much easier to believe that these two have come up hand in hand through long ages, each minute change in one being productive of a change in the other, than to imagine that a brown beetle living amongst green stuff gradually became green, so as to mimic the plant on which it lived. Given a long enough period of this, and heredity will come into play, the one will grow so accustomed to follow the changes in the other, that it may continue some time after the need to do so has passed away. This would afford a possible but not a satisfactory reason for some of the marvellous instances of adaptation apparently gaining little advantage by their mimicry. The proof or refutation of such a theory lies in such dim and remote antiquity that it is really but idle speculation.

If, however, one dispenses with the words *accidental variations* and substitutes something which implies memory, intelligence, or a conscious striving after a given form or colour one eliminates the contemplation of such odds against the accumulation of infinite minute variations, all trending in the same direction, as would amount to a mathematical impossibility.

Sexual selection has not been touched on. It is easy to believe in an accumulation of variations selected in this way finally leading to the most weird and remarkable effects but not perhaps to mimicry. At first sight the odds against such variations arriving at the perfect likeness of a natural object might appear infinitely more remote than the survival of the fittest theory. Whereas the latter at least alleges that it is the fittest or the most like the object aimed at who survive, in the former the variations selected are purely according to the caprice of the selector. However, here we have an intelligent being who may have some motive or some ultimate idea faintly connected with its selection.

The influence of environment must have its effects

on animal life as it does on the human being. The poets and lovers of all nations are given to comparing the charms of those they admire to the natural objects around them. "Straight as a cedar of Lebanon," "beautiful as the eyes of the camel," and so on. By a stretch of imagination one might imagine the insect also consciously or unconsciously comparing its species to food or natural objects which surround it.

The resemblance or fancied resemblance to some natural object might be the cause of selection and such a cause would be far more likely to remain constant in one direction for a certain time than accidental variations. Moreover, there would be a conscious striving after a given form or likeness.

Again the influence of environment might affect the colour and form of a creature. There might be some dim, subconscious memory of the shape and colour of the plant it had always fed on, that might induce in the insect a series of infinitesimal modifications which, when accumulated, arrive at the result we see.

If I had to believe in some unproved theory to account for these likenesses, I would much rather believe in some such as this, wild as it is, for it would fit in better with facts as I observe them. It would at least account for the very free and easy way that insects neglect to take full advantage of their adaptations. That is to say, a theory, to my mind, should explain : —

1. The cause of these wonderful adaptations in the insect world.

2. The reason why so many of them are apparently perfectly useless to their possessors.

As, however, it is not necessary for me to believe in anything, I wonder only more and more Why? and How?

INDEX

Abdi Hassan, head man, 168.
Aberdare range, elephant hunting on the, 3–17.
Abyssinians, respect for the buffalo among, 87; method of shooting buffalo practised by, 87–88; begging habits of, 284; thievery among, 295.
Africans, limitations of existence of native, 205–207; improvidence of, 207–208; curious family relations of, 208–209; degree of skill in bushcraft, 209–210; poor eyesight of, 210; vagueness as to time and distance, 211–214; occupations and ideas of labour among, 214–216; division of labour unknown to, 216–218; lack of trustworthiness of, 219; extreme tolerance characteristic of, 221; courtesy exercised toward white men by, 222; density of, concerning the unusual, 280–281; proverbs of the, 281–283; begging by, 283–284; conception of courage among, 285; qualities and characteristics in warfare with white men, 309 ff. *See also* Servants.
Ambatch rafts, 95, 98–100.
Ants, observations of, 346–350.
Arabs, comprehension of black man's failings by, 181.
Athi River, animals in region of the, 259.
Awemba country, measurement of distances in the, 214.

Banana wine, yeast from, 297.
Bandanas for savage wear, 77.
Bangweolo, Lake, hunting near, 33.
Bantu servants, 155, 158, 165, 168, 205 ff.
Bees, possibilities for study of, 344–345; question concerning protective colouration in, 366–367.
Beetles, study of, 350–351; protective colouration in, 364–366, 368 ff.
Begging characteristic of natives, 283–284.
Bongo, hunting the, 325 ff.; habitat of the, 326–328; method of penetrating forests, 329; food of, 334.

Bravery, native Africans' ideas of, 285.
Bruce, Captain, 25.
Buffalo, hunting the, 80 ff.; danger of hunting, as compared with other game animals, 81–82; restrictions on shooting, 83; adventures with, 84–87; destruction of, by rinderpest, 88; fallacy of subdivision of, by horns, 88–91; lighter colour of females and young, 91; dependence of, on water, 91; quicker response of, to sense of smell than to that of sight, 91–93.
Bugs in Africa, 352.
Bushbuck shooting, 240–241.
Bushcraft, superiority of Africans over white men in, 209.
Butterflies, African, 351.

Camping, practical suggestions on, 295–308.
Canoe, the native African, 103–104, 106.
Caterpillars, opportunity for study of, 351.
Chambesi River, plague of tsetse flies on the, 341.
Children, viewpoint of savages regarding, 208–209.
Chupaties, receipt for making, 297–298.
Clerk, erudition of a Mganda, 223–224.
Clothing for life in the wilds, 307–309.
Courtesy of natives toward white men, 222.
Cox, Captain, 259–260.
Crocodiles at Fajao, 108–109.
Crow, the Indian, 265.

Dinkas, fish-spearing by, 109.
Dirre Daua road, experiences on the, 290–292.
Distance, vagueness of native Africans as to, 211–214.

Ears of elephants, the fold of, 276–277.
East Africa, hunting in, 2; lack of trackers in, 19; rhinoceros hunting in, 32; pleasures of hunting in highlands of, 257, 258.